Aspen's Fundraising Series for the 21st Century

Direct Marketing for Nonprofits

Essential Techniques for the New Era

D1597229

Aspen's Fundraising Series for the 21st Century

Aspen's Fundraising Series for the 21st Century

Direct Marketing for Nonprofits

Essential Techniques for the New Era

Kay Partney Lautman, CFRE
President
Lautman & Company
Washington, DC

AN ASPEN PUBLICATION®
Aspen Publishers, Inc.
Gaithersburg, Maryland
2001

This publication is designed to provide accurate and authoritative information in regard to the Subject Matter covered. It is sold with the understanding that the publisher is not engaged in rendering legal, accounting, or other professional service. If legal advice or other expert assistance is required, the service of a competent professional person should be sought. (From a Declaration of Principles jointly adopted by a Committee of the American Bar Association and a Committee of Publishers and Associations.)

Library of Congress Cataloging-in-Publication Data

Lautman, Kay Partney.
Direct marketing for nonprofits : essential techniques
for the new era / Kay Partney Lautman.
p. cm. —(Aspen's fundraising series for the 21st century)
Includes index.
ISBN 0-8342-1959-X
1. Direct marketing. 2. Nonprofit organizations. I. Title. II. Series.
HF5415.126.L38 2001
658.8′4—dc21
2001018844

Orders: (800) 638-8437
Customer Service: (800) 234-1660

About Aspen Publishers • For more than 40 years, Aspen has been a leading professional publisher in a variety of disciplines. Aspen's vast information resources are available in both print and electronic formats. We are committed to providing the highest quality information available in the most appropriate format for our customers. Visit Aspen's Internet site for more information resources, directories, articles, and a searchable version of Aspen's full catalog, including the most recent publications: **www.aspenpublishers.com**
Aspen Publishers, Inc. • The hallmark of quality in publishing
Member of the worldwide Wolters Kluwer group.

Editorial Services: Ruth Bloom
Library of Congress Catalog Card Number: 2001018844
ISBN: 0-8342-1959-X

Printed in the United States of America

1 2 3 4 5

This book is dedicated in memoriam to
Harold Oram and David Ogilvy
and to
mentors and friends
Dick Taft and Richard Armstrong

Table of Contents

Preface

WHAT IS DIRECT RESPONSE FUNDRAISING?

Most fundraisers don't really understand what direct mail or direct response fundraising is. They think of direct mail as "junk mail," telemarketing as obnoxious, and neither as appropriate for their organizations.

To think that a letter for a good cause could be called "junk" is horrifying. Besides, it *isn't* junk! Indeed for many people, such mail keeps them up to date on causes they love and support, and brings them opportunities to help organizations doing other work in similar areas.

It is difficult for me to imagine that people who receive mail from nonprofit groups regard such letters as "junk." I *have* to believe that they see the letter for what it is: correspondence about a legitimate need.

The recipient realizes, of course, that the letter will request money as it did before. *But if the donor does not regard his or her check as "junk," then it follows that the letter requesting that gift was not "junk" either.*

Here are two examples of organizations that do not send "junk" mail, but nevertheless have highly successful direct response campaigns.

A local organization with which I work on a pro bono basis receives approximately $80,000 annually through direct mail. This is accomplished through modest acquisition mailings of 50,000 pieces, four renewal of support mailings, and several annual newsletters with response envelopes enclosed. This program, with about 1,000 active donors, is the smallest successful direct mail program of which I know.

Now, $80,000 may not seem like much to some, but it goes pretty far with this organization whose budget is about a million dollars. But the mail program has done far more than raise money. Indeed, it has raised public awareness of the problem it addresses and has raised many badly needed volunteers.

At the other end of the spectrum, a national organization derives over $13 million annually from some 200,000 donors, originally attracted through a major direct mail acquisition program. The organization has also developed a productive monthly giving program, a high dollar program, and planned giving and bequest programs—all through direct mail. Its renewal rate is almost 80 percent thanks to a seven-part renewal series and telemarketing, and its five-million–piece new member acquisition program is thriving, as it must to keep up with natural attrition.

Whether you mail 50,000 or 500,000 appeal letters, you are still conducting a direct mail campaign. Most nonprofits fall somewhere in the middle of these two, raising one to five million dollars from between 20,000 and 70,000 donors or members. The size, style, and success of each campaign represents (1) the likes and dislikes of the people in the institution, (2) the institution's dedication to and financial investment in the program, and (3) whether they avail themselves of the knowledge and skills offered by direct mail fundraising professionals—not necessarily consultants, but professionals.

Financial success ultimately depends on whether the development office recognizes the fact that potential major donors and bequests will not come from some magic place "out there" but from their own donor file. They must research their file on a regular basis, and cultivate their donors in order to reap the highest rewards of direct response.

The truly successful fundraiser is one who recognizes that, in most cases, when a donor sends a large gift in response to a letter, that gift may be upgradable—sometimes significantly.

The donor has told you that he or she cares. The rest is up to you.

Acknowledgments

As I was writing this, my second book on direct mail fundraising, I realized how little and how much things have changed, and although my career in fundraising has spanned over 30 years, I still need a little help from my friends.

For their excellent suggestions and for their time, I would like to thank my staff, especially Fran Jacobowitz, Lisa Maska, and Tiffany Neill. Additionally, I would like to thank Patricia Edwards, Marion Richardson, and Pam Lautman for their help in assembling the book.

Others who helped with the book include Tracey Lea of Share Group, who contributed to the telemarketing chapter, Laura Giesenhaus of Production Solutions on the list chapter, and Valerie Bloom of the Millard Group on the production chapter. I am especially grateful for the expert guidance of Holly White on the chapter on card, calendar, and other premium programs.

I warmly thank all Lautman & Company clients for the experience of working on their behalf, especially those who gave unhesitating permission to include in this book some of our work for their organizations.

The book is dedicated to the four people who had the greatest impact on my career. I entered the fundraising field under the tutelage of Harold Oram to whom I am ever grateful for teaching me about "The Good, the True, and the Beautiful." David Ogilvy helped edit my last book and taught me how to apply marketing to fundraising.

Dick Taft, longtime colleague and friend, not only published my first book, but hired Lautman & Company to work with him on one of the most exciting projects of my career. Richard Armstrong is a friend and the most talented writer I know, inspiring my best work.

Everyone at Aspen Publishers, who commissioned this book, was supportive and understanding and I would especially like to thank William Reinhard, Ruth Bloom, Beatrice Wolman, Laura Sobers, and Kathy Litzenberg.

I also would like to thank Hank Goldstein and Gale Publishing (formerly The Taft Group) for allowing the use of some text from *Dear Friend: Mastering the Art of Direct Mail Fundraising*, published in 1983 and again 1991, and now out of print.

Finally, Bob Lautman, my husband and friend of 34 years must be thanked just for being himself, which is to say, the best!

Kay Partney Lautman

Chapter 1
What Really Matters in Direct Mail

CHAPTER OUTLINE

- The Five Important Elements in an Appeal
- Is Direct Mail for You?—A Quiz You Can't Afford Not To Take

This chapter contains the most important things you need to know about direct mail fundraising. Most people believe that the most important elements of a mail piece are the way the letter is written and the way the package looks. This is simply not true. And as a writer and idea person, it somewhat pains me to say this.

The single most important thing in the appeal is the careful targeting of your audience. In other words, it is choosing appropriate lists of people who believe as you do and who have donated or spent money (preferably through the mail) as evidence of their interest.

THE FIVE IMPORTANT ELEMENTS IN AN APPEAL

While copy and presentation are still very important (and although several chapters contain "how to" copy ideas), copy remains third on a list of five really important elements in the appeal. They are as follows:

1. Audience/lists/segmentation
2. Basic membership offer/suggested gift
3. Copy
4. Format/presentation
5. Premiums/benefits

Now in case you don't know what each of these items are, let us go through them briefly.

1. Audience/Lists/Segmentation

No one ever convinced anyone (through a direct mail appeal least of all) to change his or her mind about a subject and then to give money. Your job is to contact people who already believe as you do, and to convince them that your organization is worthy of their support. Chapter 3 tackles the subject thoroughly. Meanwhile, if you're in a hurry or just skimming, here's my best advice:

- When it comes to choosing lists for an acquisition mailing, *do not* under any circumstances ask your board or friends for their holiday card lists, Rolodexes, etc. *Do* go to a good list broker specializing in fundraising and ask for list recommendations. This is not like getting a print bid. Spend some time with your broker and ask a lot of questions like "Why are you recommending this list?"
- Many lists are only available on an exchange (one for one) basis, so try to convince your board to allow occasional exchange of your under $100 donor list. The lists you get in exchange—as opposed to rental lists—work the best by far at a far lower cost.
- When writing to your own donors, segmentation is everything. It isn't profitable to mail every donor every appeal.

2. Basic Membership Offer/Suggested Gift

Why does one charity ask for a $20 gift, another ask for $35, and still another ask for $50? The answer, hopefully, is because they have carefully tested and chosen the right amount to request for their particular cause. Too often, it is because a board of directors feels that dues should be a certain amount or that dues haven't been raised in "too long" and that it's time for an increase. I've often heard board members declare that a $5 or $10 increase won't even be noticed; after all, it's equal to the cost of just a hamburger and soda. Maybe so, but up to 20 percent of your donors may drop out when presented with an increase, so test first in your acquisition mailings.

3. Copy

Since copywriters today receive rather impressive fees to write fundraising letters, it is no wonder that organizations want to know, "What makes a truly good fundraising letter?" The easy answer, of course, is, "A great cause makes a great fundraising letter." Even so, great causes try to improve their letters and packages in an effort to build larger constituencies and raise more money. Many nonprofit organizations detest what I would consider really great fundraising copy. I define copy as great when it immediately engages the reader, focusing on the part of the story that needs to be told (no more and no less), uses simple words and urgent language, isn't "institutional" in style, and isn't coy about asking for money.

4. Format/Presentation

Various formats are featured throughout this text, but for now you need to realize that they play a role in whether your appeal will be opened and read, and whether you will receive a contribution as a result. There are, in everyone's mailbox from time to time, regular business size (#10) appeals, oversize "flats," invitation size appeals, and everything else in between. But size is not the only element in the format/presentation. You must consider (and budget for) paper stock, number of ink colors, photographs (if any), the look of the appeal (sophisticated or homey), number of inserts (lift letter, photos, premium), type face and size, and on and on.

The most important thing in determining format is to keep it simple. No matter how complicated the offer or how extensive the order form, it is your job to make it foolproof. Make the response device easy to understand and fill out. Otherwise your prospective donor will trash the entire thing in frustration.

5. Premiums/Benefits

I often call this part of the offer the "Cracker Jack" come-on because this beloved caramel popcorn snack has, over my lifetime, promised "Toy Surprise Inside" as an additional temptation to buy.

If, over a period of two years or more, an organization you admire (but don't work for) continues to offer a backpack, you can (a) assume that the charity's returns justify backpacks as affordable enticements, or (b) that the organization doesn't know how to accurately measure long-term cost-effectiveness. Why don't you call and ask them directly? They'd probably be proud to tell you.

Selecting affordable premium offers is a tricky business. One collects other charities' mail, hoping to learn what works for them. But you only learn what the charity is offering, and not what truly works because, unfortunately, many nonprofit organizations do not stick with an offer long enough to learn its value. (And the ultimate value is whether or not the donor/member renews in the second and third years.)

IS DIRECT MAIL FOR YOU?—A QUIZ YOU CAN'T AFFORD NOT TO TAKE

Now that you know the basic five elements of successful direct mail, you should give serious thought to whether this fundraising technique is for you. After all, it's very expensive and not for the fainthearted.

The following is a series of critical marketing questions that should be addressed by every nonprofit considering direct mail for the first time. It is also a useful guide in taking the temperature of organizations already in the mail.

In the process of taking the test, you may discover that you need the help of a consultant and list broker, both of whom should be specialists in direct mail fundraising. You'll know a lot more about what to ask these people after reading this book. Here's the quiz. (You will instinctively know what the answer should be.)

1. ***Who Are We?***
   - Are we well known?
   - Is our issue "hot"?
   - Are we unique?
   - If not, who is the competition? What is their strength?
   - Who will speak for us in the mail?

2. **What Is Our Market?**
   - Who is our audience?
   - How large is our market?
   - Is our market local? National?
   - If local, can we break into a national market?
   - Do we have more than one market?
   - How large can we grow?

3. **How Should We Position Ourselves?**
   - If our name is unfamiliar to the public, does it describe what we do?
   - Should we offer membership or ask for a donation?
   - What size gift should we seek?

4. **Should We Offer Something in Return?**
   - Should we offer premiums?
   - How elaborate should they be?
   - Do we need a newsletter? Magazine?
   - How much will fulfillment cost?

5. **Are We Prepared for Failure? For Success?**
   - Do we have $50,000 for a first-time test?
   - Should we test several approaches?
   - If successful, can we afford to lose up to 50 percent of our investment?
   - If unsuccessful, can we afford to lose most of our investment?
   - If successful in the test, can we plow all income back into more direct mail for several years?

Now that you have taken the quiz, take your own pulse. Did you pass or fail? These questions go through the minds of professionals when they talk to would-be "start-up" mailers; they are questions and answers that should be honestly discussed before attempting a test.

The firm I head has had its share of extremely successful "start-up" campaigns as well as a few failures. That's because sometimes a cause is so borderline, it requires a test to show whether long-term success is a possibility.

There is no real rule as to what constitutes success in a test mailing, but in general, one aims for a .90 percent response rate or better. However, a lower percent return can be considered successful too. Unless returns drop below a .65 percent overall, it should not be deemed a failure. Even a .65 percent return can be a success if the average gift is high enough (say, $30 or more). What you truly want is to earn net income, but what you will probably have to settle for is break-even, or as close to it as you can come.

Success can only be truly determined by an organization's patience and investment capability. Direct mail is practically never "get-rich quick." I like to use the story of the asparagus garden my husband and I never planted.

We had intended to plant asparagus soon after we bought our house, but when we learned that it took three years to get an edible crop, we procrastinated. Now, 25 years later, we still have an instant gratification attitude toward gardening and we still have no asparagus.

Direct mail is like asparagus in that it takes approximately three years of investing before one earns spendable net income. But if you don't start, you'll never reap the delicious rewards.

Chapter 2
Doing the Math—Budgeting, Scheduling, and Evaluating

CHAPTER OUTLINE

- Size of the First Mailing
- Size of Subsequent Mailings
- Preparing a Budget
- Establishing a Mail Schedule
- Tabulating Responses
- Analyzing the Mailing
- How To Calculate Response Rates
- House Mailing Math

Don't be afraid of this chapter. Regardless of whether you do it yourself or hire a professional agency, your success in the mail will be determined by an understanding of the mechanics of quantities, budgeting, scheduling, and evaluation.

Scheduling appropriate quantities at the best time of year (best time for *your* organization) requires experience and good instincts. Thorough evaluation and timely reporting are critical to good decision making. Budgets and projections, of course, must be done simultaneously.

In making projections and in evaluating your returns, always remember that in acquisitions for new members and renewals of current members, a good percent return over a small increase in the average gift is preferable. Strong percent returns are what grow and maintain your file size. In house mailings for gifts above and beyond dues, you want to make good net income, which usually means getting a higher average gift than with either acquisitions or renewals.

It is a truism that when the average gift increases (as with, say, an upgrade mailing or a special appeal asking for a "stretch" gift), the percent return will decrease. The reverse is also true because high percent returns usually mean a lower average gift. Few organizations can consistently achieve both.

This chapter is devoted to helping you do the math—a process that is both exciting and creative.

SIZE OF THE FIRST MAILING

If your organization decides to test direct mail, the first issue you must address is the size and cost of the mailing. Following are three possible schedules for a national test or pilot mailing. Which do you think would be the ideal size of the pilot mailing?

- **Test #1:** 75,000 names from 15 lists of 5,000
- **Test #2:** 75,000 names from 3 lists of 20,000 each and 1 list of 15,000
- **Test #3:** 30,000 names from 6 lists of 5,000 names each

	Test #1	Test #2	Test #3
# of Names	75,000	75,000	30,000
# of Lists	15	4	4
% Return	.9%	.9%	.9%
# of Gifts	675	675	270
Average Gift	$20	$20	$20
Income	$13,500	$13,500	$5,400

At first glance, Test #1 and #2 results appear equal. In both, you add 675 new names to your donor base. But in Test #1, you learned about the profitability of 15 lists, those that worked and those that did not—valuable information to be used as a guide in selecting future lists.

In Test #2, however, you tested only four lists and learned very little about potential markets. *A larger rollout based on such a limited list test would be at very high risk.*

Test #3 is a poor choice for the same reason as Test #2—you didn't test enough lists to learn anything about your market.

In today's highly competitive market, it is the rare cause that breaks even on acquisition mail. Still, recovering as much of the cost as possible remains everyone's goal. Now, you may wonder, "If Test #1 is the best, why not mail 100,000 or 150,000 as the test?" Well, some mailers do. Certainly, larger quantities enable you to reduce printing costs and test even more lists. On larger mailings, you also can test letters or envelopes or other variables economically. But until you have the experience that comes with many years of mailing—and thus have developed an intuition for projecting the likelihood of success on an initial 150,000-piece mailing—why double the risk?

For most organizations new to direct mail, 75,000 is a sufficient test quantity to gain maximum knowledge at minimum risk on a national mailing. If yours is a local mailing, you will want to test 30,000 pieces initially (6 lists of 5,000) and no more than 50,000 (10 lists of 5,000).

SIZE OF SUBSEQUENT MAILINGS

Almost any organization has a sufficient potential audience to test 75,000 names. How large your universe is for continuation mailings in the first, second, and subsequent years must be learned. Your list broker's best estimate is what you will use initially.

Some organizations with mass appeal can mail to an almost unlimited number of prospects (many millions) each year. Other organizations with great, but not mass appeal, can mail a million to five million annually. Still others with more limited appeal, or an appeal of a local nature, should lower their sights to less than a million acquisitions per year.

List brokers and direct mail fundraising consultants can help you with projections—not just for your test mailing but for subsequent mailings. Based on test results, a direct mail consultant should prepare a proposed continuation plan that projects costs, number of new donors, and gross and net income.

Here's a rule of thumb you can use: The experts say that if you are making a net profit on acquisitions, you aren't mailing enough. This is because the purpose of the acquisition is not to make money but to build your donor file. Thus, if you break even or even lose a little money on acquisitions, you are doing fine because it is with subsequent gifts that you will begin acquiring net income. And the larger the file, the more income you can expect.

On the other hand, if you are losing substantial money on your acquisition mailings (say, you are not recovering at least 65 to 70 percent of your cost), then you may be mailing too much, as proven by the dismal results on many of your acquisition lists. It takes a couple of years to figure out just how much your organization should and can mail, based on available quantities of good lists, rates of return on acquisitions, and the amount of net income earned when mailing to your house file.

PREPARING A BUDGET

Now that you have decided to mail 75,000 pieces in your test mailing, you need to establish a budget for direct costs. These include printing package components (i.e., letter, carrier envelopes, reply envelopes, and possibly one other component), postage at the nonprofit rate, lettershop, merge/purge, and list rentals. Not included in direct costs are back-end expenses, such as receipt of postage-due mail, list computerization, and acknowledgment letters.

While all of these items can be completely bid out except for postage, it is recommended that (as of 2001) for a quantity of 75,000, you budget $400 per thousand (per M), a total of $30,000. If you are using a professional writer, add $2,500; a professional artist costs about the same. Total expenses are thus estimated at $35,000 (more if you hire a consultant).

ESTABLISHING A MAIL SCHEDULE

Now for the lesson on when to mail. Have you always heard that summer is a poor time in which to mail? That December is the best? That you should avoid mid-April because of the income tax deadline?

For every rule, there's one that can be broken by a particular organization. In sending acquisition mailings, however, it is usually wise to avoid the three weeks before Christmas during which time donors will be receiving numerous appeals from the organizations they already support. This is clearly not the time to test your cause on a new prospect. That is, unless your organization serves children, which can render this rule null and void.

Some organizations can mail successfully in June and early July, but rarely in August. In general, try to avoid July and August until you know more about the general viability of your mailings. The best months for acquisition mailings are January, February, March, September, October, and November. The spring and summer months (April through August) are the poorest. This is not a theory. Results prove it.

In establishing a timetable, try to avoid the months of April and May for your first test (not because spring isn't as good as fall, but because it takes six weeks of returns before you will have enough results to make an interim analysis of your mailing). By this time it is June, which is not the optimum time for mailing. You will now have to wait until September for your rollout (or continuation mailing), and will have lost momentum. The ideal test months are January (for an April rollout) and, best of all, early September (for a November rollout).

TABULATING RESPONSES

The task of tabulating responses is the most exciting part of the entire program. Opening envelopes and watching checks fall out is extremely satisfying.

Don't be alarmed that the first responses you receive contain complaints, impolite requests to "take me off your list," and envelopes stuffed with junk, including appeals from other organizations. People who feel the need to vent in this manner react faster than those who take your appeal seriously. Unfortunately, you must pay the postage due on these returns, but generally it does not add up to a large sum.

Most such "mail" is not worth responding to and can be trashed. Be on guard, however, for legitimate complaints. If properly answered, complaints can be turned into contributions—often sizable. We recall one instance where an almost indecipherable note was scrawled across a conservation organization's business reply envelope stating that the writer had read that a board member had been on safari killing endangered species. A letter of explanation was sent to the writer and several weeks later, the complainer responded with a check for $1,000.

Responses usually begin slowly and build over several weeks before starting to decline. Then by the middle of the third week (or 15 days), you should have received one-half of the expected total income. This 15-day halfway point (or doubling day as it is

often called) will vary from organization to organization. After you have been in the mail for a year or so, you can begin to predict total income with more accuracy based on what you have learned to be *your* doubling day. Do not, however, count days from the mailing date, as third class mail delivery is unpredictable. Count instead from the date of the first gift received.

If your donor list is not computerized when you conduct your first test, you can reproduce the form in Exhibit 2–1 on which to post all gifts.

ANALYZING THE MAILING

After 90 days of returns, your tracking report will be complete and you can translate totals into a List Report that looks something like Exhibit 2–2.

The next step is to analyze which lists worked and what they have in common. Often there is no clear answer in the beginning. But after several successful mailings in which you eliminate lists that perform poorly, retest marginal lists, and add new test lists to the schedule, you and your broker will gain greater insights. This is discussed in detail in Chapter 3.

HOW TO CALCULATE RESPONSE RATES

Use the following mathematical formulas to complete costs:
- **% Response** = Number Returns divided by Number Mailed × 100
- **Average Gift** = Gross Income divided by Number Returns
- **Cost** = Cost per Thousand × Number of Thousand Mailed
- **Cost Per Thousand** = Cost divided by Number Mailed × 1,000
- **% Cost Recovered** = Gross Income divided by Cost × 1,000

HOUSE MAILING MATH

The mechanics of budgeting, scheduling, and evaluating house mailings are less complicated.

Once your list is large enough, you will begin segmenting your file to learn whether certain parts behave differently. Thus, instead of analyzing list-by-

Exhibit 2–1 Sample Form for Posting Gifts

List Name: _____   Package: _____

Code: _____   Date Mailed: _____   Quantity Mailed: _____
Mailing Cost per M: _____   Other: _____
Date of First Gift: _____   Cut-Off Date: _____

Date	#Ret	Cum Ret	$s Today	$100 Gifts #/$ Amt	Total $s	Date	# Ret	Cum Ret	$s Today	$100 Gifts #/S Amt	Total $s
Weekly Total:											

list, you will analyze segment-by-segment. A small segmented list might look as follows:

Code	Type of Donor	$
Code A	Regular $ Donors	($20–$99.99, last 12 months)
Code B	High $ Donors	($100–$999.99, last 12 months)
Code C	Regular $ Donors (Lapsed)	($20–$99.99, 13–24 months)
Code D	High $ Donors	($100–$999.99, last 13–24 months)

By segmenting your list in this and other ways, you will learn to predict returns more accurately. You will undoubtedly find that the more recent the donor/member's last gift, the higher percent return that list segment will yield. Lapsed donors, for instance, can be profitable to mail in some donor segments because of the high average gift, but segments of lapsed donors giving small gifts will become increasingly unprofitable as their gifts recede further into the past.

By coding your donors according to the offer made, you will also be able to learn which parts of the donor file are responsive to premium offers and which are not. You will become an old hand at using the terms *recency and frequency* which, translated, means that those parts of the file having donors who give several times a year and who have given recently are your best donors. They are also the best prospects for monthly donor programs and for planned gifts. And recency and frequency combined with a high average gift (say $100 or more) identifies the best prospects for your high dollar donor program.

Another type of segmentation—devised to learn which types of package bring in donors who renew (or give a second time)—might look like this:

Code	Description
Code A	Regular $ Donors responsive to Control Package
Code B	High $ Donors responsive to Control Package
Code C	Regular $ Donors responsive to Name Label Package
Code D	High $ Donors responsive to Name Label Package

By budgeting and segmenting your own house list, you can test many things, including those that can either raise results or lower costs (more net income either way). This will be discussed further in Chapter 7 on Testing.

Exhibit 2–2 List Report: 90-Day Analysis of Test Mailing

List Name	Code	Number Mailed	Number Returns	% Response	Gross Income	Average Gift	Cost	Cost/ Thousand	% Cost Recovered
List "A"	A1	5,000	81	1.62%	$1,485	$18.33	$1,230	$246	121%
List "B"	A2	5,000	75	1.50%	$1,232	$16.43	$1,230	$246	100%
List "C"	A3	5,000	33	0.66%	$633	$19.18	$1,230	$246	51%
List "D"	A4	5,068	37	0.73%	$1,227	$33.16	$1,247	$246	98%
List "E"	A5	4,863	20	0.41%	$370	$18.50	$1,196	$249	31%
List "F"	A6	5,000	41	0.82%	$719	$17.64	$1,230	$246	58%
List "G"	A7	4,725	43	0.91%	$1,026	$23.86	$1,162	$246	88%
List "H"	A8	5,000	47	0.94%	$884	$18.81	$1,230	$246	72%
List "I"	A9	5,000	48	0.96%	$1,035	$21.56	$1,230	$246	84%
List "J"	A10	5,000	23	0.46%	$845	$36.74	$1,230	$246	69%
List "K"	A11	4,834	55	1.14%	$1,457	$26.49	$1,189	$246	123%
List "L"	A12	4,999	34	0.68%	$629	$18.50	$1,230	$246	51%
List "M"	A13	5,000	38	0.76%	$828	$21.79	$1,230	$246	67%
List "N"	A14	4,689	31	0.66%	$1,030	$33.23	$1,153	$246	89%
List "O"	A15	5,000	43	0.86%	$1,033	$24.02	$1,230	$246	84%
Misc. Returns	—	—	21	—	$595	$28.33	—	—	—
Total Returns		74,178	670	0.90%	$15,028	$22.43	$18,248	$246	82%

Note: The best lists recouped 70 percent of costs or better.

Chapter 3
Choosing Lists and Brokers

CHAPTER OUTLINE

- Locating Your Market
- What Is a List Broker?
- What the List Broker Does
- Why the List Broker Is Indispensable
- How Many Brokers Should You Use?
- Questions a List Broker Needs Answered
- How Many Brokers Should You Use?
- Testing Lists and Quantities
- Important Things To Know When Ordering Lists
- The Value of Exchanged Lists
- Still Unconvinced about Exchanging?
- How Merge/Purge Works
- How To Mail "Multis"
- Guarding against List Theft

A brilliant mailing to the wrong market will produce poor or even disastrous results. But an ordinary package directed at the right market can—and often does—produce respectable results. This is not to say that a poor appeal to good lists will always produce top results. But if you spend all your time producing an award-winning package and are uncertain about your market, you are going to be very disappointed.

Following are four laments of those who have made typical marketing mistakes:

1. *"But I mailed to lists my board members gave me. They were certain those people would be interested in contributing. Besides, they were free!"*

   MORAL: Doubtless, board members are well meaning, and we know how hard it is to turn them down. But if you want your board's praise in the final analysis, be brave enough to ask how the lists were compiled, how clean they are, and, most important, whether the people on them actually are *donors* to other organizations.

2. *"But it was a bipartisan cause. I was sure that liberal lists would work as well as conservative lists."*

   MORAL: This mailer *wanted* to believe in solidarity. But had he examined the issue in more depth, he would have concluded that it was a cause supported primarily by liberals. Instead, clinging to his idealism, he split tested liberal and conservative lists 50-50. The results? The liberal lists made a small net profit. The conservative lists recouped only 35 percent of costs.

3. *"But they should have been interested in our conservation cause. After all, they're the people who use the out-of-doors, buying all that fancy hiking and camping equipment. Maybe they don't have any money left over for clean air."*

   MORAL: A hard-earned lesson is that buyers (e.g., of catalog products, magazines) are not necessarily donors, even if similarity of interest appears to exist. This is not to say that all buyers' lists should be avoided. A few work. But let your broker guide you cautiously through the wilderness.

4. *"We weren't sure who our constituency might be, so we covered all bases taking health lists, conservation lists, youth lists, political lists, and so on. We didn't think they would all be winners but we sure didn't think we would lose almost 80 percent of our costs!"*

MORAL: If yours is an organization in search of an identity, you would do well to conduct a survey or a focus group to get a profile of your present donors or members.

LOCATING YOUR MARKET

Your market of potential donors is represented by thousands of lists that either can be rented at a cost of X dollars per thousand names or exchanged on a name-for-name basis with your own list. In either case, you arrange for one-time use only and most organizations suppress their donors of $100 or more. However, the descriptions on the list cards provided by list brokers can seem sketchy, and many lists sound alike.

How, then, do you know which lists are right for you? Following are capsule descriptions of the three types of lists available to you through a broker.

1. *Donor lists (likely to be the most responsive you can use).*
   - Organizations similar in purpose to your own, whose constituencies make donations or pay membership dues.
   - Organizations not similar, but made up of donors or members whose profiles (interests, politics, lifestyles, etc.) are compatible with your cause.

2. *Compiled donor lists not representing a single organization, with names like "Committed Liberal Donors" or "Affluent Republican Donors."*

3. *Commercial lists (the most productive will have mail responsive selections).*
   - Magazine, catalog buyers, etc., whose tastes, hobbies, and interests are indica-

tive of a potential interest in your cause.
   - Names and addresses derived from directories, newspapers, public records, voting lists, retail sales books, etc., to identify groups of people with something in common.

Even if you confine yourself to the first category (donor/member lists), you will find yourself overwhelmed by stacks of list data cards briefly describing the merits of each list. A typical data card appears on the card shown in Exhibit 3–1.

With literally thousands of cards like this to choose from (some of which have even less information), how do you know which ones are appropriate for testing? Especially when so many of them sound the same.

WHAT IS A LIST BROKER?

There are three common misconceptions about lists and brokers:

1. List brokers do not own lists. Rather, the broker is usually a middleman who brings mailers together with list owners.
2. It is a common misconception that one "buys" lists. Lists are not "bought" by either you or your broker. Rather, they are leased or rented for one-time use on a specified date for a specified fee based on the number of names you request.
3. The price of a list is not more expensive when you use a broker. Like travel agents, who are paid by the airlines or resorts, the broker's 20 percent commission comes from the list owner. You pay only the standard rental fee of between $75 and $150 per thousand names. In arranging exchanges, however, your broker will charge you a small fee of between $10 and $15 per thousand names to handle all the paperwork and phone calls.

WHAT THE LIST BROKER DOES

To earn his or her commission, a list broker does the following for you:

1. Recommends lists for a specific mailing that will have the highest probability of success.
2. Obtains approval of your package by the list owners.
3. Clears a date when you are entitled to mail.

Exhibit 3–1 Sample List Card

80,662 Donors **(1)**	$80/M **(2)**	DATE: **(3)** Xxxxxx

Tree Huggers United

Protecting our environment is the motivation that compels these donors to give. Our natural resources are important to these contributors, who have given anywhere from $5 to very large sums to express their concern for our planet.

This list has been quite successful for other appeals besides conservation, and could bring a high response rate and large average gift for your organization too.

Mail dates must be requested well in advance.

Sample mailing piece required for new mailers only.

SOURCE: **(4)**
100% Direct Mail

AVERAGE GIFT: **(5)**
$21.50

MINIMUM ORDER: **(6)**
5,000

SELECTION: **(7)**
State/scf/ZIP $3 M

KEY CODING: **(8)**
$1.50 M — 5 digits

ADDRESSING FORMAT: **(9)**
- 4-up Cheshire
- Mag tape — $25 charge if not returned in 60 days.
- Pressure-sensitive labels

DATE LAST CLEANED:
Xxxxx

(1) **Quantity:** After taking a 5,000 sample for a test, make sure the list is large enough to roll out to. (If it is three times the size of the original test, you can roll out only once in the next six months. If it is 10 times the test size, you can roll out between two and three times depending on the size of your rollout).

(2) **Cost per Thousand Names:** The best fundraising lists are expensive. At publication, 2001 list rentals ranged from $85 to $150 per thousand (M) names, with a typical good fundraising list around $85. Additional per thousand costs of between $2.50 and $5 are charged for special selects, such as females only, last 12-month donors, state, ZIP, dollar amount, etc.

(3) **Date List Card Was Produced:** Indicates how recent the information is.

(4) **Source:** This shows how list was compiled. 100 percent direct mail is the very best. If the source is other than mail, discuss with your broker those mailers for whom the list has worked.

(5) **Average Gift:** If it is below the average you are seeking, test cautiously.

(6) **Minimum Order:** A 5,000 minimum order is the industry standard. A few lists require a 10,000 sampling and a few will allow 3,000.

(7) **Selection:** This describes special selects possible and the per M charge for each. (In other words, on the list shown, you could order "Conservation Donors" in the state of New York only for a small additional charge.)

(8) **Key Coding:** May be done by your merge/purge house. Otherwise this is the per M charge to imprint your mailing key on the label. (Note number of digits allowed.)

(9) **Addressing Format:** This describes the various formats in which the list can be delivered to you and notes special charges, if any.

Some list cards also describe the gender breakout of the list (e.g., 60 percent women) and whether exchanges (rather than rentals) can be arranged. In addition, if a list has been cleaned recently, this usually is stated.

4. Issues written orders to list owners, with confirmation copies to you.
5. Follows up with owners if lists do not arrive as scheduled.
6. Sends invoices.
7. Helps evaluate list performance and—based on those results—makes recommendations for new lists to use in your continuation mailing.

Most list brokers can do the above, and do it fairly well. But the really good broker does far, far more—truly earning his or her 20 percent commission—and then some!

Of the hundreds of list brokers in the country, very few specialize in fundraising lists and the rest have limited, if any, fundraising experience at all. So to begin, you need a broker who specializes in fundraising lists. A list of such brokers can be found in Appendix F.

Even within the specialty of fundraising, many brokers have carved out categories of expertise in particular fields, such as:

- civil rights
- Jewish causes
- conservation and the environment
- health and welfare
- hospitals
- social action
- museums and cultural institutions

Thus, if yours is a membership organization in the environmental field, you would do well to ask your new broker about his or her experience in your area.

WHY THE LIST BROKER IS INDISPENSABLE

Let's face it! The broker knows far, far more about lists than you ever will because it is his or her only business. Your knowledge of a list is usually limited to the brief description printed on the list data cards. In addition to providing a brief profile of what the list represents, the list card tells you the size (universe) of the list, the cost per thousand names to rent, whether the list can be exchanged, the range of memberships or contributions included (e.g., whether the list represents $100 and over donors or donors giving less than $5), and the source of the list (direct mail or otherwise). When you think about it, that's not an awful lot of information. But it's all the information the list manager wants you to have because, in most cases, he or she has an investment in protecting the real name or source of the list, as well as other pertinent information.

On the other hand, the broker knows the following, in addition to what the list card tells you:

- Other organizations for whom the lists works
- Other organizations for whom it does not work
- Which segments of the list work best
- The type of appeal and special offers that make the list work best
- The time of year when the list works best
- Whether the list is truly clean (undeliverable addresses removed and new names added)

You also benefit from the broker's knowledge (which he or she will not or cannot reveal to you) of the following:

- Whether the list owner stacks first-time rentals with the best names
- If the list owner is a prompt shipper, or whether your list order is more than likely to arrive late
- The actual name of the organization behind the improbable-sounding one shown on the list card (in the cases of compiled lists)

Last but not least, the broker's entire business is set up to:

- Check the very latest results of organizations that used the lists you are scheduling.
- Get immediate clearance dates and confirmations.
- Follow up on late list arrivals and do something to expedite their prompt dispatch.
- Placate the idiosyncrasies of the list owners.
- Keep track, where names are exchanged between organizations on a continuing basis, of who owes whom what.

QUESTIONS A LIST BROKER NEEDS ANSWERED

The list broker will ask you many of the same questions a direct mail consultant would ask:

- What does your organization do?
- Who, other than direct beneficiaries, does your program help?
- How many people support your organization financially? How was your list built? (Word of mouth? direct mail? telephone? benefits? door-to-door? etc.)

- Is your database in-house? If so, what is it? If not, who has it?
- Are you willing to exchange your active names?
- Are you offering memberships? What are the basic dues and what are the benefits of membership? If a charity, what is the average gift to your organization? Some lists and offers pull much higher size gifts than others. It's important to have realistic expectations.
- If direct mail has been used in the past, what lists and packages were used and what were the results?

For those new to the mail as well as those who have been mailing since the invention of the envelope, we cannot overstress the importance of sharing results with your broker. Show these professionals samples of the packages that were used. Tell them about the tests that were conducted, the mail date(s), the type of postage used, and so on.

Give your list broker a copy of the list and package analysis that shows, in terms of percent return, average gift and percentage of cost recovered, which lists and packages worked, and which did not. The more information the broker has to construct the "crystal ball," the more successful your campaign will be.

Finally, your broker will request a copy of your 501(c)3 status authorizing you to mail at the special nonprofit rate. The broker will also need a sample of the letter you wish to send (for arranging list exchanges with other nonprofit organizations).

HOW MANY BROKERS SHOULD YOU USE?

We advise novices working without a consultant to work with several brokers until it becomes clear which is providing the best service, the most productive recommendations, and, last but not least, in whom they have the greatest degree of trust. In the long run, we usually recommend that an organization settle on one broker.

Here's why:

1. The exclusive broker will be able to become thoroughly familiar with your organization's strengths and weaknesses, strategies, offers, marketing plans, past successes and failures, etc. Thus, he or she will be able to make recommendations that go beyond the obvious.

2. The exclusive broker naturally is going to work harder for you, and that dedication will pay off in the long run.
3. The more the broker has at stake in making recommendations, the more he or she will research and follow up on those recommendations.
4. The exclusive broker—by virtue of being able to deliver volume orders to a list owner—is in a stronger bargaining position to negotiate the best possible terms and concessions for you.
5. The exclusive broker makes your work easier because you will not have to keep track of "who placed which order."
6. Many list brokers also offer list management services: If you have an exclusive list broker, you can often use their services for free.

Frequently, when an organization with previous direct mail experience goes to a fundraising consultant or to a new list broker, it is because the organization has hired a new development director or membership director.

The new employee, anxious to improve on his or her predecessor's record, consults with a firm or a broker prior to plunging into a campaign. But too often, these new employees—in misguided haste to prove themselves—wave aside as unimportant any past records and insist that the consultant start from scratch.

TESTING LISTS AND QUANTITIES

Most lists are available on minimum orders of 5,000 names.

Thus, if you test 75,000 pieces, you will use 15 lists of 5,000 names each. But when you plan your continuation mailings, you can use increasingly larger quantities of each original test list that worked. This is why it's good to test large lists—there is somewhere to go after the test phase.

But be cautious, especially in the beginning, until you really get to know and understand how each list works. For example, on a list that worked exceptionally well for you in the test mailing (say, it performed at a 2 percent return), your inclination might be to take the entire list on a rollout, or at least half of it. Don't do it! There are numerous cases where a list worked beautifully on a test but when rolled out, unexplainably lost money. Here is a safe alternative.

Each time you make an acquisition mailing, you can safely increase the quantity of each list by multiples of three. For example, on a good list that totals

100,000 you might first test 5,000, then 15,000, then 45,000, then go for the whole 100,000.

For a much larger list of over 100,000, be sure that all the names are *active* members or donors. You don't want to exchange or rent any names with unrealistic expectations.

Why, everyone always wants to know, do good test results sometimes go sour? Does the list owner "salt" the first order to get you to come back for more names? We would like to say that never happens, but we know that, very occasionally, it does. Therefore, it is always best to be cautious. When the first 5,000 names are given to you exactly as ordered—a pure random "nth select" across all categories of giving and across the entire nation—a rollout still can be disappointing because:

- The list had not been recently cleaned.
- Timing of the rollout is wrong, the situation has changed, or other causes have grabbed the spotlight.
- Competing mailers did not stick to their assigned mail dates. As a result their appeals arrived at the same time yours did.
- You changed your package or eliminated key elements responsible for its past success without testing.
- The list owner's computer bureau did not keep a record of the names used in the test and included them in your rollout order.

There are other reasons to reuse and retest lists other than those that performed at the very top level. The better lists make you look good, to be sure, but what are you going to do when those sources of new names dry up—after you have mailed to them again and again?

Surely you don't want to wait until then to start testing other lists. If you are serious about finding out who your potential constituents are, never stop the process of retesting marginal lists and testing promising new lists. But remember, only 25 to 35 percent of any list scheduled for a rollout should be to new, as yet untested lists.

IMPORTANT THINGS TO KNOW WHEN ORDERING LISTS

Order Lists in Advance

Too often, a new mailer will concentrate all of his or her energies on developing the package, and leave the selection of the lists until the last moment—only to find that the best lists are unavailable on the mail dates planned.

Good lists are in heavy demand; thus it is wise to place your orders as far in advance as possible. This is especially true of exchange lists because often these list owners allow only limited use (sometimes as few as 10 exchanges a year). Because of such use limitations, the wise mailer will order exchange lists up to six months in advance although lead time of two months is sufficient to obtain most lists. Commercial lists have an altogether different usage policy and it is often possible to get mail dates for such lists only weeks in advance.

But until you are a highly experienced mailer with an encyclopedic knowledge of list timetables, your broker will tell you it's best to order all lists as far in advance as possible.

Keep Your Mail Date

Mail dates are scheduled by list owners not for their benefit, but for yours. When you contract for a mail date, you have the list owner's assurance that the names you are renting or exchanging are not being used by another mailer at the same time. Failure to keep your mail date jeopardizes the success of your mailing—especially if the mailer next in line is a competitor.

If, for reasons out of your control, you cannot mail within the week allotted to you, contact your broker to see whether the following week is available. If it is, you are in luck. If not, the broker will have to clear a new mail date for you. The bad thing about this is that the next available date may be during a period when you do not wish to mail for a variety of reasons. You may be planning a house mailing or the next available date may be in midsummer or it may go into your next fiscal year.

Missing a mail date can happen to anyone, but of all the things that can go wrong on the technical end, it is the one to be avoided most carefully. This means advance planning and diligent follow-up.

Bear in mind that if you cancel your mailing at the last moment, you have deprived the list owner of an opportunity to derive income from his or her lists during the exclusive period (or window) you reserved. In such an instance, you will be obligated to pay for running charges, and you may also be charged a cancellation fee.

Check the List before Mailing

As each list arrives, make certain it is checked (most likely by your merge/purge vendor) for the following:

- *Correct list.*
- *Correct quantity.* Regardless of the number of names you ordered, chances are you will receive just under or over that amount. Should you receive 5 percent more or less than the ordered amount, your broker can obtain a credit. (Proof can be verified by submitting the count that is supplied at the end of each label or tape run.)
- *Correct ZIP selection.* If you have ordered the list on a random across-the-board select (called an "nth select"), be sure the ZIP codes you obtain correspond to the order. Similarly, if you have required that certain ZIPs be omitted or have ordered selected ZIPs, be sure that is what you receive. An error here can be fatal to a targeted geographic or demographic campaign.

THE VALUE OF EXCHANGED LISTS

If you had exchanged your list with say, eight other organizations, giving each of the eight 10,000 names in exchange for like names from their lists, you now would have 80,000 excellent prospect names to mail minus the duplicates discovered on a merge/purge (say, 20 percent). Let us now assume that these 64,000 names brought in an average return of 1 percent and a $20 average gift. You would have gained 640 new supporters, and earned $12,800 *without investing some $6,500 in rental charges.*

Despite obvious financial advantages, some not-for-profits remain reluctant to exchange lists. They typically say:

- Our donors will be bothered by other appeals.
- Our donors will be bothered by other appeals and will be angry with us for giving out their names.
- Our donors will be bothered by other appeals and will be angry with us for giving out their names and will write us nasty letters or even call.
- Our donors will be bothered by other appeals and will be angry with us for giving out their names and will write us nasty letters or even call. ***And they will stop giving to us.***

- They will give to other nonprofits *instead* of to us.

Yes, your donors will receive appeals from organizations with which you exchange names. In fact, they are already receiving such appeals. Whether these appeals "bother" your donors is a matter of debate.

Most direct mail donors enjoy receiving mail. And if 1 percent or so of your donors contribute to Organization X, that indicates that not only weren't they annoyed, but that many were actually interested in the other organization as well as yours.

"Aha!" we hear some of you saying now. "That's exactly what we were worried about. They'll be giving to others instead of to us!"

But, think about it for a moment. If you had been a longtime supporter of your local children's hospital, would an appeal from a local homeless shelter (whether or not you contribute) cause you to abandon your interest in the hospital? Of course not! The primary way an organization loses a longtime donor (other than to lowered income, death, or disinterest) is by not mailing frequently enough. You endanger your own list far more by infrequent mailings than by exchanging your list. You've got to keep reminding your constituents that you're there—doing a job they believe in!

"But what about the annoyance factor?" you persist. "Once we exchanged our list as an experiment and we received a whole slew of complaints from our donors." Almost always such a "slew of complaints" is usually quite small compared to the size of the list exchange. Would 10 complaints from your file of 25,000 donors be more than you could handle? And if all 10 stopped giving as a result of their annoyance, you will lose only 10 donors compared to the 250 new donors you receive.

That said, your donors have a right to protect their names and you have an obligation to guarantee that protection. So here's what you should do. We advise clients to send all complainants a simple, straightforward letter similar to the letter shown in Exhibit 3–2.

A letter like this puts some pressure on the member (or donor) to go to the trouble of writing to you again, thus enabling you to "weed out the grumblers from the serious complainers." Most will not respond at all and you will be surprised how many will send additional contributions—often more generous than in the past. Do not fail to thank the donor promptly

Exhibit 3–2 Sample Letter To Reply to Complaint

Dear Supporter:

We are sorry you were troubled by an appeal from [Organization X]. In exchanging part of our membership list with them, it certainly was not our intent to alienate you or to break any confidences.

The reason we exchanged names is because, frankly, our donor list is suffering from normal—but nonetheless potentially devastating—attrition.

To continue providing the services in which you believe so deeply (as evidenced by your past generous support), we must locate new donors to replace those whom we lose due to death, change in financial circumstances, or a change of address.

You will be pleased to learn that as a result of exchanging lists with [Organization X], we enlisted 340 *new members* in this past mailing alone. And because this was an exchange (and not an expensive list rental), the mailing was very economical.

Moreover, supporters of [Organization X] regard our work as worthy of help, just as you and I do. That is why they too found the exchange to be successful as it brought them new members as well.

Now I realize that you may have another concern—and that is whether [Organization X] will keep you on its list and continue mailing to you. The answer is no. The only names they keep are those who respond to their mailings with a contribution. (By the same token, the only names of theirs we keep are those who sent us a contribution.)

When you think about it, it makes sense that many who are interested in the work of [Organization X] would also be interested in us (and vice versa). Because of this, we probably will arrange another exchange next year.

If you wish your name withheld from this next exchange (or from any future exchange), let us know. I have enclosed an envelope addressed directly to me. If you use it to ask that your name not be exchanged, we will program our computer to take care of this matter.

On the other hand, as you now have a better understanding of the importance of exchanging names, you have several other options:

1. When you receive an appeal from [Organization X] or any other organization with whom we exchange, you can simply throw it away.
2. You can read the appeals from these other groups to learn whether they interest you—it might be fun to judge whether our own appeals are as good. We welcome the opinions of our supporters.
3. You can use the enclosed envelope to make a special contribution to [name of your organization].

As mentioned earlier, we are losing members through death, relocation, and general attrition. This is greatly offset by the generosity of our friends who make more than one tax-deductible gift during a calendar year. I hope that you will be one of these special friends.

Regardless of your decision, thank you for your concern and interest. We're proud to call you a friend.

Sincerely yours,

for this extra gift. In fact, a telephone call in this instance might be just the ticket!

In addition, you should ask your members/donors whether they would prefer that you not exchange their name and address. The Direct Mail Association suggests that this be done at least annually. See Appendix D for more information.

But if the "serious complainer" still wants his or her name protected from exchange, comply immediately by flagging the name on your computer with a no-exchange code.

STILL UNCONVINCED ABOUT EXCHANGING?

If, after these arguments, you are still reluctant to exchange, consider this fact. An estimated 85 percent of nonprofit organizations have been exchanging the names of their under $100 supporters with each other, for many years with little ill effect. In fact, the lists of most of these organizations were built through the practice of exchange. And so it remains today.

One final thought. If you aren't exchanging your list base in the belief that you are protecting your donors from other appeals, think twice. For most organizations, only a tiny percentage of their list truly is unique—i.e., their donors alone. So if 5 percent of your list is unique, 95 percent contribute to one or more other organizations and are therefore already on many other lists that are continually being rented and exchanged. Your own list was built, in part, through use of these names. There is just no such thing as protecting your donors. What's more, most of them are perfectly able to protect themselves. They have wastebaskets of their own.

HOW MERGE/PURGE WORKS

Because list exchanges are so common between not-for-profit organizations of like ilk, the chance of exchanging a list with a high rate of duplication is growing rapidly. That is why today, charities almost always use a deduplication process (commonly called merge/purge) for all acquisition mailings.

The merge/purge process is looking for the possibility of exact duplicates between your house file and prospect lists (and between all prospect lists) so that the intended recipient receives only one copy of the letter and so that none of your own donors receives even one copy of the prospect letter.

The process, even when done by the very best merge/purge houses, is not infallible. This section won't go into detail on how the process works. It will tell you, however, that the process reads in backward from the ZIP code, through the state, city, and street address, to the name. Thus, if your boss's mother-in-law has two residences (say, one in Connecticut and one in Florida) the merge/purge will not deduplicate her because she appears to be two separate people. And she might well be.

The merge/purge process assigns one record of one name and address to the file you will mail, not including names that already appear on your house file. Duplication rates for long-term mailers can be as high as 70 percent, but more generally are 25 percent or below.

When prospect lists are duplicated with each other, the process must assign the record to one of the lists on which it is duplicated. To give each list its fair chance at success, the process usually ascribes the duplicated records randomly among lists so that each list receives some of the duplicates.

In addition to the deduplication process, the merge/purge company keeps a separate tape consisting of one record each of originally duplicated names. The fact that the names are duplicated means that the donor contributes to one, two, three, or more charities and these can be your very best prospects.

It has become commonplace for a mailer to send the "dupe" names or multidonors, or "multis," about three weeks after the original mailing. While this tacit agreement is not written into your list orders, it has become so routine that list owners ignore the practice, and the results of the "multi" mailing often yield better results than other lists. It also helps make up for the fact that you originally paid for the full list. For more information, see the merge/purge section in Chapter 12.

HOW TO MAIL "MULTIS"

If you mail the "dupes," you have the option of sending them the same package that they received the first time (on the theory that repetition is a good thing), or if you have more than one control package, you can send the alternative package. Be sure to code these "dupes" to keep records on how well they perform, just as you would with any other list.

GUARDING AGAINST LIST THEFT

Until recently, most list owners would not ship lists directly to the organization using them. Rather, all magnetic tapes (or labels) were shipped to a third party—in most cases, the mail house or lettershop employed by the intended user.

This precaution against list theft has relaxed considerably over the past several years as methods for "salting" or "seeding" lists have become more sophisticated.

The isolated instances of list theft that do occur almost always are perpetrated by an organization's own employee(s), and even that is rare. Even beginners know that all professionally maintained lists include decoy names, which help track the use of the lists and help guard against theft. The chances of getting caught and prosecuted are extremely high.

List theft is low on your list of things to worry about in direct mail fundraising. However, if you have not done so already, we do caution you to take steps to protect your list.

In salting or seeding your list, it's not sufficient simply to insert the names of your staff members at their home addresses. Should a thief be intent on stealing your list, these names are precisely what he or she would look for and remove. Instead, or in addition to, place bogus names at the addresses of trusted associates, friends, and relatives. Or spell real names incorrectly. For example, if your name is Mary Hendler, the postal carrier will almost certainly realize that a letter addressed to M.W. Wendler at the same address is intended for you. But how would a list thief know to look it up under "W"? If you still don't feel secure using your home address on the chance that the thief would look it up (remember, he or she would have to look up the home addresses of all the staff members), we suggest you subscribe to a special service.

One of these is the U.S. Monitor Service. A monitor service operates through dummy names and addresses scattered through the country. Regardless of the segment of your list that is exchanged or rented, decoys will be included in your list order. These decoys are mailed to the appropriate address, collected, and mailed back to the service's home office, then forwarded to the list owner (you).

The list owner should then check two things: (1) that the organization mailing the package was authorized to do so, and (2) that the mailer kept the mail date that was cleared by the broker.

Chapter 4
Creating the Acquisition Appeal

CHAPTER OUTLINE

- Before You Write the Acquisition Letter
- How Much Money Should You Ask For?
- Members or Donors?
- Strategizing the Acquisition Package
- Acquisition Letter-Writing Basics
- How People Read Your Letters
- Getting Younger Donors

Acquisition mailings (also called prospect mailings) are designed to enlist the support of brand new members or donors. If your lists are well chosen and your cause is compelling, your letter and your cause will rarely be "junk mail" to the recipient. He or she is likely to be interested in the cause, but not yet familiar with or interested in your particular organization. Your job in the acquisition letter is to make the prospect believe that by giving money to your organization, his or her money is better spent than by giving it to someone else. And if you convince him or her that you bring unique qualifications and solutions to the problem, you just may gain a new donor. Even if he or she already gives to a similar cause, he or she may support you, believing it to be worthy of additional support.

BEFORE YOU WRITE THE ACQUISITION LETTER

There are a number of things you must do in preparing for an acquisition mailing. Let us assume that you have accomplished most of them, but let's name each one just to make sure:

- You have determined who will sign the fundraising letter and by whom copy must be approved—hopefully only four people— you, your boss, the letter signer (if a different person), and the program person who will read for factual material (and not for style).
- You have hired a writer and artist.
- You have obtained price quotes for copy, art, printing, lettershop, and merge/purge, and

have budgeted standard costs for lists and postage. (See Chapter 11 for more information on production.)
- You have discussed and booked your prospect lists through a good list broker specializing in fundraising. Moreover, you have scheduled the mailing to allow sufficient time to get everything done and to mail at an agreed-upon date. (See Chapter 3 for more information on lists.)
- You have registered with the attorneys general in all of the states into which you are mailing that require registration. (See Appendix C for more on state registrations.)

And there is still more.

HOW MUCH MONEY SHOULD YOU ASK FOR?

Probably the most important challenge in constructing an acquisition appeal isn't the quality of the copy, but the amount of money asked for. The initial ask (or basic dues for a membership organization) is a critical element in determining the success or failure. Ask for too little, you'll get it. Ask for too much and you won't. It's as simple as that.

If you are just starting a mail campaign, you may wish to test your entry-level gift (the smallest amount that you hope to receive as a donation or the lowest level of membership). The most common entry level asks are $20 and $25. If you conduct a two-way test, you should look for a minimum 5 percent differential in returns to prove a winner. Ten percent is more accurate still, and for that reason, tests are usually confined to a 50-50 split between the lowest and highest numbers.

There is some evidence indicating that certain types of causes can more easily seek and get a higher gift than others. For example, health, religious, and animal charities tend to get lower gifts; social action causes get medium-size entry gifts; and organizations in the arts and higher education get the largest gifts. However, organizations that typically receive a lower average gift tend to produce a higher response rate and those that get a higher average produce a lower response rate. This theory can and has been challenged, but continues to hold true.

There is also the matter of whether to ask for higher additional gift levels and whether to offer benefits or premiums. This will be discussed later in this chapter and throughout the book. For now, remember that the amount one asks for in the initial acquisition sets the tone of the relationship and dictates future gift giving.

MEMBERS OR DONORS?

After you have finalized how much to ask for, you must determine whether you want donors or members.

People who think of themselves as donors have lower expectations as to what they should receive than members have. Most charitable appeals are donor oriented. After all, it is difficult to imagine "joining" a children's hospital, a homeless shelter, or an Alzheimer's disease research organization. Or is it? If you put the words "friends of" before the name of the hospital, shelter, or research organization, it is possible to convert a donor organization into a membership organization.

If you lean toward "membership," you must decide whether to issue membership cards and pins and whether to have a newsletter. You are advised to have a newsletter regardless of which route you take in order to bond with your donors. However, cards and pins are not recommended unless your cause is also a movement, such as "Mother's March To Find a Cure," in which case "membership" seems appropriate.

The advantage of membership is that you can capture the joiners with simple renewal notices and also send appeals for money above and beyond membership dues. Some organizations such as cultural institutions are positioned just right for memberships. If you can offer benefits such as free parking, dining room privileges, discounts, special tours, etc., you should probably go the membership route and issue cards that are indeed valuable.

If you have no tangible benefits to offer, and it doesn't make sense to issue benefits, then don't. You can be a donor organization and still use "renewal language" to recapture your donor the following year. For example, you can word copy this way: "We don't take you for granted, but we do count on your renewed support each and every year."

STRATEGIZING THE ACQUISITION PACKAGE

By hiring a professional who has experience writing fundraising copy, you are off to a good beginning. The letters that organizations and causes send out asking for money are unique. They are different from foundation proposals or case statements in that they use short, emotional words; focus on dramatic situations; and almost always pull at heartstrings. If they are similar to anything, it is to political campaign speeches. As a matter of fact, if you close your eyes as you listen to a well-delivered campaign speech, you can actually hear the underlining, the dashes, the ellipses, and the parenthetical clauses. In a really good fundraising letter, you even know when to applaud.

You should provide your writer with a great deal of information (both verbal and written) as well as photographs and testimonials from people you have helped. You should also give thought to the type of appeal this will be and the strategy you might employ. There are many "types" of acquisition appeals and some of them (with modification) are appropriate for house appeals or renewals. Exhibit 4–1 lists different types of acquisition packages, reprinted with the permission of each not-for-profit organization represented.

Celebrity Appeals

I am not usually enamored with celebrity letter signers although celebrities hold an esteemed place in advertising and, on the charitable side, in special events. But rarely do people who give through direct mail attend galas. And party lists rarely attract direct mail donors. Again, different strokes for different folks. Even famous doctors, politicians, journalists, or statesmen don't always work. The main thing that "works" is a strong connection to the cause. For

Exhibit 4–1 Types of Acquisition Appeals

Package Type	Represented By
1. Celebrity Signer	The Jane Goodall Institute
2. Separate Audiences for One Cause	United States Holocaust Memorial Museum
3. Front-End (namesticker) Premium)	ASPCA (American Society for the Prevention of Cruelty to Animals)
4. Membership Benefits	Smithsonian/National Museum of the American Indian
5. Temporary Membership Card	United States Holocaust Memorial Museum
6. Back-End Premiums	Central Park Conservancy
7. Capital Campaign	National Japanese American Memorial
8. Children's Cause	Ronald McDonald House
9. Local Appeal	Community Council for the Homeless at Friendship Place

example, Senator Daniel Inouye is a credible spokesperson for the Japanese American community, whether for the National Japanese American Memorial in Washington, DC, or the Japanese American National Museum in Los Angeles, California. It's a small community and the people in it are very proud of the senator.

There are, however, a few causes that probably wouldn't be successful in the mail if they didn't have a credible celebrity involved. One with whom I worked for a number of years is the Jane Goodall Institute (for wild chimpanzees). There are so many wildlife organizations in this country that the competition is fierce. And those who specialize in only one type of animal are rarely successful in building a sizeable constituency. Had a mythical "Save the Chimpanzees" organization asked whether they could succeed in the mail, I would have said "no" and certainly wouldn't have taken them on as a client. But Jane Goodall was not just any celebrity. She had achieved revered status having "walked the walk" in saving wildlife. Thus it seemed that membership success in direct mail was, for the Institute, almost certain.

The Jane Goodall Institute package included here shows once again that photographs of animals are winners (Exhibit 4–2). The carrier envelope showed a sad baby chimpanzee with the caption, "Does It Matter What Happens to This Baby?" Apparently, it mattered to many as it worked extremely well. So too did the use of a photo of Dr. Goodall as a baby playing with a toy chimp.

Several other things accounted for the success of this direct mail launch, and they should be noted. First, the letter couples Dr. Goodall's lifelong research with personal stories about her involvement with chimps. (Remember, it is important to talk more about the people or animals an organization helps than about the organization itself.) Second, a special offer reduced the cost of annual membership from $30 to $20, for which one received membership benefits including a free chimpanzee poster.

We cannot say precisely why most celebrities fail to work in direct mail, but we can hypothesize. The main reason most people do not give is that celebrities without a strong connection to the cause seem to somehow taint the credibility of the appeal. Celebrities, no matter how big, don't stand for integrity, generosity, and self-sacrifice. The exception, of course, could be having a blind celebrity crusading for a blind cause or a celebrity whose child was disabled by a drunk driver writing on behalf of an organization that works for laws to prevent driving while intoxicated. Bob Hope was such an exception in the fundraising for the Vietnam Veterans Memorial Fund. Hope, then still entertaining the troops, signed the successful appeal because no one had yet heard of it or of Jan Scruggs, the veteran who spearheaded the campaign.

A word of caution: A nonprofit cannot mail at the nonprofit postage rate if it uses the name of the letter signer alone, even if the address is that of the organization. Thus Bob Hope's name had to appear over the name, Vietnam Veterans Memorial Fund, and its address.

The following shows what is and is not permitted:

Not Permitted For Nonprofit Postage	*Permitted for Nonprofit Postage*
Bob Hope 123 Main Street Anytown, USA 00000	Bob Hope Vietnam Veterans Memorial Fund 123 Main Street Anytown, USA 00000

Exhibit 4–2 The Jane Goodall Institute (top, front of envelope; bottom, back of envelope)

Does it matter what happens to this baby?

A9603C

John Q. Sample
123 Any Street
Anytown, US   12345-6789

Jane Goodall

THE JANE GOODALL INSTITUTE

for Wildlife Research, Education & Conservation

P.O. Box 599 • Ridgefield, CT 06877

continues

Exhibit 4–2 continued

THE JANE GOODALL INSTITUTE
for Wildlife Research, Education & Conservation

Dear Friend,

Does it matter what happens to this orphaned baby chimpanzee?

I believe it matters very much. You see, I've spent more than thirty years of my life studying chimpanzees in the wild. I've gradually learned the secrets of their lives. Gained their trust. And come to appreciate and love them for who and what they are.

Over the years, I've learned that chimpanzees are like us in many ways. They can reason and solve problems. They form lasting affectionate bonds. They feel the same kind of emotions as we do. And yes, they feel pain.

That's why it's so difficult for me to look at this picture. Because I know what this little fellow has been through. This is Merlin a year after he lost his mother. He is huddled like a socially deprived human child. He has pulled hair from his legs and belly -- just one of the psychotic or abnormal behaviors that characterize such motherless babies.

Recently, six infant chimps, looking even worse than Merlin, were entrusted to our Institute by government officials who had confiscated them from Zairian hunters. It is easy for me to imagine the scene when they were captured.

An infant sleeps, secure on his mother's lap, high in the trees. Suddenly a gunshot shatters the peace of the forest. The female, mortally wounded, crashes to the ground. Her infant still desperately clings to her. She has always protected him from harm -- but now he is torn from her lifeless body.

An adult male charges from the undergrowth, racing to the aid of the screaming child. He too is shot.

The infant is doomed. His wrists and ankles are bound with wire and he is dropped into a suffocating burlap sack. Helpless, terrified, increasingly dehydrated, he is brought across the lake to Tanzania. The story was similar for all six baby chimps.

Thanks to the courage of the Tanzanian officials, the hunters were arrested. The little orphans were dazed and in shock, bewildered, grieving for their mothers. One of them died -- too hurt, too sick, to be saved despite the desperate efforts of those trying to nurse the infants back to health.

continues

Exhibit 4–2 continued

It is ironic that we humans inflict so much cruelty upon the one creature who is our closest living relative in the animal world.

"How like us are they, really?" you may ask.

Chimpanzees share, with us, over 98 percent of their genetic makeup. Their brains are more like ours than those of any other living species. There are amazing similarities in social behavior, posture and gesture, emotions and intellectual abilities.

Did you know, for example, that chimpanzees in the wild actually make tools to help gather food? Some laboratory chimps have been taught ASL -- American Sign Language. They are able to combine signs to create new words. I met one chimp, for example, who spontaneously called a cucumber a "green banana" and another who called Alka-Seltzer a "listen drink."

You'd think we would be reaching out to these remarkable animals, trying to communicate with them and learn more about them. Instead, we torture them. Kill them. Steal them. And even sell them.

Yes, some will be bought as "pets" for the home. Dressed in human clothing, for awhile they seem cute. But at adolescence they are stronger than a man. They become destructive in the house. They are confined to tiny cages, or chained by the neck. Or worse...

They may be sold to research labs. Injected with viruses and carcinogens, they live out their lives in small, sterile steel cages, without the comfort of companionship.

Other orphans are destined for "entertainment" -- ours, of course, not theirs. They are trained with the aid of lead pipes or burning cigarettes. Often their teeth are pulled so they can't bite.

Perhaps the "luckiest" ones will wind up in zoos. But for every zoo that exhibits chimpanzees in a large enclosure, many more confine their chimps in cages like prison cells. Bereft of family, deprived of love, stupefied by boredom, they soon become frustrated, apathetic and psychotic.

It is because I so often have to visit chimpanzees in these captive settings that I am trying desperately to increase public awareness of their plight. It keeps me awake at night, for the contrast between these pitiful captives and the wonderful, free beings of the African forest is stark.

continues

Exhibit 4–2 continued

They are so grateful for a little human contact and love. They reach out to me from their cages in search of a hug or a kiss. And when I turn to leave, they scream and bang the walls. I am haunted by the desperation in their eyes. When I walk away, my own eyes fill with tears.

Most tragically, all this suffering and death is being inflicted upon an animal that is already close to extinction.

When I first arrived in Africa as a young woman who wanted to study chimpanzees in the wild... there were hundreds of thousands of chimps living across the equatorial forest belt. Today, there are probably less than 250,000 in the wild.

The relentless march of human expansion is taking its toll on the chimpanzee. As forests are destroyed for human use, the population of chimpanzees has diminished to the point where it can barely sustain itself. They are hunted for food as well as for the live animal trade.

And so, although I long to continue my study in the peace of the forest, I must leave that research to my students. Chimpanzees have taught me so much, given me so much, that now I must try to pay back.

That's why I formed the Jane Goodall Institute in 1977. And that's why I'm writing you today to ask for your support.

JGI chimpanzee sanctuaries in Tanzania, Uganda and the Congo provide orphaned chimps with a place to live out their lives in peace and safety. Meanwhile, we're also working hard to improve the fate of chimpanzees held in captivity...

Our "Chimpanzoo Project" is designed to assist zoos in their efforts to improve the habitats in which chimpanzees are exhibited. We also work closely with medical research laboratories to create more humane living conditions and minimize the suffering of chimps used in scientific experiments.

Perhaps the thing I'm most proud of is that the Jane Goodall Institute works with people -- especially young Africans -- to help create a new level of respect for wildlife and the environment through our "Roots and Shoots" program.

After all, when wildlife suffers, people suffer too. That's why it's so important for us to continue providing jobs for African villagers in our sanctuaries. To attract foreign exchange through the development of responsible tourism. To create agricultural and forestry projects that will preserve chimpanzee habitats. And to discourage poaching by creating new economic opportunities.

In short, through the Jane Goodall Institute, I am working to break the cycle of abuse and slaughter that threatens to drive the chimpanzee into extinction.

But to succeed, I need your help.

continues

Exhibit 4–2 continued

In fact, from the beginning, I knew that I could not support the Institute without the love and generosity of friends throughout the world -- many of whom I have never met, but who identify with my work with chimpanzees.

I hope that you will become one of these wonderful friends by joining the Jane Goodall Institute today with a membership contribution of just $30.

When you join the Jane Goodall Institute, I will send you an official JGI poster -- free -- to display in your home, office, or classroom as a symbol of your support for wild and captive chimpanzees. And you'll enjoy a free subscription to our annual newsletter to keep you up-to-date on how your contribution is being used to protect and preserve chimpanzees.

But I know of no better way to persuade you to help than to simply ask you to take another look at Merlin.

Chimpanzees like Merlin have suffered so much already. And unless you and I act now to intervene, they will suffer even more in the future.

For the sake of all chimpanzees throughout the world, I urge you to join the Jane Goodall Institute today. Thank you, dear friend.

Sincerely,

Jane Goodall

Dr. Jane Goodall

P.S.   If you join in the next 20 days, you can take advantage of our special offer of $20 for an entire year's membership (reduced from $30) with all the same benefits including a beautiful poster. Act today!

Courtesy of The Jane Goodall Institute for Wildlife Research, Education and Conservation (1-800-592-JANE), Silver Spring, Maryland.

Separate Audiences for a Single Cause

In the original membership campaign for the United States Holocaust Memorial Museum, invitations to potential members from Jewish lists utilized different strategy than membership offers to potential members from general lists. The letter targeted to Jewish lists was signed by the Chairman of the Museum Council. It told the story of the Holocaust dramatically and carefully, recognizing that some recipients were, themselves, survivors. The letter used Hebrew phrases and described what the visitor would see when he or she visited. Originally written before the Museum opened in 1991, it stressed that the U.S. government had given the land and would provide maintenance. But it also explained that getting the building built depended entirely on private donations. Finally, the basic membership ask was a gift of $36 (representing a doubling of the lucky "chai" or "life" in Jewish culture). The current control letter for the Museum owes its great success to enclosing a special membership card and a letter to tell about it (Pages 1 and 4 of this letter are reprinted as Exhibit 4–3).

A number of benefits were offered including the permanent inscription of the member's name on the *Charter* Member Donor Roll. After the Museum opened, Charter Membership was closed. Today, only memberships are offered.

While the letter to general lists was signed by the same person who signed the Jewish appeal (and while it undoubtedly reached many Jews), the strat-egy was markedly different. It also described the Museum and offered the same benefits of member-ship. But the theme of the letter sought to make Americans proud (rather than ashamed) of America's participation in WWII. And to that end it opened by

---

Exhibit 4–3 United States Holocaust Memorial Museum, Letter #1 (pages 1 and 4 only)

UNITED STATES
HOLOCAUST MEMORIAL MUSEUM

MEMBERSHIP CORRESPONDENCE
P.O. Box 90988
WASHINGTON, DC 20090-0988

Dear Friend,

If you're like me, you carry many cards in your wallet -- charge cards, membership cards, identification cards.

But of all the cards I carry, I do have a favorite.

One simple piece of plastic that says more about me than any gold or platinum card could hope to say: it is my United States Holocaust Memorial Museum Membership Card.

Each time I open my wallet and see this card, I'm reminded that I belong to a very special community of people. Men and women who have stepped forward to help remember and memorialize the six million Jews and millions of others who died in the Holocaust -- and to warn future generations of the unspeakable horror that can result when civilization and humanity break down.

Because I think that you are the kind of person who would derive the ~~same sense of responsibility and pride that I feel as~~ a member of this Museum, I'm sending you your own United States Holocaust Memorial Museum Membership Card.

I hope you'll accept your Membership Card with my personal invitation to support the Museum today.

As a Member, you will be entitled to a number of exclusive privileges, which I will describe for you in just a moment.

But first, let me tell you more about why this Museum is so important -- and why your financial support is needed to help us honor the dead, enlighten the living, and pave the way for a better future for humankind.

The challenge for this Museum and its members is three-fold. First, we must tell the history of the Holocaust. We must preserve the memories of those whose lives were lost. And, we must preserve evidence of the atrocities so that future generations may understand what happened and keep it from occurring again.

                                        (over, please)

continues

Exhibit 4–3 continued

4

Like me, you will probably feel that the greatest benefit to joining the Museum is the pride you'll feel. In addition to this feeling, those who carry a United States Holocaust Memorial Museum Membership Card are entitled to special privileges.

First of all, when you activate your card by joining, we will send you **Members-only passes to the Museum** that admit you (or your family or friends) to the Permanent Exhibition on any day you wish. You need not call a ticket service to reserve passes, and you will not have to stand in line waiting for daily passes to be distributed.

Your Card also entitles you to a 10% discount in our Museum Shop. All Members will be listed in the Museum's permanent "Roll of Remembrance." And, additional benefits are available to Members who make larger gifts. You'll find complete details in the enclosed summary of Membership Benefits.

Even if you don't use your Card right away, I think you'll feel proud -- as I do -- just knowing it's there in your wallet.

Because in the depths of their despair, those who experienced the most unspeakable evil in history dared to hope that someone, somewhere, would listen, remember, and bear witness for them.

When you carry this Card, you are that someone. Please join us today.

Sincerely,

Miles Lerman
Chairman

P.S. The enclosed card is unlike any other you will ever carry. It won't extend your credit for material goods. But it will help you acquire something much more important: the knowledge that you are helping to teach the lessons of the Holocaust, not only to this generation, but to those that will never live in the presence of survivors. Please join us as a Member of the United States Holocaust Memorial Museum today.

continues

Exhibit 4–3 continued (outside envelope)

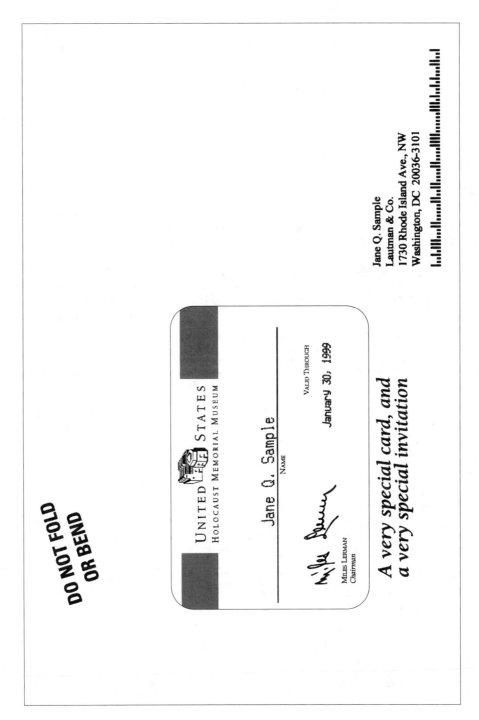

Courtesy of the United States Holocaust Memorial Museum, Washington, DC.

describing the American liberation of Nazi death camps and concentration camps. (Pages 1 and 4 of the General Letter appear in Exhibit 4–4)

The letter was accompanied by a lift letter (smaller in size and printed on different colored paper) from a man who had been a teenage soldier when he encountered the camps and how it affected him for the rest of his life. The entire package made the point that the Museum was an *American* museum and appealed to Americans' sense of fair play and democratic ideals.

Exhibit 4–4 United States Holocaust Memorial Museum, Letter #2 (pages 1 and 4 only)

UNITED STATES
HOLOCAUST MEMORIAL MUSEUM
100 RAOUL WALLENBERG PLACE, SW
WASHINGTON, DC 20024-2150

It was the testimony of American liberators that brought the Holocaust home:

"I was there. I was present. I will never forget."

-- Father Edward P. Doyle
U.S. Army Chaplain

"The same day I saw my first horror camp, I visited every nook and cranny. I felt it my duty to be in a position from then on to testify about these things in case there ever grew up at home the belief or assumption that the stories of Nazi brutality were just propaganda."

-- General Dwight D. Eisenhower

"What I saw and experienced at Dachau -- the atrocities, the cruelty -- was something which if I had not seen with my own eyes, I would not believe had happened in civilized nations. I pray to my God that this cannot happen again."

-- Douglas Kelling, M.D.
45th Infantry Division

Dear Friend,

Eisenhower knew that what he and his men told of what they saw in 1945 would be the only testimony many Americans would believe.

Thus it was that sergeants from Maine...medics from Nebraska... infantrymen from California...and a general from Kansas became not only the liberators of the Nazi camps, but the messengers of their horrors as well.

Their snapshots and diaries recorded a nightmare too horrifying to be believed, and showed us a truth too compelling to be denied. And now, 50 years later, the conscience of American citizens like you is immortalizing that truth, so its meaning will never be lost, and its relevance never forgotten.

This letter is your official invitation to take part in this once-in-a-lifetime effort, by joining thousands of Americans as a **Member of the United States Holocaust Memorial Museum.**

In a moment I will tell you why becoming a Member of this Museum will be such a rewarding experience for you. But first, let me tell you about this important national monument which opened on April 26, 1993.

Located less than 400 yards from the Washington Monument, the U.S. Holocaust Memorial Museum is one of the largest and most important Holocaust museums in the world.

Chartered by an Act of Congress, this national Museum sits on a priceless parcel of federal land. But the government did not build this Museum, nor will it provide all the funds necessary for its operation.

continues

Exhibit 4–4 continued

4

histories of hundreds of survivors. The most carefully selected collection of Holocaust evidence ever assembled in the United States.

You will make possible profound experiences of human emotion that will remain with visitors for the rest of their lives. No one who visits the Museum will be untouched. Having witnessed the nightmarish consequences of the triumph of evil, the monuments to democracy that surround each departing visitor will have new meaning, as will the ideals for which they stand.

Not since the pennies of schoolchildren erected the Statue of Liberty has our nation built such a meaningful testament to its values and ideals. It is doubtful you've ever had before, or will ever have again, an opportunity to contribute to such a profound national memorial.

Already, Americans of every faith and background have joined with us. A farmer in North Dakota sent $35. A Latino family in Colorado sent $50. A civics class in Cleveland collected $200. And the list goes on. Over 250,000 Americans from all 50 states are currently members of the United States Holocaust Memorial Museum.

Their gifts have been generous and heart-felt, but we must find many more friends in order to keep the Museum going.

Will you join us? When you become a Member for $25 or more, you'll enjoy special members only benefits, including priority distribution of same-day admission tickets to the Museum. (A full description of all benefits can be found on the Membership Acceptance Form.)

And, as our special way of saying "thank you," we will enter your name -- and a loved one's name if you wish -- on our Roll of Remembrance which will remain on permanent display in the Museum.

Fifty years ago, it took the eyewitness testimony of American liberators to make the world believe the unfathomable. Today, it requires your personal decision to preserve that testimony for all to see, experience and understand.

Please join in this historic effort today, by becoming a **Member of the United States Holocaust Memorial Museum.**

Sincerely,

Miles Lerman
Chair

P.S. While many denied the Holocaust, hundreds of photos taken by American liberators documented the truth for all time. I've enclosed photos that are similar to those permanently displayed in the Museum and a special letter from one G.I. who was there.

Courtesy of the United States Holocaust Memorial Museum, Washington, DC.

The basic membership fee requested in this appeal was $20 to encourage greater participation by non-Jews, while the benefits remained identical to the other offer.

Front-end (Namesticker) Premiums

The American Society for the Prevention of Cruelty to Animals (ASPCA) added two sheets of name and address labels to an existing control package (Exhibit 4–5). Simply by adding the labels and changing the p.s. very slightly to acknowledge their inclusion, the percent return increased dramatically. While the average gift was lowered slightly, it was not enough to offset the number of new members gained. The letter is a good example of copywriting for animal groups.

Membership Benefits

It was difficult to choose the right category in which to showcase this award-winning package for the Smithsonian's National Museum of the American Indian, first produced in 1991. However, because the original invitation is a classic membership appeal with numerous benefits (including a magazine), it was located here. The main four-page letter was signed by former secretary of the Smithsonian Institution, I. Michael Heyman. To introduce the then new director of the Museum, Richard W. West, Southern Cheyenne signed the lift note.

You are urged to look for the following in Exhibit 4–6:

- The low $20 (basic dues) "Charter Member" rate is emphasized in order to attain a high percent return. Dues of varying amounts were tested extensively before settling on $20 as having the greatest profitability ratio.
- Excellent benefits were offered, including a full color magazine, Smithsonian gift shop discounts, listing on a permanent Charter Member scroll, and more. Benefits and donor categories were emphasized again on the full color brochure. Tests with and without the brochure were conducted, with the brochure winning every time. (Brochures for nonmembership causes usually fare poorly in such tests.)
- A slightly higher dues level of $35 was also offered, promising (and delivering) a special insider's newsletter. This benefit substantially increased the average gift.

Temporary Membership Card

Temporary membership cards have been successful for many organizations including for the United States Holocaust Memorial Museum, the Central Park Conservancy, the ASPCA, and more. It is doubtful that nonmembership groups could use this approach, but it is possible.

Back-End Premiums

Sometimes membership organizations offer back-end premiums (as opposed to benefits) for joining. As you can see in Exhibit 4–7, the Central Park Conservancy in New York City offers multiple premiums for basic dues including a fold-out color map of the park, a newsletter, and a calendar of events. For dues at the second highest level, one receives all of the foregoing plus a baseball cap, and so on up to the $1,000 level, which provides attractive behind-the-scenes benefits. This package also utilizes a front end membership card that shows through the carrier window.

Capital Campaigns

The National Japanese American Memorial raised an impressive amount of money through direct mail (Exhibit 4–8). The letter described the great injustice perpetrated on the Japanese American community, and appealed to their pride in being Americans and having fought so valiantly in WWII for America. The letter is nothing like a foundation proposal for a building campaign but is as emotional as it is and practical. Note the benefits offered on page 3 of the letter. All are ways to honor the donor.

Your attention is called, in particular, to the following in the package:

- It describes the incarceration of all Japanese Americans (including American citizens) in internment camps for four years.
- It describes the heroism of Japanese American citizens (who went willingly to detention camps) and also the young men who joined the army to fight for America in WWII.
- It describes and graphically depicts the proposed Memorial in Washington, DC.
- It offers benefits, including invitations to opening ceremonies and other events as well as listing the names of donors in appropriate forums.

Exhibit 4–5 ASPCA Address Labels Combined with Response Card

 The American Society for the Prevention of Cruelty to Animals
424 East 92nd Street, New York, NY 10128 · www.aspca.org

Please Tell Us About Your Animals!
I am the proud owner of a (check all that apply):
☐ Dog ☐ Cat ☐ Other_____

YES, Roger, I want to help the ASPCA stop cruelty and save the lives of more helpless animals like Astro! Here's my membership contribution to fight animal abuse and neglect!

☐ $20 Regular Member
☐ $50 Supporting Member
☐ $100 Sustaining Member

☐ $500 Founder's Society Friend
☐ $1,000 Founder's Society Associate
☐ Other $_____

 Q Jane Q. Sample
Lautman & Company
342 Madison Avenue
New York, NY 10173-0002

Please do not peel. Tear off the reply form and return it with your check, made payable to the ASPCA, in the envelope provided. Your gift to the ASPCA is tax-deductible as provided by law.

8A99999999

DN40EM

 Q Jane Q. Sample
Lautman & Company
342 Madison Avenue
New York, NY 10173-0002

 Q Jane Q. Sample
Lautman & Company
342 Madison Avenue
New York, NY 10173-0002

 Q Jane Q. Sample
Lautman & Company
342 Madison Avenue
New York, NY 10173-0002

 Q Jane Q. Sample
Lautman & Company
342 Madison Avenue
New York, NY 10173-0002

 Q Jane Q. Sample
Lautman & Company
342 Madison Avenue
New York, NY 10173-0002

 Q Jane Q. Sample
Lautman & Company
342 Madison Avenue
New York, NY 10173-0002

 Q Jane Q. Sample
Lautman & Company
342 Madison Avenue
New York, NY 10173-0002

 Q Jane Q. Sample
Lautman & Company
342 Madison Avenue
New York, NY 10173-0002

 Q Jane Q. Sample
Lautman & Company
342 Madison Avenue
New York, NY 10173-0002

 Q Jane Q. Sample
Lautman & Company
342 Madison Avenue
New York, NY 10173-0002

 Q Jane Q. Sample
Lautman & Company
342 Madison Avenue
New York, NY 10173-0002

 Q Jane Q. Sample
Lautman & Company
342 Madison Avenue
New York, NY 10173-0002

 Q Jane Q. Sample
Lautman & Company
342 Madison Avenue
New York, NY 10173-0002

 Q Jane Q. Sample
Lautman & Company
342 Madison Avenue
New York, NY 10173-0002

 Q Jane Q. Sample
Lautman & Company
342 Madison Avenue
New York, NY 10173-0002

 Q Jane Q. Sample
Lautman & Company
342 Madison Avenue
New York, NY 10173-0002

 Q Jane Q. Sample
Lautman & Company
342 Madison Avenue
New York, NY 10173-0002

 Q Jane Q. Sample
Lautman & Company
342 Madison Avenue
New York, NY 10173-0002

Creating the Acquisition Appeal 35

Exhibit 4–5 continued

**NATIONAL MUSEUM OF
THE AMERICAN INDIAN**
Smithsonian Institution

Correspondence:
NATIONAL CAMPAIGN
PO Box 96836
Washington, DC 20090-6836
e-mail: aimember@ic.si.edu

Handle this letter carefully. Because you may be holding a powerful spirit in your hands. The spirit of brotherhood. The spirit of compassion. The spirit of understanding among all the peoples of the earth.

According to the traditional religions of many American Indian tribes, human beings aren't the only ones who have spirits inside them.

Animals, physical objects, and even the forces of nature are imbued with spirits as well. People can influence these spirits through the power of their beliefs. And by doing so, they can release potent forces capable of changing the world around them.

Is it possible the letter you are holding in your hand is imbued with just such a spirit? And if you believe sufficiently in the moral rightness of the project I am about to describe to you, is it possible you can make it come true?

Dear Friend:

I'm asking you to believe in that kind of spiritual power just long enough for me to tell you about a new Smithsonian Institution museum:

It's called the NATIONAL MUSEUM OF THE AMERICAN INDIAN. And, I'm inviting you to share in the creation of this Museum -- from the ground up -- by becoming a Charter Member today.

Established by an Act of Congress, the NATIONAL MUSEUM OF THE AMERICAN INDIAN (NMAI) is the 16th museum of the Smithsonian Institution and the <u>first</u> national museum dedicated to the history and cultures of Native Americans.

Its goal is to change forever the way Americans view the Native peoples of this Hemisphere. To correct misconceptions. To demonstrate how Indian cultures are enriching the world ... And to promote a new dialogue between Indians and non-Indians.

By visiting this Museum, Americans can learn what Indian civilization teaches us about the delicate balance between people and nature. About respect for the elderly and the importance of family. About natural healing, preservation of language, organic farming, and other timely issues.

The mission of the NATIONAL MUSEUM OF THE AMERICAN INDIAN, in other words, is perfectly in tune with the mission of the Smithsonian itself:

continues

Exhibit 4–6 continued

2

to help the American people achieve a deeper understanding of our cultural and technological heritage.

The NATIONAL MUSEUM OF THE AMERICAN INDIAN is comprised of not one, but three separate facilities. In 1994, we opened the George Gustav Heye Center, a jewel of a museum located in New York City near the Statue of Liberty and Ellis Island. Our Cultural Resources Center in suburban Maryland, which is scheduled to be completed in 1998, will serve as home to the Museum's collection. We envision this center as a state-of-the-art facility for conservation, research, and outreach.

And shortly after the end of this decade, we will open a major national Museum in our nation's capital -- next to the Smithsonian's popular National Air and Space Museum and at the foot of the U.S. Capitol.

To launch the NATIONAL MUSEUM OF THE AMERICAN INDIAN, the Smithsonian Institution has acquired the largest and most important collection of Native American art and artifacts in the world. Containing nearly one million pieces, our collection stretches in time from the prehistoric era to the present ... from the Arctic Circle to the tip of Tiera del Fuego.

Until recently, most of this magnificent collection has been stored in an antiquated warehouse in the Bronx, N.Y. But with the intervention of the Smithsonian Institution, it is being rescued, restored, and relocated. In fact, hundreds of items are already on display in our Museum in New York.

But our ultimate goal -- and the reason I'm writing you today -- is the opening of our Museum in Washington in the year 2002. Located on the last available site on our National Mall, this world-class Museum has been supported by more than 250,000 people across the country. Designed by Native American architect Douglas Cardinal, it has already earned great praise from critics and approval by the Commission of Fine Arts.

It is here that the world will finally have the chance to view Native American history and culture in the context of its own timeline. A timeline that began thousands of years before Columbus arrived in this Hemisphere and extends into the future as well.

Which brings me to an important point.

Despite what many people think, Indian cultures did not vanish with the buffalo. Like the buffalo itself, they have survived. Indian cultures thrive today in many exciting forms. And the Museum will celebrate that fact by being a living museum -- the focal point of Indian art, music, literature, dance, philosophy, and theater in the United States. In fact, the Museum will create a bridge between historical objects and more modern material, so that all are made more powerful and relevant.

Native Americans from all over the country will be encouraged to come to Washington and New York to make use of the Museum's collection, facilities, and staff support. For personal research. For religious rites. For traditional ceremonies.

And if Native Americans can't come to the Museum, the Museum will come to them.

continues

Exhibit 4–6 continued

3

Outreach efforts will be linked to a computer network combining the resources of the Museum's three facilities throughout the country and around the globe. This dynamic learning environment will expand access to the Museum's collections and exhibitions to 24 hours a day. Interactive and computer-based programs, traveling exhibitions, and audio visual materials are examples of activities already available at the Heye Center. Through community service and collaborative public programming, the Museum will serve as an important connector so that Native and non-Native communities, museums, libraries, universities, and schools can communicate more effectively among each other and with the Museum.

In this way, Native Americans can strengthen their ties to the past, even as they lay the groundwork for a more prosperous and vital future. That's why Native Americans have played a central role in planning this Museum from the very beginning ... why the inaugural exhibitions of the Museum in New York were created by Indian artists and selectors who are at last able to tell their own stories in their own words.

The Museum's Director, W. Richard West, is a member of the Cheyenne and Arapaho tribes of Oklahoma. Rick West is a prominent attorney and Stanford Law School graduate, the son of a well-known Indian artist, and an active member in many Indian cultural organizations. As such, he moves easily between two worlds.

<u>For the first time in history, a Native American is leading a national museum dedicated to the history and culture of Native peoples of this Hemisphere</u>.

I hope you share my enthusiasm for this new Museum. I hope you share my feeling that such a museum is not only morally right but long overdue.

And, I hope you'll also want to share the cost.

Thanks to a unique combination of public and private support, we have succeeded in raising the construction funds mandated in legislation enacted by Congress in 1989. <u>But a great museum must be more than just bricks and mortar</u>. And as I write this letter to you, we still have much to do before we can turn our dream into a reality ...

We must research the one million items in our collection. Move the entire collection of delicate pieces to their new home near Washington. Plan and install exhibitions for the opening of our Museum on the National Mall. Launch programs of education and outreach to Indian communities and to schools throughout the country. And much more.

Such an undertaking requires the enthusiastic support of people like you. It also requires a great deal of money.

That's why I'm writing you today to invite you to become a Charter Member of the NATIONAL MUSEUM OF THE AMERICAN INDIAN by making a personal contribution of $20 or more.

For that modest amount, you will not only have the satisfaction of being a Charter Member of this worthy effort, but you'll also be entitled to receive a number of valuable membership benefits. Among them:

continues

Exhibit 4–6 continued

4

* A subscription to <u>NATIVE PEOPLES</u>, a full-color quarterly magazine dedicated to the sensitive portrayal of the cultures and lifeways of Native Americans.

* Your name will be added to our Member and Donor Scroll, which is prominently displayed in the Great Hall of the George Gustav Heye Center in New York and, ultimately, in the Museum on the National Mall in Washington, D.C.

* A personalized membership card, which entitles you to substantial members-only discounts at all Smithsonian Museum Shops and from the Smithsonian's Mail-Order Catalogue.

* A warm and personal welcome at the first of our two NMAI Museums -- the George Gustav Heye Center in New York City. Come and see why we call this the "Museum Different," as Indian art and cultures are displayed and interpreted by <u>Indians</u> themselves. You'll also receive free admission to the Cooper-Hewitt National Design Museum, in New York City. (All other Smithsonian museums are free of charge.)

* Advance invitations to participate in NMAI outreach events and cultural programs, such as films, dances, powwows, and art shows.

* And if you can give $35 or more we'll automatically send you the <u>NMAI Runner</u> -- our insiders' newsletter on Native American projects and activities throughout the Smithsonian Institution.

Is there a voice inside you telling you it is only right and fitting that the American people build this Museum?

I suggest that what you are hearing is the voice of your spirit. The spirit of brotherhood. The spirit of compassion. The spirit of understanding among all the peoples of the earth.

Release that spirit. Let it mingle with those of thousands of other people throughout our nation. And let it further the momentum already begun to create the first national museum dedicated to Native Americans. Become a Charter Member today.

Sincerely,

I. Michael Heyman
Secretary

P.S. You can join with hundreds of thousands of people working together to build a new era of understanding. Help us preserve these important living cultures and move an incredible collection to a safe haven. There is so much still left to do, and I truly hope you'll give your full support by joining today.

Courtesy of the National Museum of the American Indian, Smithsonian Institution, Washington, DC.

continues

Exhibit 4–7 continued (reply form with tipped, on card)

000001

Here is your Central Park Conservancy Membership Card!

A7XSEDC1

Jane A. Sample
Lautman & Company
Suite 700
1730 Rhode Island Avenue
Washington, DC 20036-9999

YES . . . I want to join the Central Park Conservancy and do my part for the Park. It's up to us -- private citizens who care -- to restore, maintain, and keep our Park beautiful. I'm joining at the following membership level:

☐ **$30 Basic Member**
  ✔ Fold-out Color Map of the Park
  ✔ Newsletter with Calendar of Events

☐ **$50 Friend**
  ✔ Same as Basic Member, plus Special BASEBALL CAP

☐ **$100 Supporter**
  ✔ Same as Friend, plus Walking Tour Guide

☐ **$250 Contributor**
  ✔ Same as Supporter, plus Invitation to Park Tour led by Conservancy Staff

☐ **$500 Gardener**
  ✔ Same as Contributor, plus Invitation to Cherry Blossom Tour and Invitation to Fall Foliage Tour

☐ **$1,000 Belvedere Knight**
  ✔ Same as Gardener, plus Listing in the Annual Report and Invitations to events such as: Gala Benefits, "Windows on the Park" Cocktail Party, Family Ice-skating Party, and other special events and tours

☐ **Other $**

Central Park Conservancy

14 East 60th Street • New York, NY 10022
www.centralparknyc.org

If you want to charge your membership gift to your credit card, please see reverse.
Make your tax-deductible check payable to the Central Park Conservancy and return it along with this form
in the enclosed envelope, or mail it to: Central Park Conservancy, Box 5204, GPO, NY, NY 10087-5204.

continues

Exhibit 4–7 continued (letter, page 1 only)

Put on our cap...use our map
to find your way...
take a walk through Central Park today

Dear Friend,

Have you strolled through Central Park lately? You really should …

… because it's a wonderful place to be – again!

As you may remember, by 1979, Central Park – once New York's crown jewel – had deteriorated into a monumental disgrace.

In those days, trees were dying from neglect. Lawns were bare and brown. Benches and buildings had become vandalized ruins covered with graffiti. Lakes were choked with weeds and mud.

But, in 1980, a group of caring citizens formed the Central Park Conservancy to try to save it.

As the Chairman of the Conservancy's Board of Trustees, I am writing to ask you to join us.

Over the past 20 years, the Conservancy has restored much of the Park. We are responsible for all the care and maintenance of its greenery, buildings, and waters.

Today, our private, non-profit organization performs the work which keeps Central Park beautiful.

We seed, plant, irrigate, weed, and mow the Park's hundreds of acres of lawns, meadows, ballfields, and gardens.

Just look around the Park to see what we've accomplished …

The canopy of trees is burgeoning with renewed life … you can rest on repaired and painted benches … the ponds sparkle … and, if you see any graffiti, you can be sure that it will be removed within 48 hours.

What is especially thrilling is that this truly remarkable rebirth of our City's lovely green refuge has come about due to …

Central Park Conservancy • 14 East 60th Street • New York, NY 10022
www.centralparknyc.org
Recycled Paper

Courtesy of the Central Park Conservancy, New York, New York.

Exhibit 4–8 National Japanese American Memorial (all 4 pages)

NATIONAL JAPANESE AMERICAN MEMORIAL FOUNDATION

Dear Friend:

It has been over fifty years since more than 100,000 Japanese Americans were forced to leave their homes, their businesses, and their lives to be incarcerated in U.S. prison camps for the crime of "looking like the enemy."

Fifty long years.

Fifty years while these Americans, so unjustly treated in WWII, have waited for their patriotism to be acknowledged. Years in which aging veterans – many of them members of the most highly decorated military unit of its size in U.S. history – have waited to be honored by a country that abounds with memorials to its other veterans and war heroes.

Today, that wait is nearly over. Soon we will dedicate a memorial in our nation's capital to honor Japanese American Patriotism in World War II. A memorial that will serve as a permanent reminder that the democratic principles on which this nation was founded must be zealously guarded, particularly in times of national crisis.

This Memorial is the result of an unprecedented action in which the U.S. Congress passed a public law (PL 102-502) authorizing construction of the National Japanese American Memorial on land donated by the federal government.

While the Memorial will be visited by many Japanese American tourists, we know that because of its prominent location, thousands more will visit each year as "accidental tourists" – people who know little or nothing about Japanese Americans, our history, or the story of how shamefully we were treated during WWII. Yet it is these very tourists who, because of our Memorial, may come to a new understanding of the fragility of freedoms they take for granted.

<u>But this Memorial will not happen without your help</u>. While the U.S. government has given us a prominent tract of land near our nation's Capitol, and we have already raised the $8.6 million needed to break ground on October 22, 1999, we must still raise additional money to meet all obligations, including costs of administration, fund raising, and the dedication ceremony itself. This money will also pay for an all important education and outreach program once the Memorial is completed.

Let us describe this special Memorial to you.

The Memorial will occupy a triangular park of approximately 35,000 square feet bounded by

(Over, please)

1920 N STREET, NW SUITE 660   WASHINGTON, DC 20036
(202) 861-8845 *phone* (202) 861-8848 *fax*

continues

Exhibit 4–8 continued

2

Louisiana and New Jersey Avenues and D Street NW. It is a prominent space, just 600 yards from our nation's Capitol.

The unique design concept by architect Davis Buckley, with advice from several Japanese American architects, will tell a complex story with elegant simplicity.

Spoken through the materials of bronze, stone and water, the Memorial's message will focus on the fragility of our Constitutional rights in a democratic society and portray the story of Americans of Japanese Ancestry.

Surrounded by cherry blossom trees, the Memorial will have at its center a magnificent 14-foot bronze sculpture of two cranes – symbols of happiness, good fortune and freedom. The right wings of both cranes are held flush to the marble base by a strand of barbed wire, while the birds grasp the wire in their beaks in an attempt to free themselves. Both left wings, fully extended, reach toward the sky, symbolizing the struggle for freedom and the injustice of oppression.

Evocative landscaping and curved walls guide visitors through inscriptions and critical historical information (including a complete list of the 850 Japanese American soldiers killed in action in WWII) to the crane sculpture, and finally to a reflecting pool. Six symbolic rocks will create an atmosphere of quiet contemplation, allowing visitors to reflect upon three generations of Japanese Americans. At the same time, the rocks invite contemplation of the principles on which America is founded.

The Memorial's design and location have received enthusiastic praise not only from Washington's leading architectural critics, but also from the National Capital Memorial Commission, the National Capital Planning Commission and the National Commission of Fine Arts.

And here's the best part. Once the Memorial is built, the site itself will be maintained in perpetuity by the United States Park Service, just as it cares for the

(Next page, please)

Exhibit 4–8 continued

3

Vietnam Veterans Memorial, The Korean Veterans Memorial, the Lincoln and Washington Memorials, and other national memorials.

Now, we recognize that, like us, you may be supporting the Japanese American National Museum in Los Angeles or a memorial to Japanese American soldiers and war heroes in your own community. We urge you to continue that important support and congratulate you for it. But this particular Memorial in the heart of our nation's capital also deserves your support at this critical time.

Can we count on your help? We're hoping for thousands of gifts at the $35 and $50 level, and gifts of $100 will be a tremendous boost. And if you can afford an even more substantial gift, we will be grateful.

In addition to gratitude, the Foundation wishes to honor your participation in a more tangible way. That is why you will be kept informed of our progress ... and why, for a gift of $100 or more, we will place your name as a Charter Supporter on our <u>permanent</u> web site. If you can give $1,000 or more, we will send you a framable Certificate of Appreciation commemorating your exceptional support.

And we've saved the best for last. All donors will be listed in an easy-to-use Memorial Almanac to be published in conjunction with the dedication of the Memorial. This historic almanac, which will be offered to you as a Charter Member before it goes on sale to the general public, is certain to become an important document in your family, signifying that you helped to build this Memorial to patriotism.

This almanac will not only feature your name as a donor, it will be lavishly illustrated with photographs and drawings and will capture significant historical events. Among them will be the history of the internment of Japanese Americans ... the history of the heroism of the 100th/442nd regimental combat team in WWII ... the largely untold story of the Military Intelligence Service ... a guide to all Japanese American memorials throughout the U.S. ... and the story of how our ancestors contributed to Japanese American society.

When you take out your checkbook to send a gift of <u>any amount</u>, you will be helping to say "thank you" to the Japanese American soldiers who fought and died in defense of our country.

Your gift will also honor the courage and patriotism of the thousands of men, women and children who endured internment camps, as well as the Hawaiians who, though not imprisoned, endured prejudice and suspicion throughout WWII.

<u>All of these people have been waiting a very long time. And because time is not something they have a lot of, yours may be the last generation to live in their presence.</u>

(Over, please)

continues

Exhibit 4–8 continued

4

Your gift will also acknowledge the integrity of our nation for admitting **the great wrong** committed in the hysteria of war … for its apology through the Civil Liberties Act of 1988 … and for making this Memorial possible.

This is a cause behind which we can all unite. This Memorial will have an important meaning not only to the Issei, to whom we are deeply indebted ... not only to the generations of Japanese Americans who followed ... but to all Americans. It will forever be a symbol of our determination to heal the injustices of WWII – principally the injustice of withholding freedom from any ethnic minority. The very freedom America's own sons and daughters fought to protect.

It is also our nation's promise that we will never allow it to happen again.

Please send your tax-deductible gift today, and please be generous.

Sincerely,

Melvin H. Chiogioji
Board Chairman

Norman Mineta
Deputy Board Chairman

George Aratani
Senior Board Advisor

P.S.   Although we have the money in hand to proceed with groundbreaking, we have not yet completed our campaign. Won't you help us reach our final goal by sending a gift today?

Courtesy of the Japanese American National Museum, Los Angeles, California.

Children's Causes

The illustrated acquisition sample here is for New York City's Ronald McDonald House of New York (Exhibit 4–9). The logo is a child's drawing of a house with a heart and the copy reads "The House That Love Built," also in a child's handwriting. The story focuses on a mother who suddenly needs an affordable place to stay with her small daughter who has been diagnosed with cancer. Because Ronald McDonald House of New York offers "hotel-type" services for only $20 per night, the minimum ask was set at $20. (Perfect!) The copy about childhood cancer is frank but not maudlin, and is an excellent example of showing what an institution does by example, rather than by explanation. This is a writing lesson that more institutions should adopt.

Local Appeal

This is the only fundraising letter of my career that I have signed myself. As a member of the board of the Community Council for the Homeless at Friendship Place (CCH/FP), I undertook a small mail campaign for this local organization (Exhibit 4–10). As a neighbor (CCH/FP is just two blocks from our house), my signature had credibility even with people who did not know me personally. The success of this package is credited with targeted list selection and the neighbor-to-neighbor approach in the copy.

ACQUISITION LETTER-WRITING BASICS

Having illustrated each type of appeal with a package that is among the best of its kind, Exhibit

Exhibit 4–9 The Ronald McDonald House® of New York (page 1 only)

The Ronald McDonald House® of New York, Inc.
405 East 73rd Street • New York, NY 10021

To Ronald McDonald House, New York:

Our little girl Lisa, just four years old, was diagnosed with cancer a few days ago. We have been up night after night worrying about her, and how we will be able to pay for the treatment she needs to save her life.

We want her to have the best care possible, and her doctor says a special treatment at Memorial Sloan-Kettering Cancer Center in New York is working miracles. We want a miracle for Lisa. But we don't know how we can afford to stay in New York for so many weeks, yet we cannot send her there all by herself. We heard you could help people like us. I don't know how else we'll be able to do this for Lisa.

Will you have room for us next week?

Dear Friend,

Letters like this can break your heart, but we get them all the time. Sometimes, when we're full, we have to say "no". <u>This</u> time, fortunately, we had room for Lisa and her mother.

Before the New York Ronald McDonald House was here to turn to, parents like Lisa's would have been on their own. They would have had to stay in expensive hotels, or find a temporary apartment to rent. Some would be forced to sleep on hospital chairs or cots. And some would have to send their frightened children to New York to undergo painful treatments alone...long, lonely days and nights away from mommy and daddy.

<u>It was out of this great need that our House was born</u>. And the compassionate generosity that keeps it open is what makes us "The House That Love Built."

And as you'll see, love is exactly what greeted Lisa and her mother when they arrived here a few days after we received their letter.

Lisa's first chemotherapy appointment was early the next morning. She would need chemotherapy 10 times a month for a year. The treatments would consume hours a day, and leave Lisa too sick to travel back and forth to her home, but not sick enough to be hospitalized.

Courtesy of the Ronald McDonald House, New York, New York.

**COMMUNITY COUNCIL
FOR THE HOMELESS
AT FRIENDSHIP PLACE**

4713 Wisconsin Avenue NW
Washington DC 20016
Telephone: 202/364-1419
Fax: 202/364-8767

**I'm writing to you today as your neighbor in Northwest
Washington to share an exciting opportunity... an innovative
way to help other neighbors who happen to be <u>homeless but
who are neighbors nonetheless.</u>**

Kay Lautman

January 2000

Dear Neighbor,

You've often seen a panhandler and wondered...how did he come to this? Where does
she go when it rains or snows? To bathe or dress? To fix a toothache? To treat the flu? To just
find a friendly person to talk to?

For years I wondered the same things when I'd walk to the Tenleytown Metro station
on Albemarble Street and Wisconsin Avenue. Back then I'd literally step over the homeless
street people as I made my way through those huddled by the old Sears/Hechinger entrance to
the Metro.

I gave quarters and dollar bills to desperate people I didn't know how else to help.
Surprisingly, there were as many women as men who needed help. Even more surprising was
the fact that many of these women were past middle age and some were even elderly. Many, as I
later learned, had degrees from some of our country's finest schools.

"There, but for the Grace of God," I realized, "go I."

Their fine homes and good education and loving families had not saved them from their
descent into mental illness...alcoholism...and homelessness. In an effort to return to the comfort
of the neighborhood in which they had grown up, many returned to this area -- even if they had
to live on the streets!

But all of that began to change in spring of 1993. That is when a dedicated group of
volunteers planned the opening of a house at 4713 Wisconsin Avenue. A house that would be not
a shelter...not a soup kitchen...not a group home. Rather it was to be a center providing resources

(Over, please)

continues

Exhibit 4–10 continued

2

to help destitute people get into real housing and perhaps even back into society. It was called Community Council for the Homeless at Friendship Place (CCH/FP).

Now, helping homeless people in Ward 3 is no easier (and perhaps more complicated) than helping the homeless in other neighborhoods. Most of the people helped by CCH/FP have complex, long-term problems. They are most often in our neighborhood because they grew up here, raised their children or worked here, or because they feel safer on our streets than they do downtown. I was not surprised to learn that they are, generally, more frail than the homeless in other areas of D.C.

Over 50% are struggling to cope with a serious mental illness, and almost as many have alcohol or drug addiction as a result of having to self-medicate while on the street. **There are no mental health services for the homeless on the streets of Ward 3.**

Few of our homeless neighbors have any family ties or personal relationships. Most have tried unsuccessfully to work within conventional social and treatment systems and, because of this, almost all initially mistrust attempts to help. Only a very few seek it out voluntarily.

But CCH/FP's mission is not to sit and wait for the homeless to come into Friendship Place on Wisconsin Avenue. Our mission is to reach out to our homeless neighbor…to build trusting relationships…and provide or refer them to appropriate services.

For example, even though the long-range goal for a client may be an alcohol detox program, a job or permanent housing, CCH/FP staff meanwhile encourage him or her to come to Friendship Place and just get acquainted. And for those who are too sick or frightened to come in, CCH/FP staff and volunteers reach out with van runs bringing small necessities and a friendly voice to men and women who huddle alone in the dark.

At Friendship Place, professionals provide medical and psychiatric care, addiction counseling, job readiness/life skills training, transitional and permanent housing and most important, ongoing support and the secure knowledge that no matter what happens, there is someone who cares and somewhere to go. Over 100 neighborhood volunteers help provide that sense of real community connection and support.

In the last year alone, we have served over 300 clients…have found emergency shelter for 22, transitional housing for 77 and permanent housing for 41…jobs for 45… We have helped 52 individuals through our addictions counseling program and brought 118 newly contacted people off the streets and into Friendship Place for services. We have a wonderful house on MacArthur Boulevard for five formerly homeless women with severe mental illness and three apartments on Wisconsin Avenue.

(Next page, please)

continues

Exhibit 4–10 continued

3

We have been able to do all this because the residents of Northwest Washington and nearby Maryland -- people like you -- have refused to turn their backs on their less fortunate neighbors. Individuals, business owners, congregations and community groups have rallied to make this work possible.

Earlier I mentioned how many needy, homeless older women I'd notice before CCH/FP came to be. I don't mean to imply that we have solved the problem; we haven't. But we've made an enormous dent. <u>Let me tell you about a woman I'll call Jane.</u>

Jane lived on Macomb Street and Wisconsin Avenue -- literally on the street. We learned about her in the winter of 1998 when a good neighbor called us. Jane, who was delusional, was deteriorating on the street, refusing any kind of help and in danger of freezing because she was inappropriately dressed for the bitter weather.

Without going into all the details, we got Jane admitted to St. Elizabeth's for three weeks, during which time we were able to locate her family in California. In the process, we learned that Jane had lived in a halfway house there for the past fifteen years. But in the spring of 1998, she had stopped taking her medication, begun to believe that O.J. Simpson was following her, and gotten on the train to come to Washington, D.C., to report her "delusions" to the appropriate officials.

Our staff visited Jane while she was hospitalized, earned her trust and arranged for her brother to send her a plane ticket. Jane returned to the residence she had left many months before, and is back on her medication and doing well.

And here's the telling part of the story.

During our work with Jane, we learned that twenty years ago she had been a pre-medical student at Georgetown University and lived in Glover Park. Thus Jane had found her way back into an old, familiar neighborhood. She had come home.

<u>I only thank God that CCH/FP was there for her.</u>

Like most of the cases we take on, this outcome was not quick or easy. Happy endings require dedication and patience -- and most of all, they require money.

<u>And that, my friend, is where you come in.</u>

Will you be there for others like Jane...people who have lost their way, but whom we can help, if you will help us?

(Over, please)

continues

Exhibit 4–10 continued

4

As I said earlier, I used to give money to virtually every sympathetic-looking street person I saw -- especially during the cold winter months. But that was only instant gratification for me. Today I give my money to the Community Council for the Homeless at Friendship Place.

Believe me, it goes a lot further, and it's tax-deductible, too.

Please join me in reaching out to a homeless neighbor by sending a contribution of $35 or more today. If you can't send $35 right now, send a smaller amount to be a part of this work. On behalf of our entire "family" of staff and volunteers, thank you for being a neighbor who cares.

Sincerely,

Kay P. Lautman

Kay Partney Lautman
Co-President

P.S.   I realize that the holidays -- when most people are inspired to give -- are over. But for homeless people, the decorations and music and a hot turkey dinner during the holidays didn't change their lives.

That's what we are trying to do at CCH/FP -- change people's lives all year long. Won't you help, too? Thank you.

Courtesy of the Community Council for the Homeless, Washington, DC.

4–11 lists some "rules" of letter writing that you can refer to each time you create a draft package.

How Long Should Your Letter Be?

Virtually every representative of a nonprofit organization asks the following question at some point:

"I've noticed in the direct mail I receive that letters are at least four pages long, if not more . . . and that they use a lot of underlining and ellipses (. . .) and dashes (--). Our president would hate these things. Can you make our campaign look . . . you know . . . less like direct mail?"

Whether or not you choose to send longer letters, it is a fact that they almost always bring in more new donors and more money than short letters. This is especially true for organizations that are not household names. Organizations founded long ago that have been in the mail for many years can success-

fully use much shorter copy, but their gifts tend to be smaller.

Organizations that are household words like the Salvation Army, the American Red Cross, and the American Cancer Society usually mail short messages, often in small envelopes. After all, everyone knows who they are and what they do, and people who know and trust them tend to respond without even thinking about it.

But how many people have heard of the organization you work for? And could you effectively describe the who, what, where, when, why, and how of your organization on one page? Could you explain who you are, ask compellingly for a gift, provide moving examples of need, describe your credentials and track record, and list membership benefits (if applicable) on one or even two pages?

The longer letter is much like a visit with a potential major donor. You wouldn't ask someone for

Exhibit 4–11 Rules of Letter Writing

1. The first opening you write isn't likely to be the best. Scan the text of your completed letter for a more compelling opening.

2. State the problem, cite the enemy, or both.

3. Write about the cause: the people you serve, your needs, and accomplishments; not about the institution, its founders, or its tenets.

4. Tell stories; use case histories if possible. If you can't use real people, use real stories and disguise the people, but disclose that their names are changed for purposes of privacy.

5. Write with heartfelt emotion. If you don't feel strongly about your cause, you might consider changing jobs.

6. Use short, familiar words, medium length sentences, and variable size (never long) indented paragraphs. You don't want people to stumble and stop reading. As for using words like "and" and "but" at the beginning of sentences, bear in mind that of the first 31 sentences in the King James Bible, 30 of them begin with "And."

7. Don't attempt humor or try to be too clever. Your cause is serious and so is the act of donating money.

8. If you begin the letter with a case history or alarming news, tie up the letter at the end by referring back to the opening.

9. Ask directly for a gift at the end and somewhere near the beginning. Also refer to "need" several times without actually asking for money. Too many organizations ask too subtly.

10. Make the P.S. say something important and ask for money again. Repeating matching gift offers and time deadlines are perfect subjects for the postscript.

$50,000 in the first five minutes of your appointment would you? Instead, you would set the stage. For example, over lunch you might talk about the prospect's interest in the cause. By the time the main course arrives, you would have begun citing the need for helping more people through a new program that will cost $5 million. Then, when dessert and coffee are served, you would tell the prospect about available opportunities of giving. It will take at least that long to warm him or her up, and if he or she is interested (and certainly you will have made it interesting), he or she will want to pursue the relationship and consider your request.

There is another reason that longer letters usually produce larger gifts, and that is the perception that a longer letter describes a greater need. Whether or not the prospect actually reads every word of your letter is irrelevant. The perception is that if it takes four or more pages to state the case, it must be important.

As with most recommendations in this book, you should test letter length for your organization. If the shorter acquisition letter wins, after at least two tests, you win too because the printing cost is lower.

HOW PEOPLE READ YOUR LETTERS

A famous museum exhibitions designer, Ralph Appelbaum, explains that when he designs exhibitions, he must cater to the visitation habits of three types of people: *Streakers, Strollers,* and *Studiers.* So, too, must direct mail fundraisers.

Direct mail *streakers* are the prospects for whom we pepper the letter with occasional underlining, boldface type, and "handwritten" notations. These "readers" literally streak through your letter and read exactly those parts you have stressed, so be very careful to choose what is important, and not just what you like.

Strollers in museums don't rush through exhibitions, and tend to linger in certain places. In the mail, he or she may follow the general pattern of reading the opening and P.S. first, the closing second, and then parts of the body copy last. He or she may also look at other enclosures, especially the reply form. Such donors tend to give larger gifts than Streakers. It is for them that you have made your best case for support.

Studiers are not necessarily bigger donors, but they do seem to have time on their hands. They read and study everything and may even write to argue with you on an issue with which they disagree (or even to point out a typo you didn't catch). They may or may not send a contribution, usually depending on whether or not you answer their complaint. It is suggested that you do, because these people need to be noticed, above all else, and your reply (assuming that you enclose another gift envelope) may melt their hearts and loosen their purse strings.

There are other "studiers" out there; disguised by the fact that they don't even write to you, but who nevertheless study your case intently, deciding whether to contribute. Such people are those likely to call the Better Business Bureau to check on your rating.

GETTING YOUNGER DONORS

Organizations frequently lament the fact that their donors are getting old and that very few younger donors are replacing them.

Once, in organizing a focus group, I supplied a list of potential participants to the group leader for prescreening. A few weeks later, he reported that the list was comprised mostly of older people.

That didn't particularly bother me. After all, I knew that most donors were older. But when I arrived for the actual focus group, the leader told me that three people in the group of eight had died in the intervening two weeks.

Now, that's an old group!

But most donor lists aren't that old. In fact, the average age on most donor lists is 62 or 63. And in today's terms, when the average life span for a man is more than 72 years and more than 78 years for a woman, the mid-sixties isn't old at all.

Some not-for-profit organizations spend a great deal of time and money searching for the younger donors, using file overlays and canvassing "younger" neighborhoods. Few meet with any degree of success, simply because very few younger people are donors.

If you are looking for younger donors between 35 and 50 through direct mail, you will be disappointed too. At that age, young people are busy raising their families, buying new houses, getting ahead in business and saving for their children's education. It won't be until the children have left the nest and there is disposable income available that most people feel financially secure enough to contribute money to good causes.

The best advice I ever heard for organizations seeking younger donors was given by Hal Malchow, a respected direct mail fundraiser in Washington, DC. Hal provided me with the chart (Figure 4–1), which was part of a brilliant presentation (and which speaks for itself). His advice is: **wait**. Wait for younger people to grow up and give. Every year thousands of people celebrate their 50th and 60th birthdays. And, if you are doing your job right, some of them will become your new donors.

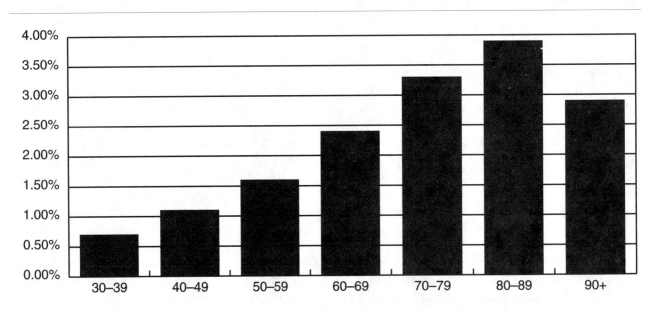

Figure 4–1 Prospect Returns by Age. Courtesy of Crowns, Malchow, and Schlackman, Washington, DC.

Chapter 5
Renewing Members and Donors

CHAPTER OUTLINE

- Asking for the Second Gift
- Frequency of Contact
- The Psychology of Multiple Renewal Notices
- First Year vs. Second Year Renewals
- Working with Lapsed Members/Donors
- Special Appeals
- Types of Special Appeals
- Converting Appeals into Acquisitions
- Thank the Donor in the Appeal
- Don't Mistake a Good Story for a Special Appeal Subject
- Don't Think an Anniversary Is the Key to Success
- Segmenting the House File for Maximum Results

Let us begin by recognizing the difference between a renewal and a special appeal. Both are sent to people already on your list who have given at least one gift. Yours is either a membership organization (say, a museum or library, with gift shop, discounts, membership cards, etc.) or it is a donor-based non-profit organization. Regardless, you are or will be sending appeals for renewal of support.

Membership organizations ask prospects to *join* and, nearly a year later, they send a magazine-style renewal series of between four and eight notices to the member until he or she renews. In the interim (before asking for renewal *dues*), the organization usually sends special appeals for gifts above and beyond dues. The number of special appeals varies, but usually they number between three and six in one year. Donor organizations that do not have an official renewal series should send appeals more frequently, (between 5 and 10), using "renewal of support" language.

ASKING FOR THE SECOND GIFT

Don't wait too long to ask your new donor for another gift. Too many organizations feel that it is bad manners to ask again too soon. But would you wait six months to ask someone you like out on a second date? By the time you get around to asking, the object of your affection will almost certainly have found another who makes him or her feel special.

It's the same in direct mail. Believe it or not, the best time to ask for another gift is within three months or less after the original donation. Of course, you have sent a warm thank you for the first gift and perhaps the new donor has received your newsletter, membership card, magazine, or whatever. But since you have not yet asked for his or her continued participation, ask now; otherwise your donor will give to another group that *does* ask.

FREQUENCY OF CONTACT

Unlike major gift fundraising, wherein you usually have an appointment with the potential donor, you have no such appointment in direct mail. Your unrequested letter arrives in someone's mailbox, and whether or not he or she responds positively depends on the state of the prospect's life at the moment.

Consider the possibilities: Perhaps he or she was just fired. On the other hand, maybe he or she got a promotion the same day your letter came. Maybe there was a death in the family. Or perhaps his or her child just graduated from college with a great job offer. Perhaps she just separated from her husband. Or perhaps he or she just won the lottery.

How do you know? You don't. But you must not assume that because the donor did not answer your first request, it means that he or she is not interested in your cause. Thus, when people say that they don't like to "impose" on their donors or members more than once or twice a year, they are assuming that the timing of their request will mesh with the donor's ability and motivation to give.

This is why organizations with the highest renewal rates send up to eight renewal notices and several appeals before calling it quits. Certainly, there are people who respond to the first bill (and first renewal notice) quickly. They save you money on subsequent renewals and relieve your anxiety. But there are people who drag their feet until *they* feel like renewing and it may take several tries to get their attention.

What is more, even people who don't renew within a 12-month period—even those who give to your organization only once every two or three years—don't consider themselves lapsed. In fact, if yours isn't a membership organization with a 12-month cycle, a publication, and other benefits, your donors *are not* lapsed after 12 months. After all, where is it written that a donor is obligated to renew annually? If you ask the average donor who has contributed three times over the past five years (but not in the past 12 months) if he or she is a supporter of Organization XYZ, the answer will be "yes" and the donor won't have the slightest idea that you consider him or her lapsed.

It is suggested that at the end of the year, if a member has not given through your renewal series but has given to one or more special appeals, that you perform a "look back," automatically renewing anyone who has contributed to any program during the year at the lowest membership level or higher. Otherwise, the donor may automatically become "lapsed," when, in fact, no lapse has occurred at all. The donor often does not differentiate between renewing a membership gift and contributing to appeals.

This is all by way of cautioning you to give your lapsed members/donors numerous opportunities in which to renew. They may not give as regularly as you would like, but they are supporters, and you should not stop appealing to them even though you have not received a response to 1, 2, 3, or even 10 mailings. Just continue mailing to lapsed donors until the mailings no longer pay for themselves (or until they don't do as well as your acquisition mailings).

Remember that it's far more expensive to get a new donor than to renew an old one.

THE PSYCHOLOGY OF MULTIPLE RENEWAL NOTICES

If yours is a true membership organization, renewal letters should focus not only on your needs, but also on benefits the member loses by not renewing, such as a free magazine subscription and invitations to events. Some mailers feel that each part of a renewal series should look much the same to be cohesive. This works well when you look at the entire series side by side as a group, but the member does not receive them all at once and each mailing must stand on its own merit. Therefore, the only prize you will receive for an elegantly matched series is in a design competition.

Just as there are direct mail streakers, strollers, and studiers, there are several types of bill payers. There are those who pay their bills the day they arrive. These are the people who will respond to one of the first two notices you send (even before their dues expire). There is no need to spend a lot of money on these notices with long letters and numerous inserts. If the member is interested, he or she will renew promptly with only a "bill" and a little urging.

After the group of compulsive "bill payers," there are those who pay promptly when the bill comes due. These are the people who pay on the second and third notices (the third notice, as you will see, is usually sent in the actual month of membership expiration and should say so clearly).

Following this group, there are the people who, for whatever reason, pay only after some urging. They probably realize that you will not give up on them easily. Heed their unspoken advice—don't give up on them. These late payers need a bit of coaxing to send their renewal dues. Thus renewal letters must be more forceful. One of the most effective techniques is to use the same copy in a late renewal letter that you used in the acquisition letter. Obviously, the donor liked that appeal, so repeating some of the language is very worthwhile.

Many final notices, be it the fifth or seventh, are created in the form of a "tell me why . . ." letter, urging the lapsed members to use your postage-paid envelope to write and say why they are not renewing.

This chapter is illustrated with a six-part renewal series. The Smithsonian's National Museum of the American Indian employs these techniques. Study the copy and formats for ideas to adapt for your own program.

The renewal chart shown below for six notices is fairly standard in the industry. As you see, the first notice (Exhibit 5–1) is mailed two months before the month of expiration, the second notice (Exhibit 5–2) is mailed the month prior to expiration, and the third notice (Exhibit 5–3) is mailed the month of expiration. Following this, the fourth, fifth, and sixth notices (Exhibits 5–4 through 5–6) (and sometimes more) are mailed in successive months. Naturally, each notice is mailed only to those members who have not yet renewed.

Telemarketing incorporated into the renewal system or used to reclaim lapsed members can be very effective. See Chapter 13 for more information on this subject.

FIRST YEAR VS. SECOND YEAR RENEWALS

Since attrition is normal on any file, you cannot expect a 100 percent renewal rate or even a 90 percent rate. After all, people move, retire, pass away, or change loyalties on an ongoing basis. What's more, first-year members renew at rates substantially lower than long-term members, so be sure to calculate these returns separately. Once members renew a second time, your ability to maintain their loyalty will increase from 40–50 percent to 50–80 percent. Exhibit 5–7 illustrates an excellent renewal series for second-year-plus members. Numbers may vary from organization to organization, but will always be better in year two than in year one, and will also decline with each successive notice.

Continually check up on your renewal series. For example, if a renewal series becomes unprofitable on the sixth notice, you will want to study the pattern for a few months and, if it holds, may deduce that five notices are all that your particular organization requires. But if you are leaving as much as 25 percent of overall membership unrenewed after five tries, you need additional notices.

If renewal notices are not pulling results in descending order, you should investigate. For example, one organization found that notice number four consistently brought in fewer renewals and less income than notice number five. Clearly, the members did not like something about the notice. When notice number four was rewritten, results improved immediately.

WORKING WITH LAPSED MEMBERS/DONORS

Most organizations that analyze their members' stated reasons for not renewing learn that money is key. Perhaps the donor is adjusting to a fixed income or perhaps he or she is calculating living expenses more carefully than in the past. Many development and planned giving directors tell us that recently lapsed members (within a year or two) make excellent planned giving prospects. This seems to be especially true of lapsed members and donors who were multiple givers (i.e., they gave several times a year). They have not stopped believing in your cause; they simply have eliminated you from their budget—*for the time being*. Recently retired people often change their wills, and if you let them know about your planned giving program (through special mailings, your newsletter, etc.), you may one day find your organization the happy beneficiary of a bequest from a lapsed donor.

SPECIAL APPEALS

People are motivated differently, so regardless of your "type" of organization, special appeals should be different from one another and should recognize the old adage "different strokes for different folks." A certain number of your donors will respond only to emergency appeals that express urgent need. Others may respond to the appeal that tells a heart-wrenching story of someone's needs (especially the needs of a child or an animal). Still, others may like to be recognized for their generosity and will respond best to what is often called a "stroke-the donor" letter that concentrates on the donor more than on the need. Still others (like it or not) respond best to premium offers, be they small items like name and address stickers; or premiums with greater perceived value, like cards and calendars; or still more prestigious items that come with membership in high dollar donor clubs.

TYPES OF SPECIAL APPEALS

Types of appeals include, but are not limited to, the following list. A sample of each type package listed is provided below with the permission of each organization.

In addition to the foregoing illustrated samples, other types of appeals can be used (Exhibit 5–8). See Chapter 6, The Letter's Not the Only Thing, for partial illustrations of different appeals.

Holiday Appeal #1

This first holiday appeal illustrated here has a Christmas theme with a "bounce-back" card (not

Exhibit 5–1 First Renewal Notice (carrier envelope and letter)

Smithsonian
National Museum of the American Indian

SMITHSONIAN INSTITUTION
PO Box 96837
Washington DC 20077-7428

Address Service Requested

Renewal Statement Enclosed

Ms. Jane Q. Sample
1730 Rhode Island Avenue, NW
Suite 700
Washington, DC 20036

R1

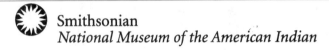

Smithsonian
National Museum of the American Indian

Office of External Affairs and Development

Dear Charter Member,

I know you're busy, so I'll be brief.

Your Charter Membership in the Smithsonian's NATIONAL MUSEUM OF THE AMERICAN INDIAN (NMAI) will expire soon.

Here are three reasons why you should renew your membership in the NMAI today:

FIRST, you'll make sure that you continue to enjoy all the benefits and privileges of membership in the NMAI – without interruption.

SECOND, you'll save yourself the bother (and save us the expense) of receiving more reminder notices.

AND THIRD, you'll continue the important work you have already begun.

When you first joined the NMAI, you became one of the very first Americans to pledge your support to our nation's first national museum dedicated to the histories and cultures of Native Americans.

Thanks to your commitment, what was just once a "good idea" is now entering the final stages of becoming one of the most important museums in the world. In fact, on September 28, 1999, we broke ground on the National Mall in Washington, D.C., and are now beginning construction. That's why we need your continuing support to help us complete the task we started together.

Please renew your Charter Membership today.

Sincerely,

W. Richard West (Southern Cheyenne)
Founding Director

P.S. Your subscription to NMAI's full-color quarterly publication, *American Indian*, along with the access to special programs that you receive as a Charter Member are benefits I know you don't want to miss. Please renew today, so your benefits will continue uninterrupted.

SMITHSONIAN INSTITUTION
PO Box 96837
Washington DC 20077-7428
www.si.edu/nmai
aimember@nmai.si.edu

Courtesy of the National Museum of the American Indian, Smithsonian Institution, Washington, DC.

Exhibit 5–2 Renewal Notice #2 (carrier envelope and letter)

Smithsonian
National Museum of the American Indian

SMITHSONIAN INSTITUTION
PO Box 96837
Washington DC 20077-7428

Address Service Requested

Renewal Statement Enclosed
Second Notice

Ms Jane Q. Sample
1730 Rhode Island Avenue, NW
Suite 700
Washington, DC 20036
IIIₐₐₐₐₗₗIIₐIIₐIIₐₐₐₗIₐIₐIₐIₐIIₐIₐIIIₐₐₐₐIIₐIIₐₐIₐII

R2

Smithsonian
National Museum of the American Indian

Office of External Affairs and Development

Dear Charter Member,

I have two pieces of news to share with you – both of them good!

The first is that your Charter Membership in the Smithsonian's National Museum of the American Indian (NMAI) expires next month.

Now, some might see this as not-so-good news, but because you have been such a loyal Charter Member, I know that you will renew right away and maintain your Charter Membership.

Which brings us to my second piece of good news. On September 28, 1999, the National Museum of the American Indian broke ground on the National Mall in preparation for the construction phase of the Museum. Perhaps you read the headlines – or saw the pictures on the front page of *The New York Times*, *Washington Post* and *Los Angeles Times*.

Construction is about to begin – and the Museum is due to open in late 2002. We want you to be with us to celebrate as a Charter Member.

We want you – and frankly, we need your continuing support to help us complete the Museum on the Mall.

That is why I look forward to receiving the good news that you have renewed your Charter Membership. I'm counting on you.

Sincerely,

W. Richard West (Southern Cheyenne)
Founding Director

P.S. Our partnership with Charter Members like you has brought us to this wonderful place where bulldozers on the Mall are indeed beautiful to behold. Thank you for your continuing support and for renewing your Charter Membership today.

SMITHSONIAN INSTITUTION
PO Box 96837
Washington DC 20077-7428
www.si.edu/nmai
aimember@nmai.si.edu

Courtesy of the National Museum of the American Indian, Smithsonian Institution, Washington, DC.

Exhibit 5–3 Renewal Notice #3 (carrier envelope and letter)

Smithsonian
National Museum of the American Indian

SMITHSONIAN INSTITUTION
PO Box 96836
Washington DC 20090-6836

IMPORTANT
Membership Card
Enclosed For:

Ms. Jane Q. Sample
1730 Rhode Island Avenue, NW
Suite 700
Washington, DC 20036

Smithsonian
National Museum of the American Indian

Office of External Affairs and Development

Dear Charter Member,

Your membership in the Smithsonian's NATIONAL MUSEUM OF THE AMERICAN INDIAN (NMAI) expires this month.

To make sure your benefits continue without interruption, we have taken the liberty of automatically renewing your Charter Membership and sending you the enclosed temporary NMAI Membership Card, which is valid for the next sixty days.

<u>All you have to do to confirm your renewal is return the enclosed statement along with your membership dues</u>.

Meanwhile, until your permanent card arrives, please sign and keep your temporary card. It entitles you to continue receiving all benefits and privileges of Charter Membership in the NMAI, including:

- A full year's subscription to NMAI's full-color quarterly publication, *American Indian*
- 10% Members-only discounts at the Heye Center's two Museum Shops, as well as discounts from all other Smithsonian Museum Shops and from the Smithsonian Mail Order Catalogue
- Permanent listing on the Museum Charter Member and Donor Scroll, on display in the Heye Center, and ultimately, at the Mall Museum
- Eligibility to participate in Smithsonian Study tours in the U.S. and abroad
- Access to Special Programs and Benefits
- Free admission to NMAI's George Gustav Heye Center in New York (plus free admission to the Cooper-Hewitt, National Design Museum)

Members contributing $35 or more receive all of the above, plus *NMAI Insight*, a semi-annual, behind-the-scenes report about the creation of the Mall Museum.

Of course, we realize you did not join the NATIONAL MUSEUM OF THE AMERICAN INDIAN just to receive an array of membership benefits. You joined

(over, please)

SMITHSONIAN INSTITUTION
PO Box 96837
Washington DC 20077-7428
www.si.edu/nmai
aimember@nmai.si.edu

continues

Exhibit 5–3 continued

because you – like thousands of other Americans – believe that creating this living tribute to the American Indian is morally right – and long overdue.

That's why I am so pleased to tell you that your membership and support enabled us to break ground on the National Mall on September 28, 1999, and begin the construction phase.

Together we are creating a national museum that will change forever the way the First Peoples of this Hemisphere are viewed. A museum that will correct misconceptions ... demonstrate how American Indian cultures are enriching the world ... and promote a new dialogue between Native and non-Native people.

By renewing your membership today, you will take us one step closer to realizing this vision.

Sincerely,

W. Richard West (Southern Cheyenne)
Founding Director

P.S. Remember, to validate your temporary membership card and to continue receiving all benefits of membership including a subscription to our all-new publication, *American Indian*, please mail us your membership renewal today. Your permanent card will be sent to you shortly after we hear from you.
Thank you.

Courtesy of the National Museum of the American Indian, Smithsonian Institution, Washington, DC.

Exhibit 5–4 Renewal Notice #4 (carrier envelope and first page of letter)

 Smithsonian
National Museum of the American Indian

SMITHSONIAN INSTITUTION
PO Box 96837
Washington DC 20077-7428

Urgent!

EXPRESS RENEWAL FORM ENCLOSED

Ms Jane Q. Sample
1730 Rhode Island Avenue, NW
Suite 700
Washington, DC 20036
||.||.||..||.||.||||.....|||.||..||.||.||..|||..||.||..|||

 Smithsonian
National Museum of the American Indian

Office of External Affairs and Development

Urgent!

Dear Charter Member,

I'm writing to let you know that your Charter Membership in the Smithsonian's NATIONAL MUSEUM OF THE AMERICAN INDIAN (NMAI) has expired.

Unfortunately, if we don't receive your renewal instructions within the next ten days, your membership and the benefits you have been entitled to as a Charter Member will end.

But the most unfortunate consequence of allowing your membership to expire will be this:

Your dream – <u>our dream</u> – of creating a living tribute to the American Indian will have been dealt a severe blow.

You joined the NATIONAL MUSEUM OF THE AMERICAN INDIAN because you understood the power of our vision to create the first national Museum dedicated to the Native people of this hemisphere.

A museum that would change forever the way the First Peoples of this hemisphere are viewed. A museum that would correct misconceptions ... demonstrate how American Indian cultures are enriching the world ... and promote a new dialogue between Native and non-Native people.

This is the vision – and the promise – of the NATIONAL MUSEUM OF THE AMERICAN INDIAN. And you still have a chance to be part of making this grand vision an historic reality if you renew your Charter Membership today.

All you have to do is fill out the enclosed Express Renewal Form and send it to me with your membership contribution. I've enclosed a special first-class, postage-paid envelope to speed delivery.

By acting quickly, you'll receive a full year's subscription to NMAI's full-color, quarterly publication, *American Indian*. You'll also continue to enjoy a Members-only 10% discount at the Heye Center's two Museum shops, as well as

(over, please)

SMITHSONIAN INSTITUTION
PO Box 96837
Washington DC 20077-7428
www.si.edu/nmai
aimember@nmai.si.edu

Courtesy of the National Museum of the American Indian, Smithsonian Institution, Washington, DC.

Exhibit 5–5 Renewal Notice #5 (carrier envelope and personalized notice)

 Smithsonian
National Museum of the American Indian

SMITHSONIAN INSTITUTION
PO Box 96837
Washington DC 20077-7428

Attention:

Your membership in NMAI expired:

December 1999

Ms Jane Q. Sample
1730 Rhode Island Avenue, NW
Suite 700
Washington, DC 20036
|ultlu.lll..lll...ull.dl..l.l..ll.l.l..l.l.l..l.ll

 Smithsonian
National Museum of the American Indian
SMITHSONIAN INSTITUTION
PO Box 96837
Washington DC 20077-7428

| **Renewal Notification** |

Membership expiration date:

December 1999

Ms Jane Q. Sample
1730 Rhode Island Avenue, NW
Suite 700
Washington, DC 20036
|ultlu.lll..lll...ull.dl..l.l..ll.l.l..l.l.l..l.ll

002122714
RSC9C5A

Yes, I want to resume my Charter Membership in the Smithsonian's National Museum of the American Indian (NMAI). Please reinstate all my membership privileges including my subscription to *American Indian.*

☐ $20   ☐ Other_____

Please mail this form with your check (payable to **NMAI/Smithsonian**) in the enclosed pre-addressed envelope.
If you prefer to pay by credit card, please see reverse.

Dear Ms Sample:

A few weeks ago, we wrote to tell you that your Charter Membership in the National Museum of the American Indian was expiring. If you have recently renewed your membership, please disregard this notice. Your new membership card should be on its way to you shortly. If you have not renewed, and we are sure this is simply an oversight, won't you please take a moment to do it now?

As one of our valued members, we want you to be able to continue to enjoy your benefits of membership, including your subscription to our new, full-color quarterly publication, *American Indian* – without interruption.

Won't you please renew today by returning the notification form above along with your membership dues? We'd like to welcome you back.

www.si.edu/nmai   aimember@nmai.si.edu

Courtesy of the National Museum of the American Indian, Smithsonian Institution, Washington, DC.

Exhibit 5–6 Renewal Notice #6 (carrier envelope and first page of letter)

 Smithsonian
National Museum of the American Indian

SMITHSONIAN INSTITUTION
PO Box 96837
Washington DC 20077-7428

Address Service Requested

We'll miss you!

Ms Jane Q. Sample
1730 Rhode Island Avenue, NW
Suite 700
Washington, DC 20036

R6

Smithsonian
National Museum of the American Indian

Office of External Affairs and Development

Dear Former Charter Member,

I got some very sad news today, and it was all about you.

I learned that you apparently have decided not to renew your membership in the Smithsonian's NATIONAL MUSEUM OF THE AMERICAN INDIAN (NMAI).

If that is indeed the case, will you kindly use the back of the enclosed form to tell me why? It will only take a minute or two of your time. And it will be very helpful to me and my staff.

Of course, if your reasons are personal and private, I'll respect that. You don't have to share them if you don't want to.

But if they have to do with the philosophy or direction the Museum has been taking recently, then I very much want to hear about it.

You see, it may be too late to convince you to renew your Charter Membership in NMAI. But it's never too late to heed the advice of a valuable Member like you.

Of course, it's possible that you never intended to let your membership in the NMAI lapse ... that it just slipped away from you.

Goodness knows that has happened to all of us! And I'm sure you have got many things on your mind other than our Museum.

But if you still believe in the importance of this living tribute to Native people of our hemisphere ...

(over, please)

SMITHSONIAN INSTITUTION
PO Box 96837
Washington DC 20077-7428
www.si.edu/nmai
aimember@nmai.si.edu

continues

Exhibit 5–6 continued (reply form)

✳ Smithsonian
National Museum of the American Indian
SMITHSONIAN INSTITUTION
PO Box 96837
Washington DC 20077-7428
www.si.edu/nmai
aimember@nmai.si.edu

Re-enlistment Form

To: Rick West

Re: My expired Charter Membership in the Everglades Circle Of The Smithsonian's
National Museum of the American Indian (NMAI).

From:

Ms Jane Q. Sample
1730 Rhode Island Avenue, NW
Suite 700
Washington, DC 20036

||l.....llll....ll....l.l..l.l.l..l.l..l.l.l..ll.l.ll.l.l

000846928
RMB9F6C

I've carefully considered your request to rejoin the NMAI.

☐ **YES** I do want to re-enlist as a Charter Member of the NMAI. Please reinstate all my membership
privileges including my subscription to *American Indian*. I enclose:

[ ] $50   [ ] $Other _____

☐ **NO**   I do not wish to remain a Charter Member of the NMAI. To help you with your membership
planning, I have briefly outlined my reason for not renewing on the back of this form.

See other side ➤

If you have already mailed your membership gift, please disregard this notice. Thank you.
Please return this form with your check (payable to **NMAI/Smithsonian**) in the enclosed postage-paid envelope.

Exhibit 5–7 Typical Renewal Notices

Notices	Timing	Typical % Return Year One	Typical % Return Year Two
First Notice	Two months prior to expiration	17%	22%
Second Notice	One month prior to expiration	12%	15%
Third Notice	Month of expiration	10%	12%
Fourth Notice	Month after expiration	7%	8%
Fifth Notice	Two months after expiration	4%	5%
Sixth Notice	Three months after expiration	3%	4%
	TOTALS:	**53%**	**66%**
Telemarketing Recapture Effort	Four to six months after expiration (or sometimes earlier)	7%	12%
	TOTALS:	**60%**	**78%**

shown) in childlike handwriting for the donor to sign and return to the House of Ruth (Exhibit 5–9). The unconventional opening of the letter may have been a surprise to readers, but kept them interested. This is good example of telling about the organization through stories and quotes rather than through description.

Holiday Appeal #2

The second holiday appeal illustrated here is for Hannukah rather than for Christmas (Exhibit 5–10). The organization for whom it was mailed is DOROT, which in Hebrew means "Generations Helping Generations," and it helps New York City's senior citizens

Exhibit 5–8 Other Types of Appeals

Package Type	Represented By
Holiday Appeal #1 (Exhibit 5–7)	House of Ruth
Holiday Appeal #2 (Exhibit 5–8)	DOROT
Other Theme Appeal (Exhibit 5–9)	Ronald McDonald House
Special Project Appeal (Exhibit 5–10)	House of Ruth
Publicity-Based Appeal (Exhibit 5–11)	AARP Andrus Foundation
Upgrade Appeal (Exhibit 5–12)	National Gay and Lesbian Task Force
Progress/Annual Report Appeal	United States Holocaust Memorial Museum
Matching Gift (Challenge Grant Appeal) (Exhibit 5–13)	Smithsonian/National Museum of the American Indian
Telegram/Emergency Appeal	Same as above
Handwritten Note (Exhibit 5–14)	Central Park Conservancy
Survey Appeal	Smithsonian/National Museum of the American Indian
(Meal) Ticket Appeal	GMHC
Bounce-Back Appeal	Citymeals-on-Wheels
Report from the Field	ACCION

Exhibit 5–9 Holiday Appeal #1 (pages 1 and 2 of letter only)

HOUSE OF RUTH
1976 — 1997

Ms. Kay Lautman
Suite 700
1730 Rhode Island Ave NW Ste
Washington, DC 20036-3101

November 21, 1997

Dear Ms. Kay Lautman:

If you asked one of the children whose mother lives here at House of Ruth what he or she wants for Christmas, you'd get some quick and predictable answers:

"A doll."

"A bicycle."

"A football."

You'd get a couple of surprise answers too...ones that tear at your heart:

"To spend more time with Mommy."

"For Mom not to cry so much of the time."

"A place where my sister and I can be together -- with Mom."

And, if you asked the moms what <u>they</u> want for Christmas this year, their wish list would be pretty much like that, too. Only they'd add a bit of realism to the list. For example:

"A place where all my children can live with me."

(over, please)

"Because a woman's place is not on the street"

5 Thomas Circle, N.W.   Washington, DC 20005-4153   (202) 667-7001   (202) 667-7047 (FAX)

#8117   A United Way/CFC Campaign Participant   #8117

continues

Exhibit 5–9 continued

2

"To get my GED certificate and a decent job."

"To regain custody of my older children."

And on and on the list might go.

Every woman who will spend the holidays at House of Ruth this year has a number of problems to solve before her dreams for herself and her children will come true. In fact, for the mothers and infants we serve, the number of issues is almost overwhelming.

The mothers have been addicted to drugs or alcohol for years and frequently give birth to at-risk babies. House of Ruth began its services for mothers and infants in response to the District's shocking infant mortality rate -- the highest in our nation! That's why these women are admitted to House of Ruth only after they begin receiving drug treatment and sustain a short period of sobriety.

In all likelihood, the woman has been abused physically, emotionally and sexually in her childhood and as an adult. She may be suffering from post-traumatic stress disorder, as well as other physical and mental illnesses that need immediate attention.

And to make matters even more difficult, these women have no regular income, few job skills, little or no employment track record and disrupted educational histories.

For years they have lived with violence, abuse and chaos. Now they want to turn their lives around. Many women come to House of Ruth because they want to put their broken families back together. Some fail, but many succeed.

Let me tell you about one such near success. I'll call her Dawn.

Happy New Year, Dawn

Dawn called House of Ruth's emergency hotline late one night about a year ago. She cried softly into the phone, telling us that she was four months pregnant and that her boyfriend's beatings had put her in the emergency room. After some coaxing, we learned that, although pregnant, Dawn was using cocaine and that she had two older children -- Bobby, 4 and Rita, 18 months -- who lived with her mother. Unemployed, Dawn was terrified at the prospect of walking out on her abusive boyfriend without a place to go.

On the other hand, she had finally realized that she had to leave in order for her and her unborn baby to survive.

Dawn did a courageous thing in calling House of Ruth that night. But she had only begun the long journey to self-sufficiency. A journey that on average takes 30 months. A most difficult journey fraught with obstacles and setbacks. A journey only for the brave.

First, Dawn entered a 30-day drug rehab program. On her release, she came to live

(next page, please)

Courtesy of the House of Ruth, Washington, DC.

in times of need. In this appeal, a case history explains the need, and in this particular case, DOROT makes an elderly person to feel less lonely during the Hannukah holiday. DOROT also sends mailings at Rosh Hashana and Yom Kippur.

It is important to realize that some holidays work better than others. Because most Jewish organizations mail on important Jewish holidays, we tested mailing at other times of the year to avoid heavy competition. It turns out that the more competitive religious seasons are usually better times to fundraise.

One holiday that works well, especially for homeless and hunger programs, is Thanksgiving. Independence Day and other patriotic holidays work well primarily for veteran and police organizations. Halloween can work for certain children's organizations as it did for Ronald McDonald House, illustrated in this chapter (Exhibit 5–11). The House hosts Halloween parties and the children are encouraged to dress up and

Exhibit 5–10 Holiday Appeal #2 (response form)

001

GENERATIONS HELPING
DOROT
GENERATIONS HELPING

171 West 85th Street
New York, NY 10024
212 769-2850

HANUKKAH GIFT FORM

☐ **YES, this Hanukkah I want to help DOROT rekindle elders' hope for the future. Enclosed is my Hanukkah gift of:**

☐ **$360** ☐ **$500** ☐ **$1,800** ☐ **$5,000** ☐ **Other $______**

☐ **I have signed the Hanukkah card. Please deliver this greeting with a Hanukkah package to a DOROT elder.**

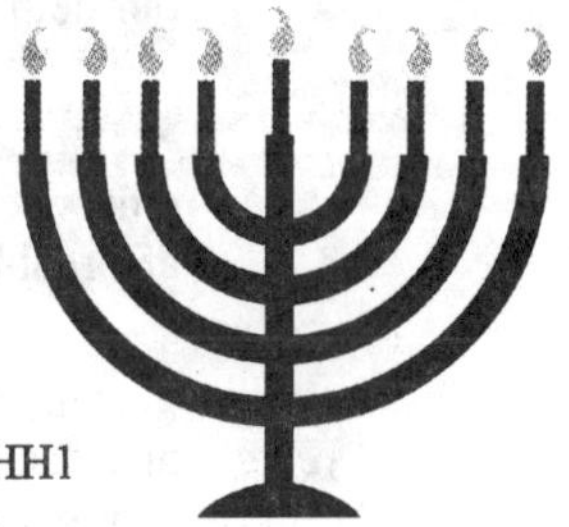

SA84HH1
37432

Mrs. Jane Q. Sample
Lautman & Company
342 Madison Avenue, Ste 2000
New York, NY 10173

See reverse side for planned giving opportunities and other ways you can help DOROT. Make your tax-deductible check payable to DOROT. If your company has a Matching Gifts Program, it can double your gift. Thank you!

GENERATIONS HELPING
DOROT
GENERATIONS HELPING

☐ I want to make a gift of stock to DOROT.
☐ Send me information on how I can receive income for life.
☐ I've named DOROT in my will.

☐ Enclosed is my honor/memory gift. Suggested contribution is $36 or more. **Please print clearly.**

IN HONOR OF:	IN MEMORY OF:
NAME	NAME
SEND NOTIFICATION TO:	SEND NOTIFICATION TO:
NAME	NAME
ADDRESS	ADDRESS
CITY	CITY
STATE ZIP CODE	STATE ZIP CODE

continues

Exhibit 5–10 continued (letter, 2 pages)

171 West 85th Street, New York, NY 10024

Dear Ms. Sample,

Hanukkah is a time of celebration. But it's hard to celebrate the Festival of Lights when you're hungry, or lonely, or worried about how you'll get to the store. And while DOROT reaches out to thousands of Jewish elders, I'm constantly aware of how many more need our help.

Homebound elders need groceries, kosher meals and help with errands. Isolated elders need companionship and intellectual stimulation. Homeless elders need safe, affordable housing.

Our Jewish elders, proud people who have taken care of themselves and their families, now face the many challenges of aging. They are becoming more frail, ill, and are losing spouses, friends, even their children. During the holidays lonely elders feel this isolation even more. Often, there is no one close by to help — no one, that is, except DOROT.

I know you care about the elders DOROT serves. I am very grateful for your past support. I ask you to continue your partnership with DOROT. Please make a special Hanukkah contribution so that we can reach out to even more deserving elders this holiday season.

Your gift to DOROT today will let us deliver a Hanukkah package to elders like Julia, who at 91 has limited vision but an unlimited zest for life.

Thanks to DOROT supporters like you, Julia will celebrate Hanukkah with traditional foods delivered by a caring DOROT volunteer during our **Hanukkah Package Delivery**. The volunteer will stay for a visit that will surely add to Julia's enjoyment of the holiday.

DOROT also adds to Julia's life in another way: we give her the opportunity to give back. Despite the many challenges she faces every day, Julia serves DOROT as a vibrant member of our Senior Advisory Council, where she brings joy to everyone she meets.

Even though many elders, like Julia, are dealing with increasing challenges — from ill health and disability to poverty and loneliness — they want to remain involved members of the community. And through DOROT, they can. To give you just two examples —

(over, please...)

continues

Exhibit 5–10 continued

*Rose, 84, is nearly blind. A DOROT volunteer reads Rose's mail aloud to her and helps her pay bills. She truly enjoys the friendship and companionship of her devoted **Friendly Visitor**. Rose also has made new friends through DOROT's **University Without Walls** (UWW) telephone conference call school for the homebound. Rose helps DOROT by serving as the leader of UWW's peer-run IN-SIGHT support group for people with visual impairments.*

*Bill, 69, was homeless when he came to DOROT for help. Through the efforts of a dedicated social worker at the **Homelessness Prevention Program** (HPP), Bill found an affordable studio apartment. Today, he helps out at the HPP as a volunteer handyman, building shelves and bookcases and making minor repairs.*

Julia, Rose, and Bill reflect the joy and renewal of Hanukkah. They face enormous obstacles every day, but despite their problems, they find a way to reach out to others. And to give back.

Their generosity of spirit inspires me. I hope it will inspire *you* to make a special Hanukkah contribution to DOROT. We need your financial support to prepare and deliver Hanukkah packages to isolated elders who have no family or friends with whom to celebrate the holiday.

We need your help to deliver pre-cooked, nutritious meals through **Kosher Meals for the Homebound** and **Shabbos Meals** ... to provide companionship and a helping hand through **Friendly Visiting** and intellectual stimulation through **University Without Walls ...** to help homeless elders find safe, affordable homes through the **Homelessness Prevention Program**.

That's why I hope I can count on you to do two things: First, please send your most generous gift to DOROT today. And second, please sign the enclosed Hanukkah card and return it with your donation. We want to include it in a Hanukkah package delivered to a DOROT elder on December 13th.

Your gift to DOROT today will rekindle our elders' hope for the future, as the Maccabees did for the Jewish people so many centuries ago. Please follow their example by making a Hanukkah gift to DOROT today!

Best wishes for a Happy Hanukkah,

Viva

Vivian Fenster Ehrlich
Executive Director

P.S. Please sign and return the enclosed Hanukkah card to DOROT by Monday, November 30. Your personal note to an elder will be included in one of our Hanukkah packages. Please give generously so that DOROT can reach out to more Jewish elders!

Courtesy of DOROT, New York, New York.

Exhibit 5–11 Other Theme Appeal (letter, pages 1 and 4 only)

The Ronald McDonald
House® of New York, Inc.
405 East 73rd Street • New York, NY 10021

October, 1999

Dear Friend of Ronald McDonald House,

Nicole wants to be a clown this year and David has decided to dress up as a pirate. Tim thinks he will be Batman, and Jenny just can't decide between being a princess or a ballet dancer.

Just like most children, these boys and girls are making the biggest decision of the year: What will they be for Halloween?

But for Nicole, David, Tim and Jenny, this Halloween is different.

You see, these children (ages 6 to 10) are living temporarily at Ronald McDonald House in New York as they battle for their lives against cancer. And this Halloween is special, because it is one of the few days of the year when each of them can simply be a child -- instead of a child with cancer.

That is why Halloween at Ronald McDonald House can last -- not for a day -- but for up to two weeks!

The days leading up to the big night are packed with special Halloween activities like pumpkin carving, mask-making and fall leaf art. Then, on Halloween night, we take the children to pre-arranged trick-or-treating at F.A.O. Schwartz and other wonderful shops on Madison Avenue. Finally, they come home to a huge Halloween party complete with music, face painting, bobbing for apples, and a costume contest, where everyone is a winner!

(Over, Please)

continues

Exhibit 5–11 continued

rent, or sleep on hospital chairs or cots. Bringing other family members along for support was too expensive, and some were even forced to send their children to the city alone!

Because of friends like you, Ronald McDonald House exists to carry these families through their darkest hours. We charge a nominal fee of only $20 per night -- just 15 percent of our actual costs. And we waive the fee whenever parents cannot afford to pay.

Thanks to you, we have been able to provide this vital service to all of the families who have come to us in need. That is why I am hoping that you will continue your support of Ronald McDonald House by sending a special gift of $20, $30 or even $100 today.

When you do, please sign and return the enclosed Halloween card with your contribution. We will decorate the House with your good wishes and loving thoughts.

Please don't wait to send your gift. We at Ronald McDonald House are counting on you -- and so are the children. Thank You!

Sincerely,

Vivian Harris

Vivian Harris
President

P.S. Actually two cards are enclosed for you to return to us -- the contribution form with your name and address, and a Halloween greeting card to sign for the children. Your signature on the greeting card (and message if you like) will tell the children and their families that you care.

continues

Exhibit 5–11 continued (card for donor's message and signature)

**Happy Halloween
to all the little
ghouls and goblins
at Ronald McDonald
House from**

_____

Sign here and return this card in the enclosed envelope

continues

Exhibit 5–11 continued (reply form)

Ronald McDonald House Contribution Form

Ronald McDonald House
of New York, Inc.
405 East 73rd Street
New York, NY 10021.

Yes! I want to help provide a home away from home for children suffering from cancer. I have signed the Halloween card for the children and enclosed a tax-deductible gift of:

☐ $20   ☐ $30   ☐ $40   ☐ Other $_____

81397   SA91E1

Jane Q. Sample
Lautman & Company
1730 Rhode Island Ave NW
Suite 700
Washington, DC 20036-3101

Please return the Halloween card and this form with your check made payable to Ronald McDonald House of New York.

Courtesy of the Ronald McDonald House, New York, New York.

play games. As Halloween has become such a major American event, it resonates well with most donors.

Special Project Appeal

One of the many services House of Ruth offers to its homeless female clients is career counseling, job training, and job placement. It was decided to make the subject one for a special appeal, but the myriad of details required were many. Thus some sort of illustration was needed to simplify the message. The technique used was the idea of the Development Director. It depicted a "Help Wanted" classified ad at the beginning of the letter and, on the reply form, showed the same ad with "Position Filled" dramatically stamped across it (Exhibit 5–12). When using a particular program for fundraising, be sure to state clearly that the donor's gift does not go only to that program unless you wish to earmark the funds. A simple way to phrase it is to say something like the following at the close of the letter. "Your gift to the House of Ruth will ensure that our job placement program as well as our many other programs will flourish." On the reply card you can say something like this: "Here is my gift to help House of Ruth support women in need of job counseling and placement as well as those in need of your many other services."

Publicity-Based Appeals

The AARP Andrus Foundation is the research arm of the American Association of Retired Persons (AARP) (Exhibit 5–13). As with most research organizations, the subject can be very dull.

The campaign had a real shot in the arm when astronaut John Glenn, then in his 70s, went back into outer space for NASA to gather data on the effects of space travel on older people. It was not even necessary to have Glenn sign the letter because news coverage of the event was so widely broadcast. Newspaper clippings can be helpful when an event is not well publicized, but in this case the additional expense was unnecessary.

Upgrade Appeal

The National Gay and Lesbian Task Force wanted to urge members to contribute $500 or more by establishing a high dollar donor club called "Bridge Builders" (Exhibit 10–1). The name of the "club" was derived from copy that described the organization's efforts as "bridge building" between itself and other gay, lesbian, and transgendered groups, as well as building coalitions with mainstream organizations.

It was agreed that the name of the organization would be prominent for recognition purposes and that the name of the club, Bridge Builders, would be subordinate. A search was undertaken for photographs of a bridge that was not instantly recognizable (such as the Golden Gate or George Washington bridges). Then, several categories of Bridge Builders were established starting at $500, and the mailing was sent to donors whose highest previous contribution was $100 or more.

Progress/Annual Report

If your organization has a good annual report, you have the nucleus of a fundraising package. Many organizations mail their annual reports with a reply envelope tucked inside, which is a good beginning. But those organizations that enclose a fundraising letter are rewarded with far more additional income. Regardless of when your annual report comes out, it can be sent as a special appeal simply by adding a letter to the package highlighting the year's most important events. Preferably it will not be an institutional letter, but one that describes the year's accomplishments by example.

Annual reports and progress reports are excellent vehicles in which to brag about your low cost of fundraising (charts and graphs are useful) and to list the names of donors who have contributed a certain dollar amount or more, beginning at, say, $100 or $1,000 or whatever amount is appropriate to your organization. If your organization does not have a regular annual report, you can create an annual or progress report with the help of project staff and the aid of good photographs.

Matching Gift/Challenge Grant

One appeal for the Smithsonian's National Museum of the American Indian utilizes both the Emergency Appeal format and the Matching Gift/Challenge Grant approach (Exhibit 5–14).

Because the Museum used actual Western Union services, this fact was used to advantage in the opening of the letter copy. There are two advantages to using Western Union over creating your own format. One is that it is very quick, so if you are in a rush, this is the way to go. All a mailer must do is provide

Exhibit 5–12 Special Project Appeal (letter, all 4 pages)

HOUSE OF RUTH
1976 — 1997

September 5, 1997

Jane Sample
Lautman & Company
1730 Rhode Island Avenue, NW
Suite 700
Washington, DC 20036

Dear Jane,

Sheila, a woman at House of Ruth, was sure she could do it. Even though she had been unemployed for two years and homeless for several months, when she saw the ad in the paper, she <u>knew</u> she'd get the job.

With a livable salary and benefits, she and her kids could find a nice apartment, and she could take good care of them.

Sheila called the company and got an interview. The interviewer was impressed: Sheila had several years of mail-room experience and she scored above average on the math and typing tests. But the interviewer did have one concern.

"Why have you been unemployed for the last two years?" she asked. "What made you leave your last job?"

Sheila didn't talk about the real problems that caused her to be fired -- lack of reliable child-care arrangements and transportation. She simply explained that she'd taken time off to have her third baby.

Relieved, the interviewer offered Sheila the job.

But within the first week on her new job, Sheila was late several times. In the second week, she missed two days of work, once because her car broke down and once

(over, please)

"Because a woman's place is not on the street"

5 Thomas Circle, N.W.   Washington, DC 20005-4153   (202) 667-7001   (202) 667-7047 (FAX)

A United Way Campaign Participant

continues

Exhibit 5–12 continued

-2-

because her baby-sitting arrangement fell through. Another time she was late because, exhausted, she overslept. By the third week, Sheila's lateness and absenteeism were causing serious concern.

<u>The fifth week, she was fired</u>.

Sheila asked herself, "Why couldn't the company understand the problems of a working mother?" She'd run into this same situation before. Sheila felt like giving up.

"The cards are stacked against women like me," she told a House of Ruth counselor. "There's nothing I can do about it!"

"Sheila, I think there <u>is</u> something you can do. There are a number of challenges that we need to consider," the counselor replied. "I'd like you to participate in and benefit from House of Ruth's Supported Employment Services so you can get <u>and</u> keep a job."

Sheila became one of the first participants in this new House of Ruth project that offers solutions to the tough problems facing women who are homeless and unemployed.

A Way Back to Work

As a supporter of House of Ruth, you know that many of the women who need our assistance are dealing with more than one major problem in their lives. It might be domestic violence, untreated illness, addiction, poor self-esteem, lack of education, or more.

Take Sheila for example. Before losing her home, Sheila had lived with an abusive husband. He lost his job and the couple couldn't pay the rent. When they received an eviction notice from their landlord, Sheila's husband went into a rage, striking her while the two children cried in the corner.

That winter night, Sheila fled to House of Ruth. After receiving counseling and taking part in support groups, Sheila decided to leave her husband. And that meant getting a job.

Sheila had plenty of confidence about finding a job. But her job history and present circumstances showed that <u>keeping</u> a job was much more difficult for her.

For almost every woman at House of Ruth, employment is a major issue. Getting and keeping a job can seem impossible when you're homeless, when you can't afford child care, when it's been years since you last worked or even filled out a job application. But good jobs are a key to self-reliance and success for women at House of Ruth.

(next page, please)

continues

Exhibit 5–12 continued

-3-

That is why we are extending ourselves to provide Supported Employment Services, despite threatened cutbacks from the District of Columbia. House of Ruth created this project in response to the needs of the women, and we believe it has tremendous potential. Let me tell you how it works:

House of Ruth's job team -- an employment counselor, a job developer, and two job coaches -- are working with prospective employers to find opportunities for women in the program. Participants will be able to consider these job openings as well as seeking out their own job leads.

The job team and each individual woman will work together to map out the journey from homelessness to work. The women will also learn practical job search skills (completing job applications, preparing resumes, conducting interviews).

But -- as Sheila's story demonstrates -- keeping a job can be even more difficult than finding one. That's why this project emphasizes ongoing support. Our job coaches will work closely with new employees on and off the job, helping them solve problems like transportation and child care, and working with them to assure good job performance.

Job coaches will also stay in constant touch with employers, so that problems from the supervisors' perspective can be dealt with before they result in termination.

And as the new employees learn how to succeed at their jobs, they will continue working on other life issues with House of Ruth's help. For example, Sheila needed ongoing counseling to deal with a history of abusive relationships, as well as treatment for clinical depression, help in finding affordable housing, and education in living skills like budgeting and parenting.

Following House of Ruth tradition, the Supported Employment Services address the whole person and her family, not just the question of getting and keeping a job.

With the advent of welfare reform, hundreds more women will be thrown onto the streets of our city when benefits are cut off. Today, more than ever, we need a program that provides real solutions to the problems of chronic unemployment and homelessness!

Help House of Ruth Provide Workable Solutions

House of Ruth's Supported Employment Project fills a major gap in our city's job programs. It is the ONLY program that supports all the needs of women who are homeless -- from addiction to housing to child care -- and the ONLY program that offers support once the women find jobs.

(over, please)

continues

Exhibit 5–12 continued

-4-

Ultimately, I hope this unique program will be the key to a better future for thousands of women and their children. For now, our goal is to see 100 women get jobs and for the majority of them to keep those jobs.

As a friend of House of Ruth, you will understand that we cannot offer these services without a significant increase in funding. That is why I hope you will help us open the doors of the working world for 100 women like Sheila by returning the enclosed reply form with a generous contribution today.

Your gift will help us bring these services to 100 women <u>and</u> sustain the current level of assistance provided to hundreds of women and children every day of every year.

<u>We need your generous support right away to expand and enhance Supported Employment Services, so I hope you will reply without delay.</u> Women like Sheila are <u>waiting to hear if they can take part in this project and start building a better future for themselves and their children</u>.

Through your past support of House of Ruth, you've made a real difference in the lives of women and children in desperate need. Please help us as we continue to develop innovative, successful programs that help all the women who come to House of Ruth transform their lives.

Sincerely,

Christel Nichols
Executive Director

P.S. Of course you want to know what happened to Sheila. With our help, Sheila met each challenge and found new solutions to her employment problems. She found reliable child care and transportation so she could make it to work every day, on time!

We then helped Sheila find another mail-room manager job. <u>She has kept it for four months. What's more, she received high marks in her first performance review a few weeks ago.</u> She talks with her job coach almost every day.

We need your help <u>today</u> to fully begin the Supported Employment Services and support all our current efforts to assist women and children in greatest need -- please return the enclosed reply form with your generous gift!

continues

Exhibit 5–12 continued (top, front of reply card; bottom, back of reply card)

HOUSE OF RUTH CONTRIBUTION REPLY FORM

5 Thomas Circle, NW · Washington, DC 20005 · (202) 667-7001

❑ **YES! Christel, I want to help more women like Sheila so they can achieve independence and provide for their families. Here is my contribution:**

❑ **$25**   ❑ **$50**   ❑ **$100**   ❑ **Other:** _____

A gift of $1,000 or more entitles you to membership in House of Ruth's President's Circle.

Jane Sample
Lautman & Company
1730 Rhode Island Avenue, NW
Suite 700
Washington, DC 20036

X999X9X
99999999

Please return this form with your check (payable to **House of Ruth**) in the envelope provided.
Your contribution to House of Ruth is tax-deductible as a gift to a not-for-profit organization. Thank You.

HOUSE OF
RUTH

You may obtain a copy of House of Ruth's annual financial report by writing directly to House of Ruth at: 5 Thomas Circle, NW, Washington, DC 20005. Residents of the following states may request information from their state agencies as follows:

Maryland: Documents and information filed under the Maryland charitable organizations laws can be obtained, for the cost of copies and postage, from the Office of the Secretary of State, Statehouse, Annapolis, MD 21401, 1(800)825-4510 (for residents of Maryland).

Virginia: A financial statement is available from the Division of Consumer Affairs, PO Box 1163, Richmond, VA 23209, 1(800) 552-9963 (in Virginia).

Courtesy of the House of Ruth, Washington, DC.

Exhibit 5–13 Publicity-Based Appeal (letter, pages 1 and 2 only)

AARP

ANDRUS

FOUNDATION

March 1999

Dear Supporter,

When 77-year-old John Glenn emerged from the Space Shuttle Discovery on November 7, 1998, at the Kennedy Space Center, he did more than just make history again.

He gave all older Americans two very precious gifts. The first is the gift of pride and accomplishment that comes from knowing that even if we are over 60, 70 or even 80, we can all be of service to our country and each other.

Second, John Glenn gave us the gift of aging-related research -- the very reason for his courageous return to outer space.

While orbiting over 300 miles above the earth, Glenn underwent 83 tests and experiments to study the effects of space travel on the human body. That's because in outer space, astronauts suffer from temporary degeneration of muscle tissue, bone mass loss, balance disorders and insomnia.

Do those symptoms sound familiar?

Such temporary symptoms are identical to <u>permanent</u> changes we undergo as we age. In the months and years to come, John Glenn's space experiments will benefit us all as we struggle to overcome the negative effects of aging.

Research efforts on aging by our national space program parallel the work of the AARP Andrus Foundation. You see, the AARP Andrus Foundation funds research that helps us better cope with the adverse effects of aging. Foundation-funded research makes life more independent, self-sufficient and just plain better in our older years.

This research is made possible thanks to valued supporters like

(over, please)

601 E STREET, NW ♦ WASHINGTON, DC 20049 ♦ (202) 434-6190 ♦ www.andrus.org

continues

Exhibit 5–13 continued

you.   Here are just a few of the vital projects we funded this year -- thanks to your help:

- A study in New York City that is finding ways for older persons with both vision and hearing loss to better cope with life's normal, everyday activities.

- A comparison of two methods of treating sleep disorders for older Americans suffering from chronic health conditions and insomnia.

- Research on the successful techniques older adults have used and found effective in coping with the consequences of chronic health conditions.

Funding for more important projects like these depends solely on your continued support. And believe me, there is no shortage of problems to tackle as we head into the next century.

With the baby boomer generation maturing and nearing retirement age, there will soon be more people over the age of 65 in the United States than ever before.

Right now, America's healthcare and financial systems are not equipped to fully provide a good quality of life for many future retirees. <u>That is why our work, and the work of brave Americans like John Glenn, is so vitally important</u>.

Last year -- our 30th anniversary -- the Foundation achieved great success in reaching doctors, national leaders and citizens like you and me with important information on aging-related issues.

But there is so much more work to do. So many more doctors, scientists and researchers need our help. More older Americans are looking to us to provide the best hope for continued independence and quality of life.

Will you please help the AARP Andrus Foundation continue to fund crucial research programs by sending a generous gift today?

The continuing debates about Social Security and Medicare, the prevalence of chronic health problems and issues of financial security imperil the quality of life we all hope to enjoy in our retirement years.

<u>But as John Glenn proved once again during his recent space flight, we are never too old to make a difference</u>. Never too old to improve our lives and push our own limits. And never too old to take a chance for a better tomorrow.

(next page, please)

Courtesy of AARP Andrus Foundation, Washington, DC.

Exhibit 5–14 Matching Gift Challenge Grant Appeal (carrier envelope)

continues

Exhibit 5–14 continued (front of telegram format)

National Museum of the
   American Indian
Smithsonian Institution
PO Box 96836
Washington DC 20090-6836

WESTERN UNION

September 17, 1997

Mr. John Q. Sample
123 Any Street
Anytown, US 12345

Dear Mr. Sample:

    We chose Western Union as the carrier of our exciting news
to convey its urgency.

    Just a few weeks ago, The Kresge Foundation announced a
grant of $500,000 to challenge NMAI members and friends to
complete our campaign for the NMAI's Cultural Resources Center
(CRC) in Suitland, Maryland.

    Let me explain why the Kresge grant is so critical at this
time and why your support now means more than ever.

    As you know, the Smithsonian Institution has embarked upon a
major campaign to complete the National Museum of the American
Indian on the Mall in the Nation's Capital, and to build a
companion resource and research facility that will serve as the
home of the NMAI collection. This companion facility -- the CRC
-- is a critical part of our plans, for as impressive as the Mall
Museum will be, it alone cannot accommodate the requirements of
the world's largest collection of Native American art and
cultural objects.

    As you also know, the U.S. Congress, in the face of budget
and revenue problems, cut appropriations for our Museum last
year. That's when we turned to our friends for help. Several
members of the foundation and business community have responded
favorably including this spectacular one-half-million-dollar
grant from Kresge. But it comes with what they call a
"challenge" and what I call a "magnificent opportunity."

    If we can raise $1.5 million of the $2 million necessary to
complete the CRC, Kresge will contribute the balance of $500,000.

    This is welcome news from a budget standpoint. But it is
even more. For winning a Kresge grant is considered by many to
be tantamount to winning a prestigious award. In making the
grant, Kresge President John E. Marshall, II, said, "We hope that

                                            (over, please)

continues

Exhibit 5–14 continued (back of telegram format)

the Kresge challenge will bring both public attention and new donor support for this historic national initiative."

This is a challenge we cannot fail to meet. Any delay in completing the CRC will further delay the opening of our Museum on the Mall scheduled for 2002 -- just four years away. We are already in the process of preparing the one million objects (squeezed into a warehouse in the Bronx since 1926) for the move to the CRC which will house the vast majority of the collection not officially on display.

With Kresge poised to give $500,000 if we raise $1,500,000, you can readily see why your special gift is critical. Please don't delay in sending it today. Thank you.

Sincerely,

John Colonghi, Campaign Director
National Museum of the American Indian
Smithsonian Institution

Courtesy of the National Museum of the American Indian, Smithsonian Institution, Washington, DC.

Western Union Nonprofit Services with approved copy, a supply of reply envelopes, a donor file tape, and the "telegram" will go out within one week or less.

The second advantage is that the words "Western Union" have real meaning for donors old enough to remember when telegrams were truly urgent. Therefore, because most donors are 63 years or older, this technique continues to work.

Unlike acquisition or regular renewal letters, telegrams have shorter copy and do not have a signature. The use of all capital letters (as found in real telegrams) is not recommended as it makes the copy difficult to read. Never send a telegram or any other type of urgent appeal when there is no real urgency, as overuse of the technique will backfire. If you are prone to having emergencies (such as international relief organizations), do not use a telegram format more than once a year or every 18 months. (As you will see below, a telegram format also illustrates the effective use of a challenge grant.)

Use of a Challenge Grant

Few things are more inspirational to a donor than a challenge grant or matching gift offer (Exhibit 5–13). In the case of the National Museum of the American Indian, a challenge grant of $500,000 was promised by the Kresge Foundation if the Museum raised $1,500,000. Often challenges can be stated similar to the following: "For every dollar you contribute, the challenger will contribute three dollars. Thus, your gift of $50 becomes a gift of $150." As with the emergency appeal, the challenge grant format should not be overused for the sake of creditability.

Handwritten Note

These packages are usually sent to high dollar donors because of the expense. The carrier envelope is actually hand addressed while the note is printed (Exhibit 5–15). A handwritten P.S. is usually tailored to the donor's past giving history and urges a contri-

Exhibit 5–15 Handwritten Note (personally addressed envelope, inside of card with handwritten message)

Mr Sample a Sample
123 Main Street
Anytown US 12345

Dear Friend,

When was the last time you took a winter walk in Central Park?
I invite you to do so now and marvel at how winter dramatically reveals
new dimensions of our urban oasis.

Without foliage, the Park takes on the quality of an outdoor
sculpture garden. You can see clearly the striking sculptural shapes of
the elms, oaks, and maples. Winter changes the Park's sounds as well as
its sights. In contrast to the commotion of the City, our urban oasis
enjoys a peaceful quiet that deepens to near silence when it snows.

<u>And while the Park itself appears dormant in winter, we at the
Conservancy are very active indeed</u>!

The Conservancy takes advantage of this short period during which
nature rests to prepare for spring and summer. Our horticultural staff
receives extra training to hone their skills. In addition, we see to the
Park's ongoing preservation. We clean ... paint ... repair ... restore
... all to ensure that our Park will be even more beautiful this coming
spring.

To make our work possible year-round, the Conservancy depends on
your financial support. Won't you please be as generous as you can?

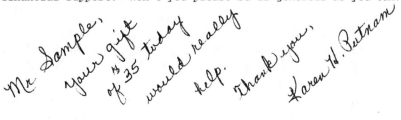

Mr. Sample, your gift of $35 today would really help. Thank you, Karen H. Putnam

Courtesy of the Central Park Conservancy, New York, New York.

bution. For example, it might say "Mrs. (name), can you increase your last year's gift to $150?"

Such notes to high dollar donors are usually mailed first class, which enhances the personal look. Money can be saved by sending smaller donors a completely preprinted version of the package (black type and blue handwriting) using a nonprofit stamp. Copy is difficult to write because it is so very short, as illustrated by the note from the Central Park Conservancy shown here. Every word counts in such an appeal, and because of the brevity, it is not appropriate for an acquisition mailing.

Holiday card art on the front of the card has not worked well for our firm's clients. Perhaps because the small square package looked so much like a greeting card and because the cover art made it look even more so, the recipient put it in the card pile rather than in the "bill paying" pile. This was not a test, so take this advice with a grain of salt. As for me, I'm convinced that holiday card art shouldn't be used in fundraising appeals.

CONVERTING APPEALS INTO ACQUISITIONS

Some of the special appeals shown could be rewritten as acquisitions to prospective new donors. As a matter of fact, there are only two donor appeals described here that cannot be converted into acquisitions. They are Certificates of Appreciation (the prospect has done nothing for which to be thanked) and handwritten notes or cards (inappropriate because of their brevity and the enormous expense involved).

THANK THE DONOR IN THE APPEAL

Renewals that stress gratitude are always well received. Phrases such as "thanks to you," "because of your past help," and "we couldn't do it without you" help get the next gift. Finally, the best renewal appeals, unless personalized, do not begin with "Dear Friend" but with "Dear Member" or "Dear Friend and Supporter" or "Dear Valued Donor" or the like. Some appeals feature the donor's name prominently. For example, Certificates of Appreciation should be designed so that the donor's name can be lasered onto the certificates simultaneously (and at no additional cost) when lasering the reply card. Personalization is all important in talking to donors. After all, there is probably nothing a person likes hearing or seeing more than his or her own name.

DON'T MISTAKE A GOOD STORY FOR A SPECIAL APPEAL SUBJECT

Long ago I created an award-winning package for a prominent wildlife organization based on children and wildlife. The colorful package contained an appropriate letter from the organization's president, and a brochure containing several illustrated children's letters to the organization. Every package component was illustrated with charming children's drawings of animals with captions in their original handwriting.

When the postmortem was done, we realized that the income goal was not met because *the appeal was about children who loved animals*, and not an appeal about animals in need of saving. This is not to say that the donors didn't like it. They probably did. But it would have made a far better magazine article. Fundraising letters, after all, need to have an enemy and a sense of urgency to inspire giving.

DON'T THINK AN ANNIVERSARY IS THE KEY TO SUCCESS

Other instances of failure are when organizations regard their milestone anniversaries as a key to fundraising success. The only people who are truly inspired by an anniversary (be it 10, 20, or 50 years) are the insiders—employees and volunteers. Thus, if the insiders get excited about the anniversary and are inspired to go out and raise money, then the anniversary can be a gold mine.

But remember—your donors rarely care. What they do care about is the people and the cause your organization helps. Certainly you should state your credentials, including how long you have been in business. But that isn't what inspires giving.

If your organization has an upcoming anniversary that you wish to publicize, you may wish to stress it in your newsletter and plan special fundraising events around it. It is suggested, however, that you limit its use in direct mail fundraising.

Here's what you can do:

- Engage an artist to incorporate the anniversary year around or under your logo (see the Elizabeth Glaser Pediatrics AIDS 10th Anniversary logo in Exhibit 6–9). Do not develop a one-time anniversary logo that renders your organization unrecognizable.
- If you wish to announce your anniversary on envelope teaser copy, do so on the back of the

envelope. This way, the front still looks like a real letter and not like a promotion.

- Mention the anniversary in your letter copy by saying something that relates to the donor such as "It is because of the ongoing commitment of people like you that we are celebrating our 15th Anniversary this year."
- Use the anniversary year as art on inexpensive premiums like name and address labels, decals, calendars, etc., but focus on the people or animals you help and not the anniversary.

SEGMENTING THE HOUSE FILE FOR MAXIMUM RESULTS

As stated earlier, "one size doesn't fit all." That means that every donor shouldn't receive every special appeal. Any organization that approaches donors with this kind of "herd mentality" will miss many opportunities to maximize giving. Proper house file segmentation is critical to maximizing the income from your direct mail program. Segmentation simply means looking at your database in terms of *what*

(types of appeals), *when* (how often and what time of year), and *how* (telemarketing or mail) groups of donors are responding.

When you select donors for a mailing, they should be grouped and coded based on similar characteristics—"segmented." The results of each segment can be compared and refined for future mailings. Basic segmentation tools include recency, frequency, and level of giving (also known as RFM). For example, all donors who have given a single gift in the past twelve months can be grouped together, and then divided into segments based on the amount of their gift. Typical segments are: $1–$9.99, $10–$24.99, $25–$99.99, $100–$249.99, etc. Then, you can see which segments respond best to each appeal. There are many ways to segment, but RFM is tried and true.

Careful tracking of these results will let you mail smarter in the future because you can eliminate those segments that do not meet your income goals. Segmentation will also help you determine the most appropriate ask amounts for different groups and help you develop upgrading strategies.

Chapter 6
The Letter's Not the Only Thing

CHAPTER OUTLINE

- The Response Device
- The (Outer) Carrier Envelope
- Designing the Reply Envelope
- Other Enclosures
- The Package as a Whole

Thus far a great deal of emphasis has been placed on the letter, be it acquisition for new member/donors, a renewal, or special appeal to current donors. However, when speaking of direct mail, the term "package" is used because the letter is not the only thing in direct mail. As you have learned, the minimum number of inserts that absolutely must accompany the letter and carrier (outside) envelope are two: a reply device and a reply envelope. In addition, other inserts may be productively used.

In this chapter, the following will be discussed and illustrated with appropriate samples with each organization's permission:

- The Response Device
- Carrier Envelope
- Reply Envelope
- Other Enclosures
- The Package as a Whole

THE RESPONSE DEVICE

The response device (sometimes called the reply card, contribution form, membership enrollment form, etc.) should always include the following:

- Name and address of your organization
- Statement enabling the donor to respond such as "( ) Yes! I want to help send a child to camp and enclose my gift of ( ) $20 ( ) $30 ( ) Other Amount _____." (Note that the suggested gifts are limited in this case to two: the donor's last gift and an upgrade amount.)

- Space to imprint the name and address of the donor (that will show through the window envelope if used)
- Clear instructions on check writing and other simplified instructions as necessary
- Statement of tax deductibility

When a donor finishes reading your letter and picks up a pen to write a check, he or she has decided to make a gift but not necessarily how much to give. The response device represents your last opportunity to make a case for the highest possible gift. Here's how to make it do the best job possible. Suggested gift amounts are generally listed in ascending order from the smallest to the largest. Some like to reverse this order or to mix up the amounts. However, this technique rarely increases the average gift.

On the other hand, the following can help you achieve the gift you are after:

- Put it first.
- Put it in bold face.
- Circle the gift.
- Print it in another color.
- Do all of the above.
- List that amount only (with the ubiquitous other $_____).
- Make the form larger.

Be sure to always include what we call "other amount." No matter how many suggested gift categories you offer (and six should be the limit to avoid overwhelming the donor), some donors will want to contribute an odd amount.

Uses for the Larger Response Device

The basics, as described above, are all that are really necessary on a response device. However, you can include something extra. Look what happens when the Marine Corps reply device (Exhibit 6–1) opens to an $8^1/_2'' \times 11''$ page, revealing an evocative photograph of the Iwo Jima Memorial and the Marine Corps Anthem. Because the form is perforated, the donor can keep the bottom part if desired.

In another example, the unfolded reply device from the House of Ruth (Exhibit 6–2), presents a holiday card to the women and children who live there for the donor to sign and return with his or her gift.

Other things a larger response device can do are described and illustrated here. The question you must address before you design your response device is, "What do I want the donor to do?" Then go about making it easy for the donor to do it. However, don't ask the donor to do more than two things, lest he or she become confused and lose interest.

First and foremost, you want a contribution. Second, you may want the donor to return an enclosure. One possibility is a signed card to share with those whom you serve like the one from House of Ruth. Another is a perforated signed petition to a politician asking him or her to act in a certain way. You may wish to test whether the requested participation and larger enclosure improves response.

The last illustration on the successful use of a larger response device was done for the Smithsonian's National Museum of the American Indian (Exhibit 6–3). This perforated form lists and promotes categories of membership and the attendant benefits of each. It is sized to fit in a $6'' \times 9''$ package and the fold is unique. The design is commercial looking and shouldn't be used for a charity where the overall look is not commercial.

A larger response device can accommodate many things. Just be sure that if the donor is to return any part of the form (other than the gift form itself) that instructions are clearly spelled out in the letter and again on the form. A response device doesn't have to be large to include additional information. For example, the back of the response form from the Jane Goodall Institute describes the benefits that come with larger gifts. And the back of the form from the

Central Park Conservancy describes how to make a gift by credit card.

Here is some technical advice regarding the response device:

- It should be on slightly heavier paper stock than the letter so that it feels substantial and different from the other enclosures.
- It should fit the carrier envelope and not slip around inside. It is critical for mail delivery that the name and address of the recipient be seen through the window of the carrier envelope.
- It should fit well in the reply envelope without the donor having to fold it.
- If folded, the fold must be at the bottom. Should it be printed upside down, the machine inserter will not be able to grab the loose edges and you will be stuck with a print job that must be (expensively) hand inserted or reprinted.
- If you have a lot of information to pack in, use a double or even triple ($8^1/_2'' \times 11''$) response device rather than using small type, which makes it hard to read.
- If it is computer generated, include an additional personal computer-generated message at no extra cost.

THE (OUTER) CARRIER ENVELOPE

Carrier Envelope Size

Most mailers use a number 10 (#10) carrier envelope because they are inexpensive and readily accessible. Larger envelopes like flats ($8^1/_2'' \times 11''$ or larger) are identified with commercial direct mail such as promotions for books, records, insurance, and other merchandise. However, based on their increased usage for certain types of appeals, it appears that by using the larger format, some organizations are meeting with success. We have used the larger format successfully for several special appeals despite the substantial additional cost. For most organizations, however, such formats are highly impractical and not worth the additional cost.

Envelopes smaller than #10 can be very successful and are not much more expensive. The monarch (#9 size) is about the smallest one can use practically. A monarch looks more personal than a #10 (often called a business size envelope). In fact, because it is not a window envelope, the monarch can look quite

Exhibit 6–1 Reply Device #1 (reply form)

Marine Corps Heritage Center
Contribution Form

P.O. Box 420, Quantico, VA 22134-0420

☐ **YES,** I wish to help build the Heritage Center where our history can be recorded, our priceless artifacts protected, and Americans can view their culture and history through the eyes of the Marines.

☐ **$50**   ☐ **$75**   ☐ **$100**   ☐ **$250**   ☐ **$500**   ☐ **Other $ ___**

AX2106A

Jane Sample
Lautman & Company
1730 Rhode Island Ave, NW
Suite 700
Washington DC 20036-3115

My gift is ☐ In honor of:
          ☐ In memory of:

_____

Please make any necessary changes to your name, rank or address at left.

email _____

phone _____
      (in case we have questions)

Please make your check payable to the **Marine Corps Heritage Center** and return it in the enclosed envelope with the top portion of this form. Gifts are tax-deductible to the extent permitted by law.

From the halls of Montezuma
To the Shores of Tripoli,
We fight our country's battles
In air, on land, and sea.
First to fight for right and freedom,
And to keep our honor clean,
We are proud to claim the title
Of United States Marines.

Courtesy of the Marine Corps Heritage Foundation, Quantico, Virginia.

Exhibit 6–2 Reply Device #2 (double reply form)

House of Ruth yes!

5 Thomas Circle, NW • Washington, DC 20005
(202) 667-7001

☐ Enclosed is my/our holiday gift to House of Ruth:

   ☐ $25   ☐ $50   ☐ $100   ☐ Other $_____

☐ I have signed my holiday card below. Please share it with the women
   and children in your program.
☐ My employer will match my special contribution to House of Ruth.
   I have enclosed the appropriate form from my employer.

Jane Sample
Lautman & Company
Suite 700
1730 Rhode Island Ave. NW
Washington, DC 20036-3101

01234567/RB96V1A

Please return this entire form with your check payable to House of Ruth.
A gift of $1,000 or more entitles you to membership in the House of Ruth President's Circle. Please make corrections in name and address as necessary.
All donations are tax-deductible if you itemize.

To Everyone at House of Ruth

Happy Holidays From

sign here

Courtesy of the House of Ruth, Washington, DC.

Exhibit 6–3 Large Response Device (front, folded at arrow)

Special
Charter Membership
Offer

↙

Enjoy these benefits
when you become a Charter Member
of the
National Museum of the American Indian

Enjoy a full year's
subscription to
Native Peoples
magazine
(see inside)

NATIONAL MUSEUM OF
THE AMERICAN INDIAN
Smithsonian Institution
NATIONAL CAMPAIGN
PO Box 96836
Washington, DC 20090-6836

CHARTER MEMBER
REGISTRATION CERTIFICATE

☐ **YES,** I want to become a Charter Member of the National Museum of the American Indian and receive all the benefits to which my membership entitles me, including a year's subscription to *Native Peoples*. Please use my contribution to build this long-overdue tribute to the Native peoples of this Hemisphere. I enclose:

☐ $20   ☐ $35   ☐ $100   ☐ $250   ☐ $500   ☐ $1,000   ☐ $_____Other

↑
*Charter
Membership
Rate*

AN18NE

Jane Sample
Lautman & Company
1730 Rhode Island Avenue, NW
Suite 700
Washington, DC 20036-1730
‖‖‖‖‖‖‖‖‖‖‖‖‖‖‖‖‖‖‖‖‖‖‖

Please detach here and mail with your check (payable to: **NMAI/Smithsonian**) in the enclosed postage-paid envelope.   C20

continues

The Letter's Not the Only Thing 95

Exhibit 6–3 continued (device unfolded)

Special
Charter Membership
Offer

Enjoy these benefits
when you become a Charter Member
of the
National Museum of the American Indian

MEMBERSHIP BENEFITS

Admission to all Smithsonian Museums in Washington, D.C. and to the Heye Center in New York City is free. Admission to the Cooper-Hewitt Museum in New York is free to Smithsonian Members. In addition, your NMAI benefits include the following:

$20 or more — GOLDEN PRAIRIE CIRCLE
Native Peoples Magazine, a full-color
 quarterly magazine
Membership Card
Museum shop and Mail Order Catalogue
 discounts of 10%
Invitations to events in your area
Your name listed on NMAI's permanent
 Member and Donor Scroll

$35 or more — RIVERBED CIRCLE
All of the above *PLUS*
The *NMAI Runner,* a special
 insiders-only publication on Native
 American activities

$40 or more — EVERGLADES CIRCLE
(family membership)
All of the above *PLUS*
Additional Membership Cards for
 family members
A free gift for each child when you visit
 the Heye Center's Museum Shops

$100 or more — SKY MEADOW CIRCLE
All of the benefits of the Everglades
 Circle *PLUS*
 Embossed NMAI Lapel Pin

$250 or more — BOUNDARY WATERS CIRCLE
All of the above *PLUS*
 Certificate of Appreciation
 — suitable for framing

$500 or more — DESERT SANDS CIRCLE
All of the above *PLUS*
 Special exhibition catalog

*For more information on benefits for
gifts of $1,000 or more, please call
Bruce at the National Campaign
office at 202-357-3164.*

*See other side for further
description of benefits.*

The National Museum of the American Indian's National Campaign logo was designed by a North Dakota Chippewa, Larry I. DesJarlais, Jr. Representing Native Americans as a holistically balanced people, the figure is placed solidly upon Mother Earth emphasizing the link between the two. The sunlike symbol reflects the sun's significance to many tribes and also represents a type of headdress.

Be kind to the earth. Please recycle

Courtesy of the National Museum of the American Indian, Smithsonian Institution, Washington, DC.

personal, like a letter from a friend or relative, or even a party invitation.

This format can sometimes be successful even for acquisition campaigns (usually for "highbrow" campaigns such as libraries, museums, and symphonies), but tests should be conducted using a change in format *only*, keeping the original copy the same right down to the P.S.

Whether To Use a Window Envelope

Regardless of the size you use, you must decide whether to use a window envelope or a closed face envelope. Clearly, a closed face envelope looks more personal—or does it? Some years ago, after most nonprofits had converted to the use of window envelopes for prospect mail, one organization with which I worked continued insisting on a closed face envelope, which meant an expensive two- or three-way match. The organization finally agreed to a small test of closed face versus window envelope. Returns were almost equal. Then in an even larger test, the counterintuitive results showed that the window outpulled the closed face envelope by a small but not insignificant margin. Today the organization sends all their prospect mail as well as most of their house mail in window envelopes.

Designing the Carrier Envelope

Naturally, your carrier envelope has your organization's name and return address in the upper left-hand corner or on the back flap. Where you put it depends on what else you put on the envelope and why.

Do you want to include, on the face of your carrier envelope:
- Teaser copy?
- A photograph or illustration?
- Nothing?

It's easier, of course, to design a plain envelope, and sometimes that's exactly the right thing to do. You've heard some people say that they *never* open envelopes with teasers. On the other hand, you've heard of many cases where a really good teaser outpulls the plain envelope. How, then, do you know what is right?

The answer is that until you actually test a teaser (on an acquisition package), you don't know for certain. But let's assume for now that you want to use an envelope with a teaser.

Ask yourself these questions:
- Do you really have good teaser copy and/or art? If not, do without.
- If your package contents don't live up to the tease, do without.

If you do decide on a teaser, here are some guidelines:
- If you are using a celebrity signer, use the celebrity's name and/or photograph on the envelope. You'll need no other message.
- Test a handwritten envelope teaser where appropriate. (See the envelope for Citymeals-on-Wheels, Exhibit 6–4.)
- Put the beginning of your letter on the envelope—just the first few lines. Or put some of the letter text on the envelope. (See the envelope for the Smithsonian's National Museum of the American Indian, Exhibit 6–5.)
- Make your envelope look like a telegram or a foreign airmail letter—but be sure you follow through inside with an emergency situation.
- Put "PHOTO ENCLOSED: DO NOT BEND" on the outside of the envelope if you're enclosing a photograph or facsimile.
- Try a manila kraft envelope for an official look.
- Never let art or copy extend below the window on the envelope. The Postal Service has a regulation prohibiting this.

DESIGNING THE REPLY ENVELOPE

There are five things to consider in designing the reply envelope:
1. size ($6^3/_4$ and monarch are standard)
2. postage paid or not postage paid (BRE or CRE)
3. color
4. text
5. teaser copy, if any

Postage Paid or Not Postage Paid

Because it costs money to receive a first class postage-paid contribution in a BRE (business reply envelope), some nonprofits are using CREs (reply envelopes without prepaid postage). Nonpaid return mail works well for most house mailings and even for some acquisition campaigns. We believe that the success rate is due to the fact that virtually all creditors

Exhibit 6–4 Envelope for Citymeals-on-Wheels

Marcia Stein

Citymeals-on-Wheels
355 Lexington Avenue
New York, NY
10017-6603

THERE IS NOT MUCH TO SAY ABOUT MYSELF. MY FAMILY IS GONE AND I LIVE ALONE.

Jane Q. Sample
Lautman & Company
1730 Rhode Island Avenue NW
Washington, DC 20036

Courtesy of Citymeals-on-Wheels, New York, New York.

---

have stopped paying return postage; thus people now keep stamps on hand. As most people send their charitable contributions when paying their bills, this works to the organization's advantage. However, we urge cautious testing before abandoning postage paid.

- Always pay for return postage on a test acquisition mailing. If you wish to find out if you can be successful without paying for postage due, test several times.
- Be cautious with test quantities. For example, on a mailing of 100,000 pieces, we would advise testing on only 10,000 pieces (2,000 from each of five lists).
- When not paying the postage on the reply envelope, test such phrases as "Your stamp here is an additional gift." It may be counterintuitive, but some organizations have found that this message *depresses* returns.

At the other end of the spectrum, some very large organizations are using "live postage" on reply envelopes. Live postage can be a single stamp or series of stamps of various denominations totaling the first class postage rate. One major nonprofit mailer is convinced about using live first class return postage—even on some acquisition mail. (Note: Most organizations cannot afford to do this and it is not an experiment to be undertaken without professional guidance and high name recognition.)

Color and Copy

Few organizations add "promotional" copy or photos to their reply envelopes, but it can be extremely effective. For example, when raising money for an emergency, it might be effective to put a phrase on your reply envelope such as EMERGENCY RESPONSE ENCLOSED: RUSH PROCESS! And if you are appealing for a special project, you might want to have your reply envelopes indicate that the gift is for a special purpose.

When it comes to choosing a color for your reply envelope, black type on white paper is the least expensive. Also, an all-white BRE will usually stand out in a package where you have used a lot of color in the other contents. Here too, you can experiment. Sample reply envelopes (BRE and CRE) are shown in Exhibits 11–4 and 11–5.

OTHER ENCLOSURES

Now that you have written and designed a letter, response device, carrier envelope, and reply envelope, do you have a complete package? Doubtless, if you put it in the mail exactly as it is, it would be sufficient. Still, you wonder if a little extra "something" might improve results.

For acquisition mailings, you can test an extra enclosure to learn whether the results are worth the additional cost. Following are seven items (among many) worth testing. Address labels are *not* simply

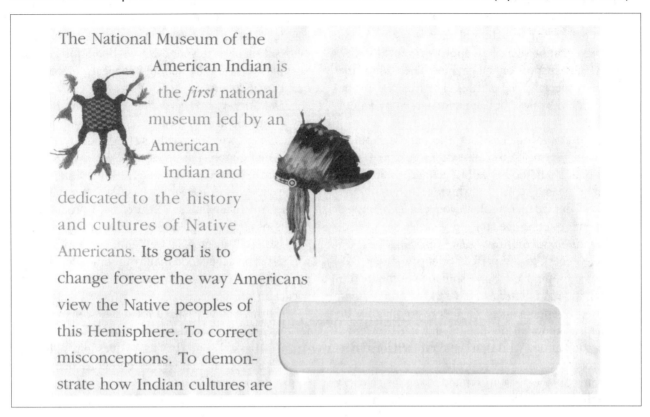

The National Museum of the American Indian is the *first* national museum led by an American Indian and dedicated to the history and cultures of Native Americans. Its goal is to change forever the way Americans view the Native peoples of this Hemisphere. To correct misconceptions. To demonstrate how Indian cultures are

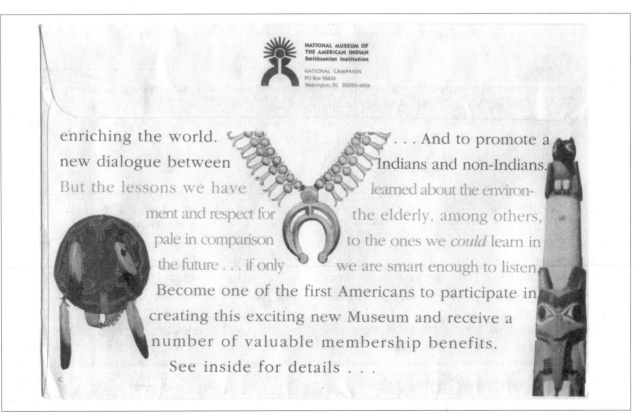

NATIONAL MUSEUM OF
THE AMERICAN INDIAN
Smithsonian Institution

NATIONAL CAMPAIGN
PO Box 96836
Washington, DC 20090-6836

enriching the world. . . . And to promote a new dialogue between Indians and non-Indians. But the lessons we have learned about the environment and respect for the elderly, among others, pale in comparison to the ones we *could* learn in the future . . . if only we are smart enough to listen. Become one of the first Americans to participate in creating this exciting new Museum and receive a number of valuable membership benefits. See inside for details . . .

Courtesy of the National Museum of the American Indian, Smithsonian Institution, Washington, DC.

additional enclosures, and are considered a type of package unto themselves.

Media Endorsements. This seal of approval can be in the form of an editorial or news story about your organization that has appeared recently in a leading newspaper or magazine. The thing that makes it especially valuable is that it is not propaganda written by you, but an endorsement by an outside party.

If you are fortunate enough to have a fabulous news story, reprint it on plain white stock; newsprint is even better. And do not fail to get permission from the paper or magazine in which it originally appeared. If denied permission, you can save money and time by quoting the story in your letter.

The Endorsement Letter or "Lift Note." Even if you have access to the perfect celebrity signer, it is sometimes preferable to have someone in the institution sign the main letter and have the celebrity sign a brief letter of endorsement. It is more credible for the president to know all the details and statistics about your organization, while the celebrity endorsement underscores the emotional appeal.

There's another reason, too, for asking the celebrity to sign the shorter letter, generally printed on monarch size stationery. It will take less time and headache to get his or her approval of shorter copy.

The Petition. If your organization is raising money to get something accomplished politically, a petition to a local or national government official can be an effective involvement device. It is regrettably true that politicians pay very little attention to "form" petitions (compared to handwritten letters). Nonetheless, petitions can be effective fundraising devices. Petitions to senators and representatives are classified as lobbying and you want to take care not to exceed your organization's stated lobbying budget. You can safely petition some other government officials, however, including the president of the United States, without the mail being classified as lobbying. Similarly, you can use petitions to corporations to make your case.

The Brochure. Fewer and fewer fundraising packages contain a brochure because in most cases tests show that packages without brochures elicit greater results at lower cost. However, there are exceptions, and cases where brochures should be used include:

- Membership organizations offering numerous benefits such as publications, products, trips, discounts, etc.
- Arts organizations that may wish to showcase items from their collections

The Newsletter or Magazine. We do not advocate sending your organization's publication(s) with an appeal to join. However, newsletters and annual reports can be effective when used in conjunction with annual or special appeals to your own file. Enclosing your publication(s) can also be helpful in appeals to renew your best lapsed donors.

The Survey/Questionnaire. When you send a survey or questionnaire as part of a fundraising package, some donors will answer the survey and return it without a contribution. This is especially true if the survey was used to obtain new donors. However, four iterations of the survey package Smithsonian's National Museum of the American Indian (Exhibit 6–6) produced best results of any package mailed for them over a seven-year period. It worked so well on house appeals that it was tested on acquisition mail with some success. (That is, it did well, but did not quite win over the control package.)

The reasons the Museum's survey worked so well for fundraising is because:

- It asked solid (but easy) questions rather than the usual lightweight questions one sees in most surveys.
- It was worded simply so as not to make the prospective donor feel uninformed.
- It did not overwhelm the request for money, which was very prominent in the letter.
- It gave a deadline so that responses could be tabulated, summarized, and given to the exhibition and public programs staff for their use.

Decals. Some organizations have found that the inclusion of a decal increases results. Other organizations have found it to increase only the package cost. If testing proves the latter to be true for you, it may be better to include the decal in your acknowledgment or "Welcome Member" package.

Messages from the Donor. Several organizations have successfully included sign and send back messages from donors in their mailings—especially holiday mailings. The holiday card from House of Ruth is one example of a "strong bounce-back" message. So is the holiday placemat from Citymeals-on-Wheels (Exhibit 6–7). The placemat is especially appropriate for organizations serving food, while the card can be used for any organization having a place of residence such as a hospital, homeless shelter, etc. If you tell the donor that you will distribute the placemats, cards, or other "bounce backs," be certain to do so. Then, for optimum results, include a story and photograph about this in your next

Exhibit 6–6 Charter Member Survey

CONFIDENTIAL

SURVEY NUMBER: 93RT543AJ1
ESTIMATED ANSWERING TIME: 5 minutes.
DEADLINE DATE: Ten (10) Days After Receipt

NMAI Charter Member Survey

PURPOSE: To solicit the advice of the American public on the creation of this Museum. In face-to-face consultations with the Native American community our question has been: What would you most like America and the world to know about you, your culture, your philosophy, your history, and your ideals?

Our questions for Charter Members of the Museum follow below. Please answer as carefully and thoughtfully as you can. Additional space is provided on the back to amplify your ideas (in words or drawings). Individual answers will be kept strictly confidential.

PART I Please mark your responses with a ☑.

1. Who do you think is the *primary* intended audience for the NMAI? (Check only one.)
☐ Native Americans
☐ Non-Indians
☐ Adults
☐ Children
☐ All of the above

2. Should the Museum focus on objects or ideas, or both?
☐ Objects   ☐ Ideas   ☐ Both

3. How do you think the exhibitions should be organized? (Check only one.)
☐ By culture
☐ By modern national boundaries or regions
☐ By tribal nations
☐ By theme
☐ By topic
☐ By historic period
☐ By current issues
☐ All of the above

4. What exhibition techniques should NMAI use? (Check as many as apply.)
☐ Books and other written study materials
☐ Live demonstrations and storytelling
☐ Recreated environments
☐ Hands-on, interactive displays
☐ High technology video and computer exhibitions

5. Should the Museum discuss topics of current social concern, such as health issues and economic problems on reservations?
☐ Yes   ☐ No   ☐ Maybe

6. Does every tribe in North and South America need to be represented in some fashion? (NOTE: There are at least 500 tribes in the Western Hemisphere.)
☐ Very important to do so
☐ Somewhat important
☐ Not important

7. Which of these programs are the most important for NMAI to provide? Rate in order from most important (1) to least important (6).
__ Easy access to collections for personal research
__ Traveling exhibitions
__ Videotape and computer programs
__ Conference center for Native American use
__ Loaning items to individual tribes
__ Fellowships and scholarships for Native American students

8. Which aspects of Indian society do you believe have the most relevance in today's society? (Check as many as apply.)
☐ Environmental values
☐ Respect for the elderly
☐ Tribal governance and conditions
☐ Organic agricultural practices
☐ Family relationships
☐ Spiritual beliefs

9. Which aspects of Native American history would you personally like to learn more about? (Check as many as apply.)
☐ Ancient history and early migration
☐ Pre-Columbian civilizations
☐ Colonial period
☐ Indian wars of 1800s
☐ Modern period
☐ The future of Indian culture and society

10. Which aspects of Indian art would you like to see highlighted in the Museum? (Check as many as apply.)
☐ Music and dance
☐ Drama and poetry
☐ Jewelry making and beadwork
☐ Weaving, pottery and other crafts
☐ Storytelling and oral history
☐ Painting, drawing and other graphic arts

11. In your opinion, what will be the most important achievement of this Museum? (Check no more than two.)
☐ Provide a new source of pride for the Native American community
☐ Offer contemporary Native American artists a showcase for their works
☐ Establish a dialogue between Indians and non-Indians
☐ Preserve the history and culture of the Native American people
☐ Demonstrate how Indian culture has enriched the world
☐ Educate and sensitize the non-Native American community

(Please continue on other side)

continues

Exhibit 6–6 continued

PART II

12. Have you ever been to (Check as many as apply):
- ☐ An Indian reservation
- ☐ Historic Indian ruins or battlegrounds
- ☐ An Indian pow-wow
- ☐ A museum of Indian art/culture

13. Have you ever visited the National Museum of the American Indian at 155th Street and Broadway in New York City?
- ☐ Yes ☐ No

14. Do you financially support any of the following? (Check as many as apply.)
- ☐ Native American Rights Fund
- ☐ American Indian College Fund
- ☐ Association of American Indian Affairs
- ☐ Native American primary and/or secondary schools
- ☐ Other museums of Native American arts/culture
- ☐ Other (Please specify.)

_____

15. Was your subscription to NATIVE PEOPLES magazine a critical factor in your decision to join NMAI?
- ☐ Yes ☐ No

16. Has NATIVE PEOPLES lived up to your expectations?
- ☐ Yes
- ☐ No
- ☐ No opinion

PART III

YOUR ANSWERS TO THE FOLLOWING QUESTIONS HELP US REACH OTHERS INTERESTED IN SUPPORTING NMAI.

17. Are you a Native American?
- ☐ Yes ☐ No
If yes, which tribe? _____

18. Your age (Check one.):
- ☐ Under age 18   ☐ 50-64
- ☐ 18-34   ☐ 65+
- ☐ 35-49

19. ☐ Male   ☐ Female

20. Your education level:
- ☐ High school graduate
- ☐ Some college
- ☐ College graduate
- ☐ Advanced degree
- ☐ Other (Please specify.)

_____

21. Can you make a contribution for the construction of the NMAI to help us during this critical launch phase?
- ☐ Yes ☐ No
(If yes, please fill out the top portion of this form.)

22. Any other ideas or suggestions? Please use the space below to share your thoughts about the proposed museum in words or drawings. (Use additional sheets if necessary.)

_____
_____
_____
_____
_____
_____
_____
_____
_____

```
DO NOT WRITE IN THIS SPACE
FOR INTERNAL USE ONLY
DATE SURVEY REC'D _____
DATE SURVEY TABULATED _____
TABULATOR'S INITIALS: _____
```

Courtesy of the National Museum of the American Indian, Smithsonian Institution, Washington, DC.

Exhibit 6-7 Example of a Bounce-Back Appeal (letter, page 1 only)

Marcia Stein
Executive Director

HAPPY THANKSGIVING

When you sign the enclosed placemat, we will deliver it for Thanksgiving -- accompanied by a turkey dinner with all the trimmings -- to a home-bound senior citizen here in New York City. Knowing that you care will mean so much to someone who is old and alone this Thanksgiving.

But first, read the shocking facts about the lack of food and nutrition in our elderly community.

Dear Friend:

Imagine being old and alone in New York at any time of year -- but especially during the holidays. Thousands of older people live right here in New York City -- not in retirement centers or nursing homes, but still in their own apartments. They've managed to do what most of us want to do as we age: maintain our dignity and independence, for as long as possible.

But many of these seniors develop permanent or temporary conditions -- a broken hip, blindness, severe arthritis -- that keep them from going out on their own. And it's to these shut-ins that Citymeals-on-Wheels delivers hot, nutritious meals.

Citymeals-on-Wheels -- with the support of thousands of New Yorkers like you -- helps our elderly neighbors by bringing meals to 12,000 doorsteps each week. Meals that they are too old or frail to shop for or prepare. Meals that many of them can't otherwise afford. Meals brought by a friendly visitor.

Meals that literally save lives.

At least half of those we serve live below the poverty line, which means they live on only about $7,500 a year. All are chronically disabled. And almost all live alone.

Believe me, the women and men we assist are grateful for our help, as shown by the hundreds of letters we receive from them. Here's a letter from Dorothy, for example.

355 Lexington Avenue   New York, New York   10017-6603   (212) 687-1234

continues

Exhibit 6–7 continued (placemat, size 8¹/₂″ × 11″)

HAPPY THANKSGIVING

Please enjoy this special holiday meal with our best wishes.
Greetings from your friends at Citymeals-on-Wheels
and

NAME AND GREETING

Citymeals-on-Wheels   355 Lexington Avenue   New York, New York 10017-6603

Courtesy of Citymeals-on-Wheels, New York, New York.

newsletter. Incidentally, the placemat is an inexpensive enclosure as it is printed on one side in only one or two colors and has no personalization. It is standard size ($8^1/_2'' \times 11''$ or 16'') and folds to fit a #10 envelope.

Report from the Field. This type of insert should read like an actual report from someone close to the organization, but not in the administrative office. It can be from an organizational representative (such as a letter requesting more supplies). It can be a "wish list" from a nurse or doctor, say in a field hospital or clinic. Like the illustrated sample from ACCION International, it can be a "Report from the Field" (Exhibit 6–8). In this instance, the report was printed on lined blue paper with photographs. Such devices can be very effective when used constructively.

Meal Tickets. If your organization feeds its clientele on a regular basis or on special holidays, meal tickets are an effective way to dramatize the need. Each ticket should represent a different size gift people make to your organization. The meal tickets for GMHC in New York City effectively illustrate this type of enclosure (Exhibit 6–9).

Certificate of Appreciation. A framable Certificate of Appreciation can be used to commemorate an anniversary, the conclusion of a campaign, and other events in your organization. However, the focus should be on the donor in both the certificate and the accompanying letter. When printed as part of the response device, the certificate can be personalized at no additional charge. The sample here for the Elizabeth Glaser Pediatric AIDS Foundation is an especially attractive certificate sent commemorating the donor's loyalty (Exhibit 6–10).

THE PACKAGE AS A WHOLE

You've worked hard to make each component in the package look just right. You can now rush to the printer, right? No, not just yet. Each part of your package may be good, but how do all the parts look together? Do the pieces complement one another? Is the whole more (or somehow less) than the sum of its parts? To find the answers to these questions, you should take a hard look at the package, as it will be seen by the potential contributor. Here are some things to ask yourself.

Does the Envelope Fit Well with the Letter?

If you are using teaser copy, make sure that the reader who has been "teased" has his or her curiosity satisfied. For example, if you have a picture of an abused animal on the envelope with copy that reads, "This dog was in danger of dying, until . . . ," don't wait until the fourth paragraph to mention the dog. If you are constantly revising the envelope and/or the beginning of the letter, it's important to make sure that you don't decide on the "perfect" envelope and the "perfect" opening, only to find that the two have little to do with each other.

Does Your Appeal Have a Theme?

Be consistent throughout. If your theme is "Give a kid a break" by sending him or her to summer camp, mention it on the response device by writing, "Yes, I want to give a kid a break! Please use my enclosed contribution for your Summer Camp Financial Aid Fund." On the BRE, instead of just having the name and address of your organization, you might include something like "Summer Camp Financial Aid Fund Contribution: Process At Once." Even if your appeal isn't this specific, you should still make sure its theme is clear throughout the package.

Do You Try To Include Too Much Information?

When doing research for your appeal, you may find that you have more information than you know what to do with. It may be tempting to try to include everything. But be careful not to bombard the prospect with too much information. You also don't want to make your appeal visually unattractive with small margins in order to get every last word in about your organization's programs. All the information in the world won't mean a thing if it is too much to read or be absorbed by the prospect.

Does the Lift Note or Enclosure Complement the Appeal?

If a credible celebrity is going to sign a lift note, make sure that what the celebrity says relates to the rest of the package. If your signer tells how one of your organization's programs helped his elderly mother (or some other person), be certain to mention that program in the main letter, or even use a photograph of the celebrity and his mother.

Similarly, if you're enclosing a news article or magazine piece describing your group, the image that enclosure conveys should represent what you've presented in the rest of the appeal. Like the pieces of a puzzle, all the pieces of a direct mail package should

Exhibit 6–8 Letter (page 1 only) with Report from the Field

ACCIÓN

More than hope, success.

June 1999

Dear Valued Supporter of ACCION,

The scenes of destruction caused by Hurricane Mitch in Honduras and the earthquake in Colombia have faded from our TV screens, but life in these and other hard-hit Latin American countries has not returned to normal. Far from it.

<u>People who were poor to begin with are now devastated as well</u>.

To help you see what they're not showing on television, I have asked the ACCION International staff to visit, over the last several months, many of the countries in Latin America hard-hit by natural disasters and economic instability. I have talked with our ACCION affiliates in Honduras, Colombia, Ecuador and Brazil. And they have spent countless hours and days with many of our clients who have lost their homes and businesses in Hurricane Mitch and the Colombian earthquake — and scores of others whose incomes are being eroded by intense economic pressures.

The enclosed report, complete with photographs, is the result. Its purpose is to update loyal ACCION supporters about the urgent need for capital to help the people of Latin America dig their way out of the massive natural destruction and economic downturn that is now exacerbating the region's endemic poverty.

Without the modest loans ACCION and our affiliates provide, these small business owners — these courageous "microentrepreneurs" — will not have the money needed to start over.

As you'll see, <u>the situation in these countries remains grave</u>. Although the lives of these people have been turned upside down, they're not down and out. I'm confident that, with a helping hand, they'll turn things around. And once you realize what is needed to help them rebuild their lives and work their way out of poverty, I'm hopeful you'll respond as you have in the past, by making a generous contribution to ACCION.

The will of these people in the face of adversity is remarkable. I've never seen more determination and pride in people coping with natural disaster or intense economic pressures. It is inspiring to witness such energy and creativity from men and women who have every right to feel shortchanged by circumstances — but refuse to give in.

Again and again, the people the staff met with — the poor microentrepreneurs who rely on ACCION and our affiliates for small loans — assured us that once they're back on their feet, they will repay every last *peso* and *real* we extend to them.

From the tortilla maker in Tegucigalpa, Honduras to the bakery owner in the heart of Colombian coffee country, these ACCION clients told us about their plans for rebuilding. They listed what equipment they'd need to buy to get back in business again. And over and over again, they thanked ACCION — and

(over, please)

ACCION INTERNATIONAL 120 Beacon Street, Somerville, Massachusetts 02143 USA Tel 617-492-4930 Fax 617-876-9509 www.accion.org

continues

Exhibit 6–8 continued

REPORT FROM THE FIELD:

May 1999

ON THE GROUND IN TEGUCIGALPA, HONDURAS
IN THE WAKE OF HURRICANE MITCH -- (November 1998)

Immediately after the hurricane, loan officers from FUNADEH, our ACCION affiliate, traveled by jeep and on foot over washed-out roads to assess the damage. They encountered small business establishments toppled by wind and homes packed to the ceiling with mud and debris.

Despite the widespread devastation in the area, they reported that not one FUNADEH client they talked to asked that his or her loan be forgiven. Instead, the people asked for more time to repay their existing loans, and in some cases for additional loans to rebuild their businesses. One group of borrowers even pooled their strained resources to take on the debt of fellow borrowers who had suffered even greater losses.

AND 3 MONTHS LATER -- (February 1999)

VIRGINIA MONCADA. 32-year-old Virginia Moncada's brick and concrete house was completely destroyed by Hurricane Mitch. The house her family is now living in was pieced together from wood she found after the waters receded. Virginia told us she has four children. She urgently needs a small loan to help improve their living conditions.

GLORIA MARTINEZ. Left homeless by Hurricane Mitch, Gloria Martinez, who had been self-employed as a seamstress before the storm, is now living with her six children in a temporary dwelling. When we visited her, she was living with ten other people in extremely crowded conditions.

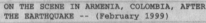

Gloria has had three loans from ACCION's affiliate FUNADEH. She used them to buy a new sewing machine and fabric to begin her own business to support her family. When our staff spoke with her, Gloria said she needs another loan to begin her business again, and replace her lost income -- so she can feed her children.

ON THE SCENE IN ARMENIA, COLOMBIA, AFTER THE EARTHQUAKE -- (February 1999)

In an immediate response to the January 25, 1999, earthquake, ACCION's affiliate Cooperativa Emprender gathered donations from its own staff members. Within days of the disaster it had managed to deliver $9,000 to two of its hardest-hit agencies in Armenia and Pereira to use as direct assistance for their own personnel -- many of whom had lost their homes.

A total of 15 community kitchens were also set up to serve the people in Armenia and Pereira. And ten tons of rice, cornmeal and beans were served to over 1,500 hungry people who had been left with little more than the clothing on their backs.

AND 4 MONTHS AFTER THE EARTHQUAKE -- (May 1999)

Thousands of Colombians who lost their homes and livelihoods in the severe earthquake are still living in shelters like this. They need loans to rebuild their businesses and start again.

Courtesy of ACCION, International, Somerville, Massachusetts.

Exhibit 6–9 Response Form and Meal Tickets

GMHC 2000 FALL FOOD CONTRIBUTION FORM

☐ Yes, I want to help provide hot, nourishing meals for people with AIDS this Thanksgiving. I've signed the meal ticket in the amount I want to contribute, and I'm returning it with my gift to support GMHC's 2000 Fall Food Appeal.

☐ $63.75   ☐ $127.50   ☐ $255.00   ☐ Other $_____

100% of your gift will go to feeding people with AIDS. Please give generously! 1704 AHAAA4

To charge your gift by credit card or to request information, please see reverse side.

Please return this form with your contribution (payable to GMHC) and one meal ticket in the envelope provided. Your contribution is tax-deductible to the full extent of the law. **THANK YOU!**

Ms. Jane Q. Sample
Lautman & Company
342 Madison Anenue
New York, NY 10173-9999

GMHC 119 West 24th Street, New York, NY 10011

THIS CERTIFICATE WILL PROVIDE NOURISHING MEALS FOR PEOPLE WITH AIDS

I am making a contribution of $63.75 to provide hot, nutritious meals for 3 people with AIDS for a week.

1704   AHAAA4

Ms. Jane Q. Sample
Lautman & Company
342 Madison Anenue
New York, NY 10173-9999

SIGNATURE

THIS CERTIFICATE WILL PROVIDE NOURISHING MEALS FOR PEOPLE WITH AIDS

I am making a contribution of $127.50 to provide hot, nutritious meals for 3 people with AIDS for two entire weeks.

1704   AHAAA4

Ms. Jane Q. Sample
Lautman & Company
342 Madison Anenue
New York, NY 10173-9999

SIGNATURE

THIS CERTIFICATE WILL PROVIDE NOURISHING MEALS FOR PEOPLE WITH AIDS

I am making a contribution of $255.00 to provide hot, nutritious meals for 3 people with AIDS for 1 month.

1704   AHAAA4

Ms. Jane Q. Sample
Lautman & Company
342 Madison Anenue
New York, NY 10173-9999

SIGNATURE

Exhibit 6–10 Certificate of Appreciation and Response Form

ELIZABETH GLASER PEDIATRIC AIDS FOUNDATION
2950 31st Street, Suite 125, Santa Monica, California 90405
www.pedaids.org

Yes, I want to help the Elizabeth Glaser Pediatric AIDS Foundation continue their vital work to find a vaccine for pediatric AIDS, to raise AIDS awareness and to support families struggling with HIV. I enclose:

☐ $100   ☐ $250   ☐ Other $_____

Mrs. Jane Q. Sample
Anytown   64067
U.S.A.   S69A1F

Please detach and return the top portion of this form with your check, made payable to the Elizabeth Glaser Pediatric AIDS Foundation, in the envelope provided. Your gift is tax deductible to the extent allowed by law. Thank you!

To request information, please see reverse side.

DETACH HERE

A decade of progress,
a decade of promise

THE ELIZABETH GLASER PEDIATRIC AIDS FOUNDATION

Gratefully Acknowledges

Jane Q. Sample

For outstanding support on behalf of children with HIV/AIDS.

Susie Zeegen
Co-founder

Kate Carr
Chief Executive Officer

A Decade of Progress, A Decade of Promise

Courtesy of the Elizabeth Glaser Pediatric AIDS Foundation, Santa Monica, California.

fit together to create a picture of your organization and why it merits the donor's support. That may mean you have to spend more time rearranging the pieces, but it will be worth it when the entire package is as good as the individual pieces that make it up.

Does Your Appeal Have Integrity?

Before concluding this chapter, it is important to mention how crucial it is that your appeal be presented honestly. While you must prepare a package that will motivate people to support your organization, you must be careful not to damage your credibility by using false or misleading statements.

Here are five dangers to watch out for.

1. Don't take credit for something you didn't do.
2. Don't use misleading information to support your case.
3. Don't overdo the guilt or fear factor.
4. Don't make false claims about how contributions will be spent.
5. Don't use fictional case histories attributed to an actual person. Typical case histories are suitable, but must be described as typical. Never use a person's real name without written permission.

These five dangers aren't the only ones you are likely to encounter in creating your appeal. Remember to cast a discerning eye on what you're sending out and ask yourself if what you are claiming is really true. If the answer is no, it's best to change it. Not only is this the moral thing to do, it also is the most practical in the final analysis. It isn't worth it to risk your own or your organization's integrity.

Chapter 7
Testing for Fun and Profit

CHAPTER OUTLINE

- Everyone Can Test
- What's in a Winning Package?
- In What Quantities Should You Test?
- In What Proportions Should You Test?
- What Size "Lift" Makes a Difference?
- What If the Test Package Partially Works?
- How Are House Appeal Tests Different?
- Benefits and Premiums
- Brochure
- Credit Card Charge Option
- Endorsement or "Lift" Letter
- Envelope Teaser Copy
- Insertion Order
- Letter Length
- Letter Signer
- Package Size
- Photographs
- Art
- Postage
- Reply Envelope: Postage-Paid BRE vs. CRE
- Temporary Membership Card
- Name and Address Labels
- Typeface
- Underlining and Call-Outs
- Basic Membership Ask Amount
- Conclusion

EVERYONE CAN TEST

Many organizations believe that they cannot conduct direct mail tests because of insufficient quantities. This is rarely the case. If you are expecting a minimum return of 200 gifts from any one mailing, you can test *something*. This is because 100 is the magic number that is statistically quantifiable.

Thus, on a house mailing to just 5,000 members/donors (from whom you expect a 4% return) you can make a quantifiable test if you just divide your list in half. And on an acquisition mailing to just 20,000 prospects (from whom you expect a 1% return), you can also test by dividing your merged lists in half.

What you want to learn by testing is what makes a package the best it can be—something we all think we know, but often don't. Only through testing will you learn whether the envelope teaser copy is as good as you think . . . whether that pithy shorter letter can really outpull a longer version . . . whether the inclusion of photos depresses response and much more.

WHAT'S IN A WINNING PACKAGE?

#1. *More often than not, a new member/donor acquisition package will contain:*

- a four-page letter, printed front and back, signed by the chief executive officer

- a postage-paid business reply envelope (BRE)
- a #10 business envelope with a nonprofit live stamp
- the reply/gift form that carries the prospect's name and address and briefly restates the message

#2. *The package might contain:*
- Outside envelope teaser copy
- A front-end premium if the mailing is 150,000 or more; if the mailing is smaller than 150,000, obtaining a good benefit/cost ratio would require something less expensive such as a bookmark or decal

#3. *The package would not contain*:
- a brochure (unless there is a good reason)
- a lift letter (unless dictated by politics)
- photographs (unless it is about animals)
- a credit card payment option (at this time)
- an additional offer of *any* kind (you want the prospect to focus on making a gift)

#4. As for a house appeal, the difference between it and an acquisition package is that one would almost never put teaser copy or photos on a house appeal envelope, a courtesy reply envelope (CRE) would be used instead of a BRE, and the letter might be shorter (certainly different) than the acquisition—usually 3 pages is sufficient. However, some successful house appeals are up to 10 pages in length.

How do I know this? I know through many years of testing almost everything there is to test for hundreds of organizations of every type—large and small, local and national, in the fields of education, the arts, health, the environment, and social services. And, the way you will know which techniques and styles work best for your organization is to test them.

The following pages document 16 things that are worth testing on most charitable direct mail. There are other things that can be tested too, but these 16 are the most important.

IN WHAT QUANTITIES SHOULD YOU TEST?

As stated earlier, to gain statistically valid reports, you must receive a sufficient number of gifts (100) from any given test segment.

If your mailing quantity is sufficiently large, you can test more than two things. In fact, as long as you design a test correctly, you can test as many variables as size, budget, and your ability to analyze the tests allow.

IN WHAT PROPORTIONS SHOULD YOU TEST?

Some mailers feel that testing 50–50 percent provides adequate results, but it is not recommended.

The purpose of testing a new approach is to increase results, but test ideas can also depress results, and sometimes what you learn seems entirely counterintuitive. So just in case the new test loses, why not hedge your bets and mail the control package to 65 percent of your file, thereby testing that new idea on only 35 percent of the file? (Just be sure that the smaller portion can theoretically yield at least 100 gifts—hopefully more, for valid, winning results.) For accuracy, make sure the test and control groups are the same size as shown in Table 7–1.

Thus if you want to test two new ideas on a mailing totaling 30,000 pieces, your control package will go to 19,500 people and your two new tests will go to the remaining 10,500 people split two ways, or about 5,250 people per panel. To have verifiable results (i.e., to reach 100 percent responses), you need an overall 2 percent return in small test panels of 5,000 or 10,000—a number you should easily surpass on a house appeal, but one you rarely reach on an acquisition.

WHAT SIZE "LIFT" MAKES A DIFFERENCE?

If a test gets virtually the same percent return as the control, but gets an increased average gift of $5 or more, you should check to see if there are any anomalies in the returns such as one or two gifts of more than $100 (or higher if, as a rule, you get an exceptionally high gift average such as $75). But if your average gift is like most organizations—between $20 and $35—$100 gifts should be discounted when determining test winners.

What you are looking for in a test is a lift of at least 5 percent in returns and in gift average. If test

Table 7–1 Testing the Validity of Mailings

Valid Test—Compare these two panels for results

Total Mailing	Control	Test	Balance
100,000	25,000	25,000	50,000

Invalid Test—You cannot compare two groups of different sizes.

Total Mailing	Control	Test	Balance
100,000	25,000	50,000	25,000

results look promising, you should retest as soon as possible. If results hold up on the second test, you can feel confident in rolling out this version of the package to the entire file on the next go-round.

WHAT IF THE TEST PACKAGE PARTIALLY WORKS?

Don't be greedy. You don't have to get both a percent return increase *and* a larger average gift to declare the test a winner. In fact, when one goes up, the other usually goes down or stays the same. Further, if yours is an acquisition mailing, and if it is a large one, you can check to see if one package works on particular lists and not on others. If you can detect a pattern, you can try mailing two or more control packages to two or more distinct list types. This approach can work well, but is only affordable for larger mailers.

HOW ARE HOUSE APPEAL TESTS DIFFERENT?

Most tests are conducted on acquisition mailings because in house file mailings of the same appeal are rarely sent twice. Therefore, if a particular enclosure in a test package wins—and it's a one-time occurrence—you are gaining almost useless information for future mailings. However, if you consistently test the same thing (and for most organizations, this would mean at least four mailings per year), you can learn a great deal. For example, if you test teaser versus no teaser on house appeal envelopes; window envelope versus closed face; or two-page versus four-page letters and the results consistently show that no teaser wins, or that window envelopes tie with closed face, or that two-page letters do just as well as longer letters, then you can increase returns and save money because all of your winners are the less expensive way to go. Just don't make any of these important decisions based on a one-time test.

Exhibit 7–1 offers a listing of "package elements" to test. Each element is discussed in more detail and some are illustrated with samples.

Some of the test suggestions listed require additional discussion, which follows.

BENEFITS AND PREMIUMS

While these two words are often used interchangeably, for purposes of clarification, we will call *benefits* those rewards that you receive after giving a gift or joining, and what we will call *premiums* are rewards you get up-front in the fundraising packages, which you receive regardless of whether you give.

Front-End Premiums

Front-end premiums include, but are not limited to, decals, bookmarks, stamps, note cards, calendars, certificates, namestickers, and the like—almost always something designed to be used and inexpensive to produce (despite the fact that the item's perceived value is much higher than the actual cost). Such premiums can be used in house file mailings, in acquisitions, or both. Using a premium for both decreases the per unit cost and is thus more cost-effective. See Chapter 9 for more on premiums.

Back-End Benefits

The typical benefits of membership in an institution are:
- membership card
- newsletter and/or magazine
- free admission
- discounts in shop or by mail
- lapel pin

Benefits are not exclusive to membership organizations, although some types of benefits—especially membership cards—are more appropriate for membership organizations than for donor organizations. Additionally, there are literally hundreds of other items offered by many nonprofits (especially those that do not have a campus or building) including tote bags, baseball caps, umbrellas, books, maps, and signed prints. There is no proof, one way or another, that the addition of "fancy" benefits, increases giving at the basic levels of membership. Sometimes a benefit will work and other times not. What seems to work best are "behind the scenes" benefits, especially for upgrading members to higher levels of giving.

Think of special invitations to events, a special entrance or use of a dining area, naming opportunities, hard-hat tours, and the like. People like to be singled out, to hear their name called, to be special in some way. Just look at theatergoers looking in the "Playbill," to ensure their names are included as sponsors and to learn in what category their friends might be.

Exhibit 7–1 Worthwhile Tests To Conduct

Tests	*Examples*
Basic Membership Price/Ask Amount	Determine whether a larger or smaller "ask" will increase income long-range.
Benefits (back end)	Premium/benefits vs. none or one vs. another or stronger emphasis on a certain premium.
Benefits (front end)	Decals, bumper stickers, etc. vs. no premium, or one front-end premium vs. another.
Brochure	Delete brochure from package, or try adding one. (An ideal place to list benefits).
Credit Card charge option	Test accepting checks and credit cards vs. checks only.
"Ask Line"	Ask amount circled, most recent contribution vs. highest previous contribution, long ask string vs. asking for only two basic amounts plus "other."
Endorsement or "lift" letter	Include "lift" with main letter vs. main letter only.
Envelope/Teaser copy	No message vs. a "grabber" teaser or art or one teaser vs. another.
Insertion Order	Vary the first thing the prospect sees on opening the envelope.
Letter length	Two pages vs. four or more.
Letter signer	Celebrity signer vs. in-house signer with title of authority.
Name and address labels	With labels vs. without labels.
Package size	Smaller vs. larger size with virtually identical content.
Photographs	Photos in body of letter copy vs. no photos at all.
Postage	Third class meter vs. indicia vs. live stamp.
Reply Envelope (Postage-paid BRE v. plain CRE) or even vs. live stamp(s) on reply envelope	BREs do not require the donor to affix postage as the CRE does. Use of live stamp(s) on a reply is also an option.
Temporary Membership Card	These usually show through a window of the carrier envelope.
Typeface	Courier vs. Times Roman; also underlining vs. no underlining.
Underlining and Call-Outs	These emphasize the most important points.

BROCHURE

Years ago, virtually every direct mail package included a brochure. This was true in the days of the short letter where the brochure contained the additional information that wouldn't fit in the letter, but no longer. Like the advice given under the topic of letter length, it is suggested that you omit the brochure and use a four-page letter. While fun to design, a brochure rarely adds anything except cost to an appeal and its presence often depresses returns.

There are exceptions, such as for membership organizations that offer a lengthy array of membership categories and benefits, or museums requiring photographs of objects and exhibitions, etc. By and large, however, brochures are passé in direct mail. *A word of warning:* Never, ever send a brochure on its own without a letter. If in doubt, you can test it.

CREDIT CARD CHARGE OPTION

It may surprise you to learn that in this modern age, the jury isn't in yet on the use of credit cards in direct mail. While it may be convenient to the donor, there is some backlash against fraudulent use of credit cards. It is not as simple as saying that credit cards work for some organizations and not for others. We have seen credit cards sometimes work and not work within the *same* organization. You are advised to test credit cards at least four times throughout the year on acquisition packages as well as house appeals and renewals. Make your decision on the information gained in general.

The reason for the failure of credit cards to catch on could be the fact that most donors are over 62 and do not move easily into the modern, fast-paced world. Direct mail is an old-fashioned communication device, not given to jazzy art or to modern techniques. Within a few years, credit cards may be commonly accepted by everyone just as bar coding has now come to be accepted. But now is now and the future is not yet here. So test. And test again.

ENDORSEMENT OR "LIFT" LETTER

A "lift" letter is a second letter of a smaller size and length, from someone who has a different perspective on the issue or cause being discussed. It can be a thank you letter from someone served by your institution, a letter from a celebrity who is relevant, or some other new message from a person other than the signer of the main letter. Its purpose, hence its name, is to "lift" response to your mailing. Like the brochure, its inclusion can easily be tested against leaving it out. They have worked and they have failed. Use your best judgment as to whether the additional message is motivating, then test it.

ENVELOPE TEASER COPY

House Renewals and Appeals

It cannot be overemphasized that on most house appeals (with the exception of the renewal series) teaser copy and art on the carrier envelope reduces income significantly by reducing the percent return, the average gift, or both. The theory as to why this is so is: When a current donor or member sees teaser art or copy (which looks commercial), he or she assumes that it is not a "real" letter from you or your organization. So it is trashed, unopened, more frequently than the plain business style envelope that looks like a real letter.

On the other hand, organizations having a renewal series of up to 10 in number, usually find that "renewal language" teaser copy on packages in the series usually work better than plain envelopes. You must assume that people don't want to lose their membership privileges or their association with your organization. And envelope teasers that state that a renewal reminder is enclosed tend to get opened. You can use language like "Your Membership Expires This Month" or "Final Renewal Notice" or "Special Benefits If You Renew Early," or "Annual Renewal Enclosed." For more information on establishing a Renewal series, see Chapter 5.

Acquisition of New Members/Donors

On acquisition copy (solicitation of new members/donors) teaser copy can be a powerful tool in getting the envelope opened, but not always. For every teaser on acquisition envelopes that improved results, there are plain envelopes that won the tests over teaser envelopes. You must test for yourself.

Let's not forget that when something shows through a window envelope such as a Temporary Membership Card or Name and Address Labels, that is also a teaser because it is trying to entice the recipient to open the letter. (See the section on temporary membership cards later in this chapter.) For example, see the sample AARP Andrus label package (Exhibit 7–2).

Exhibit 7–2 Envelope Teaser Copy and Letter (page 1 only)

601 E Street, NW
Washington, DC 20049

Non-Profit
U.S. Postage
PAID
Permit #377
Frederick, MD

Free Gift Enclosed!

Jane Sample
Lautman & Co
1730 Rhode Island Ave NW
Washington, DC 20036

AARP

ANDRUS

FOUNDATION

May 1999

Dear Friend:

We are delighted to send you these personalized address labels. They come with a message of hope I'm sure you'll want to hear.

For over 40 years, Americans have grown to rely on AARP for many services, including those related to health and aging. Now, Americans are helping the AARP Andrus Foundation undertake important research that will enable older people to maintain their independence and quality of life.

Some of these research projects include safe driving, coping with vision and hearing loss due to conditions associated with the aging process, and targeted memory training.

I'll describe more health-related projects in just a moment. But right now, I don't want to overlook some equally important research studies that we fund that are critical to the issue of <u>financial independence</u>, such as:

* Examining the impact of proposed changes to the Social Security system;

* Identifying the economic impact of Alzheimer's disease on family caregivers;

* Determining trends in private savings and pension options.

These are just a few of the hundreds of projects and programs the AARP Andrus Foundation supports. Together, they account for nearly $33 million spent by the Foundation to make the mature years what they really should be for everyone. But, <u>I</u> need <u>your</u> <u>help</u> to continue this work.

There are more than 32 million people in America today who struggle daily with the challenges of growing older. It's likely that you already know someone -- a family member or close friend -- who is facing the loss of independence and ability to live alone because of health or financial reasons.

(over, please)

601 E STREET, N.W. • WASHINGTON, D.C. 20049 • 202-434-6190 • www.andrus.org

Courtesy of AARP Andrus Foundation, Washington, DC.

INSERTION ORDER

Sometimes, but rarely, there is a marked difference in returns if you vary the first thing the prospect sees when opening the envelope. It's difficult to guess which piece in your package has the most appeal, but I would suggest that if you use teaser copy on the carrier envelope, the first item seen should relate to the teaser. If you are not using any teaser, probably the first thing should be a typed letter on your letterhead with good margins, indented paragraphs, and solid ink coverage. In other words, something inviting to read.

LETTER LENGTH

Perhaps the most questioned element in direct mail fundraising is the length of the letter. Hopefully, the following will explain why longer letters usually produce more donors/members and the most money. Most mailers—especially new mailers—are not household words. If they were, they wouldn't need to explain so much to prospects. Famous organizations like the American Red Cross and the Salvation Army can, and do, mail small packages with short letters that say very little. Such organizations don't get a large gift average (usually under $15), but they do get more gifts than most because they are well known and respected.

Most organizations, however, have to make a case for their cause—their need, qualifications, and expectations. This, combined with human-interest stories and the request for financial support, are necessary to sell the cause. Rarely can all this be compacted into a one- or two-page letter, and even if it could be, you don't want to do that. Here's why: The longer the letter (whether or not the prospect reads it all), the greater the perceived need, and the prospect is inspired to give more to address that need.

The main reason for the longer letter is simply that it raises more money than it costs. This doesn't mean you can't and shouldn't test a shorter letter. If your appeal can be adequately described in two pages, you should try to shorten it simply because you will save money on paper and printing. Just make certain that the short and long letters are virtually the same—that the beginning, ending, and P.S. are identical.

If you are making a longer letter into a short one, carve entire paragraphs out of pages two and three, the least read pages. If you are going from short to long, add information to pages two and three, perhaps including additional important points from your brochure. But change the letter only. Don't change anything else in the package so that you can verify "letter length" results. (For more information on letter length, see Chapter 4.)

LETTER SIGNER

Some people believe that there is magic power in who signs the letter. I believe there is far more magic in the person's title, unless the signer is extraordinarily impressive on his or her own merits. Recently, the longtime president of an organization with whom we had worked for many years retired. We had no choice but to send mail over the new president's signature and were afraid that the constituency had so closely bonded with the old president that returns would fall off.

What happened? Nothing. As logical as our worries may have sounded, the donors responded to the title and not the name, even though it was a less familiar name. And this experience occurs again and again.

There have been occasions when I have put all my hopes into a celebrity signer and I'll never know if I was right. The most memorable of all was in starting a mail campaign for the Vietnam Veterans Memorial, when we held out for Bob Hope. The reason was that back then no one had ever heard of Jan Scruggs, the young founder of the Fund, or indeed that a small group of veterans planned to build a memorial on the National Mall. That is why we felt a well-known spokesman would do better. The mailings did so well that whether or not the signer made the difference, well—it didn't matter any longer. But one thing was for sure. Once prospects became donors and received mail from the president of the organization who told stories of having been a Vietnam veteran himself, they gave and gave again.

PACKAGE SIZE

It is rarely worthwhile to test the same package components in two different sizes (say, #10 vs. 6″ × 9″). Changing the format can freshen the look and perhaps save a dying control package from obliteration, but rarely does testing two sizes merit the extra cost. The best thing is to choose the "right" size for a particular package in the first place.

Most appeals work quite well as a conventional #10 package, while others call out to be baronial or invitation style. Still others, like those for building funds, benefit from a 6″ × 9″ size and even large flat 8¹/₂″ × 11″ packages where blueprints or architectural renderings can be included. (But beware: In big cities of apartment dwellers, these larger formats can get crushed in small mailboxes, not to mention that they require more postage.)

PHOTOGRAPHS

The inclusion of photos in a package relates closely to whether you intend to use a brochure. If you do not, there are only three other places to use them: in or throughout the letter, on the reply form, or as loose photo-size reproductions (separate from the letter). With the exception of animal causes, most direct mail appeals fare better with the written word only. The inclusion of even one photograph on page one of a letter makes the appeal look more commercial, no matter how appealing the photograph.

The most effective use of photos is on the response card, but since space is limited, make it count! Don't use collages or montages, which are confusing to the reader. The use of loose photographs (especially with handwritten notes on the back as one would send to a friend) are extremely effective for the right package, but are expensive. Therefore, the lift in response should be considerable to make them worthwhile.

One caveat: If you are out to win a prize for your package, photographs are almost indispensable, for otherwise how can you capture the judge's attention? Fortunately, the giving public rarely decides to send money based on artistic merit. This plainer approach may bore your boss or client, but it saves you money and raises more too.

ART

In testing a plainer look for charitable appeals, do not confuse this look with premium-based appeals such as namestickers, calendars, cards, or certain other special appeals such as those for capital campaigns or building funds. Artwork is important to most premiums, just not always required on carrier envelopes. Artwork is also important in describing capital campaigns because you will want to send floor plans, architectural renderings, etc. to the donors and prospects. In some cases, you will want to send these in full color, but not always. For organizations that receive small average gifts, full color can

look extravagant. For museums and other institutions receiving larger gifts, full color may be entirely appropriate. Winning a prize is not the goal. Remember that what you are trying to do is to convince the donor that the project is being done as he or she would want it done and that you need help and involvement in order to succeed.

POSTAGE

While a few organizations sometimes use first class postage on acquisition mail, it is rare and not economical. The main reason for the use of first class postage is to speed delivery. This is because postal regulations allow the delivery of nonprofit mail up to three weeks after the drop date. While it doesn't usually take this long, it can. That (and the fact that first class postage is unnecessary to raise money) is why most acquisition mail is sent at the nonprofit, third class rate. As to whether to use live stamps as opposed to meter, it is up to you. We give a big thumbs-down to indicia mail unless the package already is extremely commercial looking. The difference is so slight in returns that the savings of metered mail over live stamps (which are much slower to affix) can be negligible. You really can't go wrong either way.

As for the house file, continuous testing has shown that first class postage—even when sent only to high dollar donors—can lower the returns because of the high cost (even if more people do give). The reason most organizations apply first class postage in writing to high dollar donors is to create an aura of important mail. Usually such mail is also fully personalized and sent in closed face envelopes. I believe, however, that what makes a letter look real and personal is no longer the first class stamp, but an envelope that is free of teasers and art. But you will want to test postage to donors for yourself. As for prospects, stick with third class, nonprofit, and try to qualify for as many postal discounts as possible (see Chapter 11).

REPLY ENVELOPE: POSTAGE-PAID BRE VS. CRE

In mailing to their own house files, nonprofits can do as well with a CRE as with a BRE. Donors seem quite willing to apply their own stamp to send a gift to a familiar cause. However, in acquiring new donors or members, it generally pays to spend the additional money to pay for the return postage.

You may ask, Why do many organizations apply first class live stamps to reply envelopes to their own high dollar donors if the donors are willing pay the postage to send a check?

It is rarely necessary to pay return postage on any house file mail. However, some organizations traditionally send their reply envelopes to major donors prestamped, and the donors have gotten used to it so it "might" hurt a given mailing slightly not to stamp the envelope. Still, it's hard to imagine someone writing out a check for $500, and then deciding not to send it when forced to apply a stamp. But stranger things have happened.

It's all about appearances. On a wedding invitation, the sender usually includes a live stamp on the reply envelope. In truly formal weddings, however, one doesn't even include a reply card or envelope; however, if that happened in direct mail, we'd go broke!

TEMPORARY MEMBERSHIP CARD

The technique of showing a membership card in acquisition copy has improved returns for such different organizations as the ASPCA (American Society for the Prevention of Cruelty to Animals) and the United States Holocaust Memorial Museum, among others. Samples of the outside envelopes with cards showing through the window are shown in Chapter 4 (Exhibit 4–2 and Exhibit 4–6). Bear in mind that the real membership cards are in full color.

NAME AND ADDRESS LABELS

The other type of acquisition package that continues to work quite well is the name and address label package or "namesticker packages" as they are often called. In the beginning, these ubiquitous labels were designed as three dimension stacks, either single or double, that usually showed through the carrier window. Today's labels usually come in sheet form, and are larger and more elaborate, with those in full color or in gold or silver foil working best. It's not a complicated thought process that leads to using photographs of kitties and puppies on labels for animal organizations. But what do you use for organizations that don't have the obvious to offer? Or what if your logo is not particularly suitable or beautiful? Through testing, we have learned that nonrelated items attract many people (and donations). You can use birds for non–animal appeals, flowers for non–horticultural appeals, and, of course, seasonally,

you can use nonreligious symbols such as bows, holly, or snowmen in either color or in foil. For example, the AARP Andrus Foundation used dogs and cats and nature scenes.

TYPEFACE

This is not a critical test, but an easy one to perform. In most tests, Times Roman wins but not always; Courier still works for some organizations. Don't use fancy fonts, including italics, in the body copy. It simply isn't legible and will get trashed more often.

UNDERLINING AND CALL-OUTS

Some development professionals are of the opinion that smaller donors under $100 like underlined sentences and bold face and that high dollar donors detest it. Underlining on letters should not be overdone—it's for emphasis only. But judicious use of underlining and bold face guides the reader through the critical parts of the letter. Ralph Applebaum, a famous designer of exhibitions and museum interiors, has said that he designs simultaneously for streakers, strollers, and studiers. In other words, some people spend an hour in an exhibition, others two or three, and some visitors return repeatedly to visit a favorite area again. In direct mail, we too have streakers, strollers, and studiers. We can segment our donors all we like, by giving amount, frequency of giving, longevity, etc. But there is no way we can tell whether they streak through or stroll through our letters.

We can hypothesize that most streakers are smaller dollar donors and studiers are major donors. But is that really so? A streaker could have so strong an interest in what you are doing (and trusts you so much) that he or she needs to read very little. A studier could be an average size donor who likes to critique copy or punctuation or give you a hard time about whatever strikes his or her fancy. In any event, remember that the underlining and other emphasis are to help guide the streakers and strollers. As for the studiers, since you don't know who they are until they write to you, you can't spare them the dreaded underlining.

BASIC MEMBERSHIP ASK AMOUNT

The most important thing has been left for last so that it isn't buried in the middle as you skip read. (You too may be a streaker or a stroller.) How much you ask for in the letter and on the reply form (that is the first and lowest amount you ask for) is vitally important. Some organizations can ask for and get a high basic gift. The arts and education in particular are thought of as high-ticket items and the audience to which you will address such appeals is usually affluent. Local organizations tend to get higher average gifts than national organizations, just as well known charities (think Red Cross, Salvation Army) get smaller gifts, but many more of them. It makes sense.

If you are just now starting to build a donor file however, don't presume to know too much. The first thing you might test is entry level—say $20 and $30. Make the second ask amount $10 higher than the first, and offer a very special personal benefit for the extra $10 to keep the gift average up. Always remember: The majority of people will give you the smallest amount you ask for. Always. But enough will give at the second level that it may increase the size of your average gift. For example, the Smithsonian's National Museum of the American Indian (NMAI) asked for $20 as its basic gift because the Smithsonian Institution itself charged only $20 for base membership. Wishing to secure a larger average gift, however, a $35 gift level was inserted and a very special premium was offered at that level. It was special because it was not a "thing" (you already got the magazine and membership card and museum discounts at the $20 level). It was special because it was a newsletter that took you "behind the scenes at the Smithsonian"—a newsletter through which you would gain an "insider's look" at the work being done in the Native American community. The result? The average entry-level gift shot up to $28—exactly between the $20 and $35 levels.

Emphasis on Ask Line

You can make it $20, $30, $50, $75, $100 and stop there. Or you can add $200, $500, and $1,000. In general, when acquiring a donor, you just want him or her to give a small gift now and upgrading can come later. Also, too many choices may keep the prospect from giving at all. When you test the ask line, always add the famous box called "( ) Other amount $_____."

CONCLUSION

In testing the foregoing package elements, take care that you design a valid test. This requires that the next test package be as similar to the control package as possible, except for the variable you are testing, then:

- Mail test segments at the same time.
- Use the same postage on both.
- Keep everything except what you are testing exactly the same.
- Code lists carefully.
- Test in sufficient quantities for verifiable results.

If you don't test correctly, you will never know whether those address labels or that movie star's signature were the right way to go or not. In short, when testing any component of a package, make every effort to leave the rest of the package as it was, including premium offers, postage, graphics, envelopes—everything!

Chapter 8
Card, Calendar, and Other Major Premium Programs

CHAPTER OUTLINE

- Program Description
- Perceived Value
- Choosing Art
- Writing Copy
- Results To Expect
- Packaging
- When You Care Enough
- Premiums in Acquisition Packages
- A Word of Warning

Some years ago, a new approach to obtaining additional gifts from members and/or donors came upon the fundraising scene. While the profitability of the program was exceptional, some people (like me) scoffed at the blatant use of premiums as fundraising "gimmicks." Let me describe the program and tell why I am devoting an entire chapter of this book to it.

PROGRAM DESCRIPTION

An organization or its agent would design a series of greeting cards or a beautiful wall calendar to give—not sell, mind you—*give* to donors and/or members. But while these were, in fact, gifts, the recipient was nevertheless asked to make a tax-deductible contribution to the nonprofit sending them. (There really is no such thing as a free lunch.) This was entirely legal from every standpoint. In fact, the cost of producing the gift itself ($1 to $2 at most) was well below the IRS standard of $7 for "goods or services received."

The organization stood to make a considerable sum of money and the donor received a gift with a "perceived value" of more than $7. The pioneer organizations that undertook the program fared as well as direct mailers in the 1960s, garnering gigantic percent returns. As an avalanche of "look-alikes" glutted the market, returns dipped. Yet such programs, when crafted strategically in terms of timing, product, and ask, still do extremely well.

Here is how the mechanics work:

- The first letter announces that a special gift will be sent to the donor from the nonprofit. There is an opt-out clause in small type on the reply card (usually on the back, but we recommend the front) giving the recipient an opportunity to refuse the gift. An astonishingly low percentage of recipients utilize this option.
- The second letter is sent six weeks later with the gift. The images on the cards (or calendar) have been carefully chosen to both reflect "popular" taste in art and, when possible, to relate to the organization's mission (for example, children's art for a children's hospital or nonthreatening wild animals for a conservation organization). The letter and reply form ask the donor to verify the gift was received in good condition and simultaneously to send a gift to the organization.
- The third and final letter is sent some six weeks later, "just to make sure" the gift was received. Again, donors who didn't contribute to the two earlier appeals are asked for a gift. All are sent reply envelopes.

So now you know. While I initially disdained the use of premiums as fundraisers, I have found them to be extremely effective as an adjunct to traditional direct mail. They can also be in good taste when the themes relate directly to the purpose of the organization. They are especially useful when an organization's programs are difficult to describe or when programs can obtain images that address their purpose (such as animal organizations that can use drawings of puppies and kittens or any type of baby animal, or mother-infant pictures for that matter). My own firm now creates premium programs for a number of clients including the Central Park Conservancy in New York City, the AARP Andrus Foundation (the illustrations are a good example of images to use when your program does not fit a particular card or calendar-worthy image), and the American Society for the Prevention of Cruelty to Animals (ASPCA), the program for which is a perfect example of what people love: kittens and puppies.

In partnership with an expert in the field, Holly White, in Falls Church, Virginia, the ASPCA was the first organization for which our firm produced calendar and card programs and the organization for which we originated and created a brand new premium: gift-wrap paper with gift tags. After mailing card and calendar programs for several years, we hoped that this diversification would be novel enough to boost premium revenue, which over time was experiencing some fatigue. To our delight this item has been enormously successful and is being adapted by numerous organizations, just as the card and calendar programs have been adapted by others.

The following steps are suggested for beginners:
1. You must be able to fit a two- or three-part series into your existing mail schedule without overworking the file. Granted, not everyone on your file will receive the package, but a large percentage will, so you must schedule each mailing regardless of type at least six weeks apart so as not to truncate returns to each previous mailing. (See Chapter 5 for a good mail schedule that utilizes a two-part premium series in addition to membership renewals and other special appeals. This hypothetical organization mails between 7 and 10 times annually to its members/ donors.)
2. Your active donor file of $15 plus donors in the past 18 months should total at least 20,000.
3. Mail the entire file initially, segmenting the names by clumps of gift sizes such as, $15–$19.99, $10–$24.99, etc., and how recently a gift was given, 0–6 months, 6–12 months, etc.
4. Evaluate mailing results, immediately ex-

cluding donors who asked to "opt out" (not to receive the gift) as well as any segments that did not break even. If you have an acknowledgment program in place, it is a good idea to include a reference to the premium program to which they gave. You often get a second gift this way.
5. The next time you undertake a premium program, mail first (with appropriate coding) to those donors who responded to the original program. You will be well rewarded financially. Then retest donors who did not participate, but whose file segments made money. This may or may not prove profitable, so keep the test size small.
6. Now you have a list of donors who are premium-responsive. You can mail premium offers to them even more successfully in the years to come. To that you should add all of your new donors/members, following steps 2, 3, and 4 above to learn which are premium-responsive.

PERCEIVED VALUE

The segmentation just mentioned is critical for, as we know, different people respond to different stimuli. People who like to attend parties respond best to invitations. Benefit lists rarely, if ever, work in direct mail. Similarly, there are always people who want something in return for their gift and know that there are many organizations out there who offer something—be it T-shirts, baseball caps, tote bags, umbrellas, music and video cassettes, etc.

Since certain people are so premium-responsive, and since there are so many potential premiums (more, even, than those listed above), why is it that nonprofits aren't using T-shirts or music cassettes as premiums in these programs? Why only cards, calendars, and gift-wrap paper?

The answer is a combination of perceived value and practicality as a mailing piece. While a beautiful 12-month wall calendar, a box of greeting cards, or a cellophane wrapped packet of gift wrap and matching cards should cost under $1.50 for the item itself (all are made of paper), the other items cost at least $3 or more, thus considerably reducing profitability. Also, it is relatively easy to obtain photos and describe, for example, Central Park in four seasons—fall, winter, spring, and summer—and all the work involved in keeping the park so beautiful all year long. What is more, these paper products (note cards, calendars, and gift wrap) are ephemeral: They get used up. The calendars last the longest and perhaps that is why calendars tend to get a slightly larger average gift than other premiums. It has a longer shelf life and thus a higher perceived value. The products become so popular with some people that they seek to purchase additional copies.

Cost-effectiveness is everything. So remember, when tempted to spend more money to use bleeds, to make the paper stock nicer, or the size larger, or have expensive original art done, consider cost-effectiveness. Such extra expense does not usually increase response. Rather it only lowers net profit.

CHOOSING ART

Here are a few rules about choosing themes, writing copy, and selecting commissioned art for your products.

To begin, remember that because a wall calendar is something people hang on their walls, it's something they must look at every day. So heed the following advice. The more pleasing the subject matter, the better the response will be. Color is more than worth the cost because we live in a color world today. Do not choose art based on what your boss likes or even what you like. Just remember, Norman Rockwell and Grandma Moses are the country's most popular artists, not those great artists whose retrospective exhibitions draw long lines around the block. People who go to museums are art lovers and not necessarily your donors. You have no way of knowing whether your donors like Picasso, Van Gogh, Remedios Varo, Paul Klee, or any one of a thousand other greats who could be named.

The chances are much, much better that they like Norman Rockwell or Grandma Moses. The chances are even better that they will like art by someone who isn't famous at all, but whose art or photograph is pleasing to them. "Art" seems to be most popular for greeting cards and gift wrap, while color photographs are the most popular for wall calendars.

WRITING COPY

In writing the letter(s) that precede, accompany, or follow the actual premium, be sure to emphasize that there is "No Obligation" to send a gift. Do not include a photo or drawing of the gift itself because marketers have discovered that the "mystery of not knowing" adds to the perceived value of the gift.

Letter #1, announcing that the gift is coming,

should be the one into which you put the greatest effort. The gift itself will be judged on its own merits and your best prose is meaningless. You do, of course, need to be enthusiastic in your letter with phrases such as, "Here is the wonderful Tenth Anniversary Calendar you've been waiting for. I have been eager to send it to you because I know how much you will enjoy it and remember us, month after month. The gift is without obligation, of course … it's my way of thanking you for all that you have done for us in the past. But while a contribution isn't required in exchange for the gift, our winter months would be a lot easier if you found it possible to send something now, while you are thinking about us."

Serial Style Copy

Some years ago, it was believed that if a suspenseful story ran through all three phases of your series, readers would open each and every package to see what happened next. Organizations that used this method usually sent all three mailings to every name on file, regardless of whether the donor had already given to an earlier appeal. (This dubious practice did garner multiple gifts from a small part of the file, but as the cards or calendars were touted as "gifts," we feel it is advisable to delete the "ask" when sending the cards to donors who gave to the first mailing.)

In any event, the "serial style" copy has been tested numerous times against a letter that essentially tells the same story, but includes the story's conclusion in each and every letter instead of saying, "I'll let you know what happened to the poor little match girl in my next letter."

Test results have shown that the serial style packages perform about the same as the letters that are self-contained (that is, in which the ending of the story is not withheld). Since such letters are more difficult to write and because most mailers are now sending (or testing) a two-part series, this style is no longer necessary. You can let those who do not open all three mailings (and that is most of them) in on the punch line with just one reading of your letter.

RESULTS TO EXPECT

Response rates to the three appeals tend to work as follows: The second package containing the gift of cards, calendar, etc. does the best; the first package announcing and describing the gift does second best; and the third appeal, playing on guilt because maybe the recipient used one of the cards and didn't send a gift, comes in last, but is still moderately profitable. Some mailers have pretty much reduced the number of mailings in the series by eliminating the third appeal or the first appeal. One choice of which to eliminate is usually dictated by the overall mail schedule and which mail months are available. This is primarily because (a) an organization can send an appeal on a nonrelated subject that performs better than a follow-up and (b) the organization doesn't appear to be dunning the donor. At the current time, we recommend only Parts 1 and 2 to most nonprofits.

PACKAGING

Testing can determine the packaging that works best for your organization. You can test boxed cards against cards packaged in 6″ × 9″ envelopes. You can test art and teaser on the carrier envelope or box. You can test inserts or special "extra" gifts in the second or third packages. If your file is large enough and you can afford it, you can even test cards versus calendars or calendars versus gift wrap, etc.

Test results vary from organization to organization. Exhibit 8–1 lists some tests conducted and possible results.

WHEN YOU CARE ENOUGH

Every organization grapples with the issue of whether to put its own "hallmark" on the back of the cards. That is, whether to include the organization's logo, name, and, perhaps, address. One's first instinct is to include it, and thus spread the word. You should

---

Exhibit 8–1 Tests Conducted and Possible Results

Some Tests Conducted	*And the Winner Is .....*
Boxed cards vs. envelope carrier	Boxed cards usually win in percent return and gift average, but seldom in percent cost recovered. If image is important to you, boxes are the way to go. I'm prone to them myself.
Art and teaser on boxed cards and envelopes vs. organizational logo only	Art showing all or part of card art inevitably wins against the plain carrier.
Large envelopes (flats) for calendars with art vs. logo only carriers	Logo only (name and address) outpulls envelopes with art. Test if you can.
Extra gift (sticker sheet, wallet-size) calendar, bookmark, etc.) vs. the product only	This often produces the best results in the third package to premium-oriented donors.
6 greeting cards vs. 8 vs. 10, etc.	Perceived value is key, so more is usually better. However, for the sake of net income 9 is best, three each of three designs that complement each other and, if possible, relate to your cause. (And don't waste your money putting more than 9 cards and envelopes in a carrier envelope instead of in a box.)
Low dollar vs. high dollar donors	People who are premium-responsive are good prospects regardless of income level. And since you don't know who they are until you evaluate mailing results, think twice before eliminating them.

always put your name and a short legend on a calendar. In fact, you can devote a full page or two on the back of the calendar to tell your organization's story. After all, only you and very few others will read this copy.

Unlike the calendar, cards do not remain with the donor. The greeting cards are sent to friends and associates whom they may—or may not—wish to tell about their association with your organization. For example, if yours is a prestigious arts organization, or a conservative environmental organization, donors may wish to be associated with your cause.

On the other hand, causes that are potential "downers" such as diseases or controversial causes, may not wish to include their name on the back of the cards. If quantity is sufficient, we recommend testing. It's one of the simplest and most economical tests you can undertake in a card program. When we tested this, we found it can go either way, but without a test to verify your instincts, we recommend playing it safe.

Finally, if you decide to include your name and a legend on the card, keep it simple. One thing we know for certain is that people often continue their longer personal notes on the back of cards. Thus filling up more than an eighth of this space makes the card less usable.

PREMIUMS IN ACQUISITION PACKAGES

Using any premium product in acquisition is usually only affordable if you are already printing them for mailing to your house file. Certainly, you do not want to build a file that is composed exclusively of premium-responsive donors. This would mean having to offer premiums with each and every mailing. Eventually you would have a premium file instead of a donor file. However, if you include premium mailings in the "mix" of what you send to donors, you should at least test the cost-effectiveness of using products in acquisition. Please note that you are testing cost-effectiveness and not responsiveness. It is almost guaranteed that your percent return will increase and your average gift decrease with the use of cards or a

calendar. Thus you must ascertain whether you can afford to use premiums in acquisitions.

Some prospect lists are more premium-responsive than others are. You absolutely must track the donors who respond to premiums to learn how well (and to what appeals) they renew the following year. If renewal rates are high with the donor segments acquired through premiums, try renewing donors by adding a premium offer to half of your renewal package. If you can only make renewals effective by offering more premiums, you must decide whether or not to pursue premiums in acquisition. The other route to go is to segment those donors acquired through premiums and mail to them only when you have a premium offer planned.

A WORD OF WARNING

It is critical that the program not be left completely with the supplier. Some organizations take over the entire program, including receipt of money and file segmentation. They seek to make the process of locating premium-oriented donors seem mysterious. It isn't. They reap enormous profits if the checks are not made out to your organization and mailed directly to your headquarters or to your lock box.

Just remember—reputable fundraising firms never, ever receive a client's money, nor do they pay their bills. When you remain in charge of costs and income, you're in the driver's seat.

Exhibits 8–2 through 8–5 illustrate samples of premium packages (reproduced here in black and white), reproduced with the permission of each nonprofit organization listed here.

Sample Premium Packages. (See Exhibits 8–2 through 8–5.)

Package Type	Represented By
Cards	GMHC (Exhibit 8–2)
Calendars	Smithsonian's National Museum of the American Indian (Exhibit 8–3) and WIMSA (Exhibit 8–4)
Gift Wrap	AARP Andrus Foundation (Exhibit 8–5)

Exhibit 8–2 Package Type—Cards (letter, page 1 only)

FIRST IN THE FIGHT
AGAINST AIDS

GMHC

April, 1998

Dear Friend of GMHC,

Here it is!

Here's the set of Spring Notecards that I promised you in my last letter. It's our gift of thanks to you for all the support and friendship you've given us in the past.

These cards are yours to keep without cost or obligation. But I do want to ask you for one small favor:

Please return the enclosed reply form to let us know that you received the notecards and that they arrived in good condition.

<u>And if you possibly can, please include a generous contribution to GMHC as well</u>.

In our work, we see so much suffering and death throughout the year that the arrival of Spring -- with its theme of renewal -- has a special significance to us.

Despite the fact that we are dedicated to fighting a deadly disease, GMHC is a place where people come to embrace and celebrate <u>life</u>.

Take these notecards, for example. They were designed and painted by three talented GMHC clients who participate in our Therapeutic Recreation Program. As you can see, the paintings are strikingly different from one another. But the enthusiasm and creativity evident in each demonstrates the wonderful diversity and energy of our clients.

Let me tell you about two of the artists whose work was selected for our Spring Card Program.

Louis Miller, who painted the lovely floral watercolor, has been a GMHC client for three years. He's a familiar face at the GMHC dining room, where he

Gay Men's Health Crisis   The Tisch Building   119 West 24th Street, New York, NY 10011-1913   212-367-1111

continues

Exhibit 8–2 continued (sample of card box)

continues

Exhibit 8–2 continued (sample of card #1)

FIRST IN THE FIGHT
AGAINST AIDS

Original Art by a GMHC client.

Founded in 1981, Gay Men's Health Crisis is the nation's oldest and largest AIDS organization
providing direct services to men, women and children with AIDS in New York City,
and education and advocacy worldwide.

Knowledge = Power … Get the Facts about HIV and AIDS
Call the GMHC Hotline – It Could Save Your Life
(212) 807-6655 • TDD (212) 645-7470 (hearing impaired)

©1998
740D-1

41542-G
LITHO IN USA

continues

Exhibit 8–2 continued (sample of card #2)

FIRST IN THE FIGHT
AGAINST AIDS

Original Art by Robert Diaz, a GMHC client.

Founded in 1981, Gay Men's Health Crisis is the nation's oldest
and largest AIDS organization providing direct services to men,
women and children with AIDS in New York City,
and education and advocacy worldwide.

continues

Exhibit 8–2 continued (sample of card #3)

FIRST IN THE FIGHT
AGAINST AIDS

GMHC

Original Art by Louis Miller, a GMHC client.

Founded in 1981, Gay Men's Health Crisis is the nation's oldest and largest AIDS organization
providing direct services to men, women and children with AIDS in New York City,
and education and advocacy worldwide.

Knowledge = Power ... Get the Facts about HIV and AIDS
Call the GMHC Hotline – It Could Save Your Life
(212) 807-6655 • TDD (212) 645-7470 (hearing impaired)

©1996
740D-3

41542-G
LITHO IN USA

Courtesy of The Gay Men's Health Crisis, New York, New York.

Exhibit 8–3 Package Type—Calendars (letter, page 1 only)

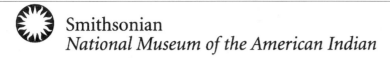

Smithsonian
National Museum of the American Indian

Office of External Affairs and Development

Jane Sample
Lautman & Company
Suite 700
1730 Rhode Island Ave., NW
Washington, DC 20036   November 1999
|.|.|||..||....||.||.|.|.|

*When a child asks, "What did you do to celebrate the year 2000 and the new
Millennium" you can reply: "I did something very special; something to make
the world a better place for you. I helped build the National Museum of the
American Indian — a place to honor the indigenous people who have given so
much to our country ... who sacrificed and suffered in the process ... and who
continue to help define what it means to be an American."*

Dear Charter Member,

Enclosed is a special gift for you — the Smithsonian's National Museum of the
American Indian Charter Member wall calendar for the Year 2000. The theme "Children:
Uniting Generations," was deliberately chosen to represent the departure of the old Millennium
and the dawn of the new — and the continuum of generations, year by year, from one era to
another.

What could be a better symbol than a calendar to convey my gratitude for your support
in the last century, and my hope for that support to continue in the new?

If you have not already done so, I encourage you to take a few minutes to look at the
beautiful photographs that appear on each page of the calendar. When you do, you'll find
yourself face-to-face with my Native past — the smiling eyes of a Hopi boy at his pueblo in
Arizona, circa 1914; the wistful face of a Cheyenne girl in traditional dress; and the serious
concentration of a Seminole boy from 1915.

But alongside this past, you will see the present and the future of my people as well —
the staff of the NMAI with their children or young relatives.

Viewed together, these photographs represent the continuation of life and the passage of
cultural knowledge from one generation to the next.

Even before it has opened, the National Museum of the American Indian is a part of that
chain of cultural heritage. And, if putting that Museum together has had such a positive impact
over the last years, just imagine what its contribution will be when it opens in late 2002.

SMITHSONIAN INSTITUTION
PO Box 96836
Washington, DC 20090-6836
aimember@ic.si.edu   www.si.edu/nmai

continues

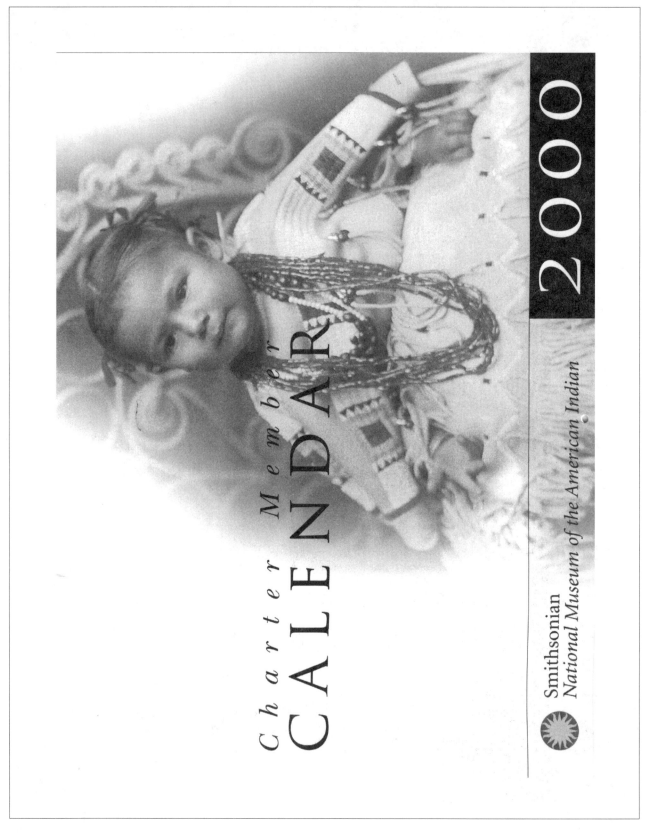

continues

Exhibit 8–3 continued (page 1 of actual calendar)

JANUARY 2000

SUNDAY	MONDAY	TUESDAY	WEDNESDAY	THURSDAY	FRIDAY	SATURDAY
	Walter A. Burlack, age 17 months. Son of Glenn Burlack (Lumbee), Administrative Specialist/Administration.		DECEMBER 1999 S M T W TH F S 1 2 3 4 5 6 7 8 9 10 11 12 13 14 15 16 17 18 19 20 21 22 23 24 25 26 27 28 29 30 31	FEBRUARY S M T W TH F S 1 2 3 4 5 6 7 8 9 10 11 12 13 14 15 16 17 18 19 20 21 22 23 24 25 26 27 28 29		1 New Year's Day Kwanzaa ends
2	3	4	5	6	7	8
9	10	11	12	13	14	15
16	17	18	19	20	21	22
23 Martin Luther King, Jr. Birthday (observed)	24	25	26	27	28	29
30	31					

WWW.SI.EDU/NMAI

NATIONAL MUSEUM OF THE AMERICAN INDIAN

continues

This is My War Too!, 1943,
by Dan V. Smith

She's Helping to Win ... How about You?, 1943, by John Falter

Be A Marine, 194?, Anon

Woman's Place in War, 1944,
by Ramus

You Are Needed Now–Army Nurse Corps, 1943, by Green

The Girl of the Year is a SPAR, 1943, by Bentley

Don't Miss Your Greatest Opportunity, 1944, by John Falter

Are You a Girl with a Star-Spangled Heart?, 1943, by Bradshaw Crandell

Share the Deeds of Victory – Join the Waves, 1943, by John Falter

Join the Navy Nurse Corps, 194?, by Whitcomb

WASP Victory, 1978, by David Strand

Mine Eyes Have Seen the Glory, 1944, by Schlaikjer

WOMEN IN MILITARY SERVICE FOR AMERICA

★ ★ ★ ★ THE WOMEN'S MEMORIAL ★ ★ ★ ★

MEMORIAL FOUNDATION

Dept. 560 ★ Washington, DC 20042-0560 ★ 800-222-2294

PRINTED IN THE USA BY
CONCORD LITHO CO., INC.
CONCORD, NH

30305-A
©1993

Courtesy of the Women in Military Service for American Memorial Foundation, Inc., Washington, DC.

Exhibit 8–5 Package Type—Gift Wrap (letter, page 1 only)

AARP Andrus Foundation

Mr. John Q. Sample
123 Main Street
Anytown, US 12345-6789
IIl...II....II....II.I.I.II....I.I.II....I.I.II....I.I.II

April 1999

Dear Friend,

It is my pleasure to send you your special AARP Andrus Foundation
Spring Gift Wrap and to wish you "Happy Springtime!"

Please accept your gift wrap as a personal gift from me to you ...
a gift of thanks for your support of the Foundation. But your gift wrap
is far more than a simple "thank you" gift. It is a symbol of my
gratitude for all you have done to support the Foundation.

Just as nature is bursting out all around us in color, warmth and
life, the science of aging is moving ahead ... renewing our ability to
live well and enjoy better health and independence as we age.

- Women all over the country are learning new, effective
  ways to prevent and detect breast cancer.

- Older Americans are finding more ways to
  achieve financial independence in retirement.

- Health care professionals are learning more about the
  special needs of older people and the many assistive
  devices that are available for those who have difficulty
  getting around or remaining independent in their home.

All of these things will help us renew our ability to live well and
enjoy better health and independence as we age. Doctors, scientists and
researchers from around the world are focusing their work on finding
solutions to the effects of the aging process.

As you know, the research the Foundation funds covers a wide range
of projects that interest you -- from financial issues to chronic health
problems. And each of these programs has two major factors in common:

Every research program is geared toward
improving the quality of life for thousands
of older Americans ... and none of them
could happen without your financial support
of the AARP Andrus Foundation.

(over, please)

601 E STREET, NW ♦ WASHINGTON, DC 20049 ♦ (202) 434-6190 ♦ www.andrus.org

continues

Exhibit 8–5 continued (sample of gift wrap)

Courtesy of AARP Andrus Foundation, Washington, DC.

Chapter 9
Monthly Donor Programs

CHAPTER OUTLINE

- Doing the Math
- Creating Motivation
- Naming the Program
- Initial Invitation
- The Best Prospects
- Monthly Billing
- Bonding with Sustainers
- Member Attrition
- Delinquent Pledgers
- Annual Upgrading
- Electronic Funds Transfer
- Credit Card Option

Monthly donor programs (also called sustainer programs) are of enormous importance to most non-profits for the following reasons:

- They substantially upgrade the size of the donor's gift(s).
- They hold great appeal for seniors on fixed incomes and others who can't afford to write single large checks.
- They build loyalty and long-term relationships.
- Because of the long-term relationships, monthly donors are the most likely to include your organization in their wills.

If you have a donor file but don't yet have a monthly donor program, this chapter can help increase your bottom line.

DOING THE MATH

A highly motivated donor giving $20 to each of three appeals per year will contribute $60 annually. But if that person joins a monthly donor club, giving at only $10 per month—that's $120 per year—a 100 percent upgrade.

Results vary from one organization to the next, but as a general rule, somewhere between 3 and 5 percent of a donor file is sufficiently dedicated to your cause to enroll in a monthly donor program.

Let's assume that 3 percent of your current donor file will join such a program, and that the average pledge and subsequent monthly gift will be in the $10 to $20 range. The rate at which most pledgers fulfill (actually send their monthly gift) is about 70 percent. Thus, if your file has at least 20,000 active (past 18 months) donors with gifts between $10 and $499.99, you can project that 3 percent of them will give an average of $15 initially. Because about 70 percent will fulfill their pledges after the first gift, you will keep about 420 sustainers. And over a period of 12 months you should gross approximately $75,000. Even if your active donor file has only 10,000 names, such a program can be worthwhile.

The cost of maintaining a monthly giving program is a function of its size: The larger it is, the more likely that you will need a special "sustainer clerk" whose job it is to maintain the program. But for small undertakings, a monthly giving program can be efficiently run by a conscientious part-time volunteer or by an existing staff person devoting one day a week to the job.

CREATING MOTIVATION

In order to persuade a donor to write out a check every month, you must be able to clearly and concisely articulate why you need a steady reliable flow of funds and how you will spend the money each month.

As fundraisers know, donors don't like to pay for everyday needs like the rent, the light bill, or salaries. Instead, donors prefer to give to hands-on programs and to realize instant gratification for their gifts. So, try to make the need something familiar to the donor; something that gets used up and needs replacing. Thus, if you need money for groceries to feed the hungry, gasoline for the school bus to bring poor kids to special schools, fuel to keep furnaces going to warm people in colder climates, or disposable diapers in a hospital for babies with AIDS, you have exactly the kinds of programs to which people respond best with monthly contributions.

NAMING THE PROGRAM

The best monthly donor programs are created as a sort of "club" within each organization, which donors "join." Such clubs usually take a special name such as *Leadership Circle, Friends for Life,* or *Best Friends.* However, don't name your club so exotically that it becomes unrecognizable. In the sample invitation provided as Exhibit 9–1, the American Society for the Prevention of Cruelty to Animals (better known as the ASPCA) appropriately named its program, ASPCA Guardians.

Art that utilized the existing ASPCA logo (but which incorporated the new word, "Guardians") was created. The final product still looked like the ASPCA, but the new "club" now had its own identity.

You are cautioned against creating a new identity whose name and image is far afield from the main organization. After all, the donor was originally motivated to give to your cause. Now that he or she is giving you even more money, you want him or her to continue to feel a part of that overall cause.

INITIAL INVITATION

Once the basic case statement has been formulated and packaged, the initial invitation to join is mailed.

The sustainer invitation may look very much like a special appeal in that it contains a letter, a response slip, and a reply envelope. The carrier envelope should look as personal as possible (no teaser copy, please, although "RSVP" is often good) and should be close-faced and mailed first class with a stamp or stamps if the budget will allow.

Study the ASPCA sustainer package carefully for ideas you can use including, but not limited to, the following:

- The letter begins on an intimate note with the writer confiding to the member that, "This is a letter I could write *only* to you."
- The letter praises the donor for being special.
- The letter tells how a monthly pledge will be used.
- The reply card offers a "paperless" electronic funds transfer and a credit card option in addition to a pay-by-mail option.
- A formal invitation is enclosed (after careful testing, this addition boosted returns for several organizations).
- The letter and reply card describe the special gift one will receive for joining. Note: A poster, certificate, pin, paperweight, or other appropriate token will not cost much, but will be perceived as meaningful.

THE BEST PROSPECTS

Naturally, not all of your members/donors are good prospects for a sustainer program. It isn't cost-effective to bill donors who respond with monthly gifts of less that $5. On the other hand, since a year's income from one monthly donor is likely to be over $100, you don't want to solicit donors who regularly write single large checks.

The best prospects for a program like this are current multidonors (those donors who have given multiple times during one year) of gifts between $5 and $99.99. If you are successful with these segments, you can move on to test high dollar donors (those contributing between $100 and $400) as well as recently lapsed segments of the file.

MONTHLY BILLING

As returns are received, a master billing form is created for each monthly donor to keep track of his or her individual pledge payment each month.

The basic elements of the bill include: name, address, original (or upgraded) pledge amount, donor ID number, payment history, and a place for personalization. A generic monthly bill appears in Exhibit 9–2.

The monthly bill should be mailed first class about five days before the end of the month, timed to arrive so that the pledger pays it along with his or her regular monthly bills. Such bills must be mailed on time, at the same time every month.

Each month, as returns are received, someone in your organization posts the information on the master billing form and returns the form to its file.

Exhibit 9–1 Monthly Donor Letter

January 13, 1998 / 8:00 P.M.

Dear Friend,

This is the time of night when I allow myself the luxury of worrying.

For most of the day, I'm much too busy to worry. In my five and a half years as President of the ASPCA, there have been many urgent responsibilities that demand my attention.

Meeting with our animal hospital director and ASPCA law enforcement officials are two jobs that can't be set aside. Other time-consuming activities include reviewing proposed legislation, approving copy on publications and attending meetings with city officials and ASPCA board members.

But now -- at 8:00 p.m. -- when I'm almost ready to lock up my office and go home for the day, I think about all the animals who desperately need our care.

Many pets come to us frightened and some urgently need veterinary care. Some are neglected, abused, or simply unwanted. It's up to us -- the ASPCA -- to find them loving, adoptive homes.

And like anybody who owns a pet who is sick or in pain, I worry. I worry about how many will find those loving homes and how many will die. And most of all, I worry about how we'll pay for tomorrow's routine expenses of running this massive enterprise called the ASPCA.

That's why I stayed in my office just a little later than usual tonight to write you this letter. It's the kind of letter I could only write to <u>you</u>.

Why only you?

Because, quite frankly, lots of people respond to letters about the abuse of laboratory animals, factory farming, and fur-trapping -- concerns we're actively working to remedy. But only a precious few understand the need for the kind of ongoing commitment to the care of animals -- <u>all</u> animals -- which also characterizes our daily work at the ASPCA.

The American Society for the Prevention of Cruelty to Animals
424 East 92nd Street, New York, New York 10128
www.aspca.org

M1

continues

Exhibit 9–1 continued

Unlike many other national organizations, we've also committed ourselves to helping find homes for companion animals in our immediate community -- which just happens to be one of the neediest communities in America -- New York City!

That's why I'm writing to invite you to join a small, select group of ASPCA members who have undertaken a special challenge.

The group is called the "ASPCA GUARDIANS," and it is comprised of people who have pledged a small monthly amount to help us cope with the constant flow of animals who need our help.

When I say "constant flow," I'm not exaggerating!

Every year, we provide adoption and veterinary services to tens of thousands of animals. That makes our veterinary hospitals some of the busiest in America!

And to help control animal overpopulation, we offer reduced-cost spay/neuter services -- a vital part of the ASPCA mission.

When a forlorn kitten or sad-eyed puppy needs a new home . . . when a carriage horse in Central Park collapses from exhaustion, it's the ASPCA who comes to the rescue.

When there's a cockfight in the Bronx . . . when a goat is hidden away to be killed in a ritual sacrifice . . . when a drug dealer beats his dog to make him mean, it's the ASPCA who investigates the crime, makes the arrest, and saves the animal.

When a family wants to share their love with an unwanted animal, it's the ASPCA that provides veterinary care for the animal, screens the adoptive family, and makes the placement that's so important to the life of that animal _and_ that family.

The ongoing costs of arranging adoptions, conducting investigations, subsidizing our spay/neuter services, and managing our veterinary hospitals are enormous. They are never-ending. And they are always on the rise.

Our biggest financial challenge, in fact, is simply to find a dependable source of funds that can help us meet these ongoing expenses.

Unless we succeed in keeping our heads above water, it's impossible for us to achieve such long-range national goals as promoting the use of non-animal laboratory tests as humane alternatives, protecting endangered species, and reducing the undeniable abuses of factory farming.

continues

Exhibit 9–1 continued

That's why we formed the ASPCA GUARDIANS, and that's why I'm urging you to join this special group today.

As an ASPCA GUARDIAN, you will be asked to pledge a small monthly contribution of $5 or more that we can count on to help us pay our bills. By giving as much as $15 a month, for example, you'll pay for such things as:

* Antibiotics, suture material for spays, vaccines, and bandaging material for wounds. (Almost 40,000 animals were treated last year -- many at reduced fees.)

* Pet education workshops and basic dog training classes . . . animal-assisted therapy programs . . . and subsidized spaying and neutering to help end the scourge of pet overpopulation.

* And all the costs related to our cruelty investigations and law enforcement, including such things as inspecting pet shops and zoos; rescuing and rehabilitating wild animals; protecting carriage horses; monitoring circuses and rodeos; and "busting" dog and cock fighting.

Whether you give $25 a month or $5 a month, the size of your contribution is not as important as the regularity of it.

<u>Because by committing yourself to a specific amount each month, you'll not only be helping us keep up with our monthly bills . . . you'll also enable us to plan for the future</u>.

Will you accept the challenge?

Will you make a monthly commitment to help care for the thousands of animals who come to us each month?

I know you give to the ASPCA out of love for animals, not because you expect something in return. But to thank you for joining the ASPCA GUARDIANS, I'd like to send you a handy 8 1/2" x 11" magnetic memo board and pen with erasable ink. It will fit perfectly on your refrigerator and will be a daily help to you when making grocery lists, leaving messages for family members, or writing reminders of things to do.

Of course, you'll continue to receive all the membership benefits and privileges to which you are normally entitled -- including your subscription to our magazine, <u>ASPCA Animal Watch</u>, your membership card and the privilege of voting at our annual meeting.

continues

Exhibit 9–1 continued

Most importantly, you'll have the good feeling of knowing you personally are giving comfort and care to the sick, the injured, and the frightened animals who need the ASPCA's help every day.

These are the ones I worry about every night, and tonight I'm asking you to share the responsibility.

Please don't turn your back on them.

Please make a monthly commitment to the animals by becoming an ASPCA GUARDIAN today. Thank you.

Sincerely,

Roger A. Caras
President

P.S. I've asked the Senior V.P. of the ASPCA's Bergh
     Memorial Animal Hospital to prepare a brief memo
     outlining some of our hospital expenses for a typical
     month. I think you'll find it interesting.

continues

Exhibit 9–1 continued (monthly donor reply form)

The American Society for the Prevention of Cruelty to Animals

Dear Mr. Caras,

I accept your invitation to become a member of the ASPCA GUARDIANS. To help pay for the ongoing expenses of comforting and healing the thousands of sick, injured and unwanted animals who show up at your door each month, I agree to make a monthly pledge of $5 or more. I pledge:

☐ $10   ☐ $15   ☐ $20   ☐ Other Amount: $ _____

Enclosed is my first monthly check for: $ _____

07091287   S8A1M1

You will be sent a pledge reminder for this amount each month. The option to pay by credit card or by NoChex is available on the reverse side of this form. You may cancel or alter the amount of your monthly pledge simply by notifying us.

     Lautman & Co.
     1730 Rhode Island Ave. NW
     Suite 700
     Washington, DC 20036

M1

Please return this card with your check in the enclosed pre-addressed envelope.

When you become an ASPCA GUARDIAN, you will receive this handy 8½" x 11" magnetic memo board and pen with erasable ink. It's our way of saying *thank you* for your commitment to help the animals.

A financial report is available from the New York State Office of Charities Registration, Albany, NY 12231

424 East 92nd Street, New York, New York 10128
www.aspca.org

Please turn over for more information about paying

with our **NoCHEX** or

CREDIT CARD options

continues

Exhibit 9–1 continued (back of reply form)

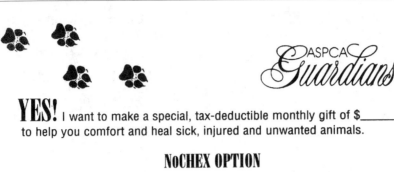

YES! I want to make a special, tax-deductible monthly gift of $_____ to help you comfort and heal sick, injured and unwanted animals.

NoCHEX OPTION

Yes! I am choosing the NoChex plan to devote more of my gifts to the animals.

NoChex Authorization: I authorize my bank to transfer $_____ from my checking account each month. In the event that I wish to discontinue my pledge, I will write to ASPCA's Development Department. A record of each gift will be included on my bank statement and will serve as my receipt.

*Please be sure to enclose a check for your first contribution.

Signature _____ Date _____

CREDIT CARD OPTION

Yes! I am choosing to pay by credit card, so more of my gifts will be devoted to the animals. Please charge $_____ each month to my:

☐ MasterCard   ☐ VISA   ☐ American Express

☐☐☐☐ ☐☐☐☐ ☐☐☐☐ ☐☐☐☐ ☐☐ ☐☐
Card Number   Expiration Date

Signature _____ Date _____

- -

▲ Detach top portion and return with your check.   Keep bottom portion for your records. ▼

Your copy of NoChex Authorization

Monthly pledge amount: $_____

Date: _____

I authorize my bank to transfer the amount pledged above from my checking account each month. In the event that I wish to discontinue my pledge, I will write to ASPCA's Development Department. A record of each gift will be included on my bank statement and will serve as my receipt.

continues

Exhibit 9–1 continued (carrier envelope)

The American Society for the Prevention of Cruelty to Animals
424 East 92nd Street, New York, New York 10128
www.aspca.org

Lautman & Co.
1730 Rhode Island Ave. NW
Suite 700
Washington, DC 20036

continues

Exhibit 9–1 continued (inserts)

Your monthly support will help provide care for animals like these. Won't you become a GUARDIAN today?

The Board of Directors of

The American Society for the Prevention

of Cruelty to Animals,

America's foremost champion

of Animal welfare, is honored

to announce your election to

Guardian Membership

with all its

exclusive privileges and

benefits.

RSVP

Exhibit 9–2 Sample Generic Monthly Bill

Sustainer

$20.00
Pledge due (see below)

Ms. Jane Q. Sample
123 Main Street
Anytown, U.S.A. 12345

Extra gift this month

TOTAL ENCLOSED

Please show any change in your name or address.
Please return this portion of the statement with your check.

Pledge Amount: $20   **Sustainer:** $20

Date Due	Amount Pledged	Status	Date Rec'd	Amount Paid
1/21/00	$20	Paid	1/17/00	$20
2/21/00	$20	Paid	2/15/00	$20
3/21/00	$20	Paid	3/16/00	$20
4/21/00	$20	Paid	4/15/00	$20
5/21/00	$20	Prepaid	4/15/00	$20
6/21/00	$20	Prepaid	4/15/00	
7/21/00	$20	open		

Thank you for your monthly gift, which brings hot food to our tables day after day, week after week.

Sincerely

Pam Smith
Executive Director

BONDING WITH SUSTAINERS

Although you should remove a new sustainer from your regular file of donors eligible for renewals, appeals, and other solicitations, do not drop out of the donor's sight. Instead, send a "stuffer" with all monthly bills.

A "stuffer" is simply an enclosure and it is critical because it is the link that keeps the monthly donor interested enough to continue writing you monthly checks. Stuffers should be different from one another, and by utilizing materials you already produce, you save money and keep the sustainer well informed.

For example, if you have a quarterly newsletter, send it as a stuffer with the bill for each of those four months. If you have an annual report, send it as the stuffer. That takes care of five months. Then, at least quarterly, write a short letter to the monthly donors telling them how much they are appreciated for their gift to your program.

For the final three months, send existing materials used in other parts of your mail campaign, such as a decal, bookmark, greeting cards, calendar, etc.

It is recommended that you not send routine special appeals to donors who are already contributing monthly. However, you can send your year-end appeal as well as any emergency appeals, and this group of donors will respond exceptionally generously.

Sustainers are close family and should be treated as such. The more you can make them feel like insiders—a part of the cause, a member of your inner council—the more generous they will be in the long run. That is why bills should be personalized.

Generally, personalization with monthly giving programs takes two forms, both of which are important. First, you should be prepared to personalize the bill with a special message each month. If time limitations prevent you from personalizing each bill (e.g., "Mrs. Smith, I hope you will take a moment to read the enclosed editorial written by [name of board member] about our wonderful new program."), at least take the time to write "Thank you" or "Happy Holidays" or some other message on the bill. If you have volunteers, handwriting is best. If not, notes can be typed or computer generated.

MEMBER ATTRITION

No matter how well run your monthly giving program, there is one inescapable reality: The donor base that you build up initially will erode over time. That is why you will want to convert new donors into monthly pledgers.

There are three potential ways to accomplish this:

1. Invite each newly acquired member or donor into the special monthly club as soon as he or she first gives your organization an initial gift. In fact, the acknowledgment letter can be used to prepare the donor for the subsequent sustainer invitation. For example, "P.S. Please look for a letter from our president who will be writing soon to describe an exciting new program called Best Friends, which we think you'd like to know about."

2. Less aggressive organizations prefer to wait approximately a year and invite those who have renewed their annual support at least once or who have made multiple gifts within the year. If you prefer this method, you can state your reason for inviting the donor as follows: "Because of your demonstrated loyal interest and most generous support, we want you to know about an exciting program we call Best Friends."

3. The third way is to send an annual invitation mailing (to the appropriate dollar segments) regardless of when the donor's last gift was made.

DELINQUENT PLEDGERS

The best-run sustainer programs have pledgers whose hearts are bigger than their wallets. Keep track of sustainers who habitually fail to respond to their monthly bills. After three to four successive months of not fulfilling, delinquent pledgers should be telephoned to ask them to reinstate. If they don't rein-

state after such a call, they should be taken out of the program and put back in the house master file.

ANNUAL UPGRADING

As devoted as monthly givers are, often they'll do more. Once a year, all monthly pledgers—with the exception of those who have recently joined the program—should be asked to increase their monthly pledges. The response to this request varies widely from one organization to the next, but on average 10 to 15 percent of your sustainer file will increase the size of their monthly pledge. You can ask for the upgrade right on the bill form or you can enclose a special letter as your stuffer that month. If possible, use increased prices as a reason for asking. For example, "Because the price of fuel has increased by 20 percent, I hope that you can increase your monthly pledge by that same amount."

ELECTRONIC FUNDS TRANSFER

A fast-growing alternative to monthly billing manually is electronic funds transfer (EFT).

EFT has many applications, such as direct deposit of payroll, Social Security, and pension checks; point-of-sale terminals; bill paying by phone; home banking; and preauthorized bank transfers.

The major benefit of EFT to nonprofits is donor pledge fulfillment and donor retention. This is because the EFT donor doesn't have to write a check each month and therefore doesn't have to make continual decisions about whether to continue supporting you.

A donor can simply preauthorize monthly automatic payment of membership dues and/or pledges to charitable groups. For preauthorized charitable giving, the donor signs a special form and returns it to the charity along with a check for the first month's payment. The check gives its bank the checking account numbers necessary to facilitate the electronic transfer of the monthly debits. EFT is really akin to payroll deduction, allowing a gift to fit conveniently into the contributor's budget.

The steady and predictable cash flow provided by an automatic monthly contribution plan is helpful to many nonprofits in their budgeting and financial planning. And as EFT gains increased acceptance, it is sure to play an increasing role in fundraising in years to come.

A few organizations have had success with programs that invite members to contribute monthly *only* via EFT or credit card. The response to such invitations is somewhat lower, but because the fulfillment rate is close to 100 percent, it is often more economical. If you already have a monthly donor program, and have established that a "paper" appeal works, you might want to test the viability of converting your sustainers from a billing option to a "paperless" program as a way of renewing their pledge. See Appendix H for a list of EFT service providers. You won't get all of them to switch over, but those who do will stay with you much longer.

CREDIT CARD OPTION

In discussing paperless options for monthly donor programs, the focus has been on EFT rather than on credit cards. The latter is definitely an option, and the methods for setting up a program remain much the same as with EFT.

Credit cards, however, have certain drawbacks that EFT does not. For example, most credit cards expire after two years. Thus if your sustainer joins halfway through the credit card cycle, the card could expire one year later and you will have to enroll him or her all over again. (Easier said than done.) The more important drawback is that people regularly lose, cancel, or even change credit cards. In fact, changing cards has become almost routine because lower interest rates are being offered constantly.

It's up to you. You can offer the monthly billing option only, or you can offer either EFT or credit card options, or both—or all three. Whichever way you go, you are almost certain to earn more money for your organization by starting a monthly donor program.

For additional information on monthly donor/sustainer programs, you are referred to *Hidden Gold*, a book by Harvey McKinnon (Bonus Books, Chicago, Illinois).

Chapter 10

Special Donor Programs (High Dollar, Bequest, and Capital Campaigns)

CHAPTER OUTLINE

- Bequests and Planned Gifts
- How To Launch a High Dollar Program
- Capital Campaigns through the Mail
- Synergistic Programs

There still exists in fundraising the belief that if you ask a donor for a small gift, you can't return to ask for a large one. In other words, you've blown your chance.

While this may be true in certain types of fundraising, it is not true in general.

In fact, if a donor has been contributing $250 annually for four years, you might assume that he or she is a great prospect for your high dollar club where gifts begin at $1,000. And if he or she joins the club as the result of a letter of invitation, he or she may be a candidate for an even larger gift which should be solicited in person, if possible.

In effect, this donor has raised his or her hand indicating an interest in your organization, but isn't going to give more unless you ask.

Some years ago, I worked with a special, small college whose particular mission enabled them to raise substantial money through the mail. When the development department received a gift of $100 or more, the donor's name and address was given to the appropriate field representative for follow-up. For gifts of $500 and more through the mail, the name was often given to the president of the college to pursue in his travels.

The field reps loved contacting people through such leads because it gave them a reason to call on a person. Many rewarding contacts were made this way, and many of those contacts resulted not only in

larger gifts, but also in bequests or other forms of planned gifts.

BEQUESTS AND PLANNED GIFTS

It is virtually impossible to ask people who do not know your organization to put you in their wills. Thus you must have an established donor base before you begin building a bequest program.

Bequest programs rarely satisfy the fundraiser looking for instant gratification. The best planned giving experts are patient people who understand the art of cultivation. They know that the best prospects for planned giving are not necessarily the larger donors. Rather, they are smaller donors who have consistently supported an organization over the years. And the longer the period of support, the more likely the donor is to write you into his or her will.

Many fundraisers have learned that their recently lapsed donor file (say, donors who have not contributed in the past 24–36 months) are good sources for bequest gifts. Many people agree that perhaps some older donors stop giving when they go on fixed incomes. But although their donations may decrease or even stop, they often write organizations near and dear to them into their wills. Thus, it is not uncommon to have a large bequest come from a lapsed donor who made modest contributions of under $100 several times per year.

How To Launch a Bequest Program

Most planned gifts come in the form of bequests. If yours is a major institution, you already have or should hire a consultant or employee specializing in deferred giving. If you are a small organization, you can start a modest program on your own. It is recommended that you take a course on the legalities and mathematics of planned giving so that you can answer basic questions knowledgeably.

First and foremost, establish such a program by giving it a name. For example, if your organization is called The Arts Institute, you might name your program *"The Legacy Program of The Arts Institute."* You might also want to name a chairperson or co-chairs who have themselves put you in their will.

Announce your program in your newsletter or annual report and never stop writing about it in your newsletter. The most effective way to do this is to tell stories about people who have named you in their wills or made other deferred gifts. To get the stories (and permission to write about them), you will have to do some digging and some visiting, but it will be well worth the effort. Be sure to make the stories human by having the donors tell why they care so much about your organization, and how they want to see your work carried out after they are gone. Do not be squeamish about talking about bequests and death. Just observe the rules of good taste.

As already stated, the best prospects for deferred gifts are long-time donors, especially those who give several times each year. If you have a monthly donor program, you can be sure that these donors are excellent prospects. Thus, you should segment your donor or member file according to longevity (how many years a donor has been giving), frequency (how many times a year he or she gives), and recency (how recently the person has given). This latter criterion runs somewhat counter to the earlier statement that lapsed donors make good prospects. I would approach lapsed donors last, but I haven't changed my mind about their viability.

If you have a donor file of 50,000 people, probably as many as 25 percent will qualify as good prospects because they have given in the past two years on a regular basis. Thus, your mailing will consist of roughly 12,500 pieces.

Your letter, signed by your new Planned Giving Chairperson(s), need not be long. In fact, since those to whom you will be writing know you so well, you might want to limit it to two pages.

In writing on behalf of a ballet company, for example, you might say something like the following:

We each have our own reasons for loving the ballet. But one thing we can agree on—the ballet must endure into the future so that others can experience the excitement you and I have been privileged to enjoy.

That is why Mrs. Thomas and I have written the Metropolitan Ballet into our wills—so that our children and our grandchildren can continue to enjoy and support this great institution. And that is why I hope you will join us in considering putting the Metropolitan in your will too.

I know that bequests aren't anyone's favorite subject. But I also know that the ballet is one of your favorites. So the next time you contact your accountant or lawyer, won't you discuss the possibility of a legacy to us? If you would like more information on a particular program, please call me directly at the number below or call Jane Smith, Development Director. Either of us would be happy to speak to you.

Naturally, you will want to tailor the letter to your own organization, but in all cases, it is important to acknowledge a mutual caring about the organization. Some groups include a card that the recipient can return to the nonprofit. While returns from such cards are not a clear indication of how many people will actually follow through, they can be helpful. If you decide to include such a card (or a brochure), you might want to include the following check-off boxes:

☑ Please telephone me about putting the Ballet in my/our will(s).
☑ I/we have already included the Ballet in our wills.
☑ I/we plan to include the Ballet in our wills.

And don't forget to include an envelope to ensure the donor's privacy in returning the card.

Offering Bequest Program through Acknowledgments

If you have no budget for special mailings to bequest prospects, you can tell them about your program at little or no cost. When you acknowledge all gifts made over the period of a year, you reach almost everyone in your donor file. Thus it is a simple matter, after thanking the donor for his or her gift, to add copy similar to the following:

Because we have received so many requests for information about our bequest program, I'm taking the liberty of assuming that you may also be interested. That is why I want to tell you how you can ensure that future generations develop the same love of the ballet as you have.

HOW TO LAUNCH A HIGH DOLLAR PROGRAM

The high dollar programs here refer to giving at the upper end of your program (but do not cross over into truly high dollar programs wherein the prospects are visited or otherwise personally solicited).

Direct mail high dollar programs generally start at $500 or $1,000 and go no higher than $10,000—depending, of course, on the organization. What is high to one organization may be low to another; so you decide.

Starting such a program is simple in concept. Problems happen only when the development office (for fundraising) and the membership (for direct mail) departments function separately. However, assuming that everyone is on the same page, here is what you need to do to launch such a program:

- Name the program, but be sure to incorporate your organization's name into it. For example, in talking about a high dollar program, you might call it "Friends of Universal College" or "Guardians of the American Hospital" or "The John Smith Society of Happiness Park." (The latter assumes that John Smith was a prominent and well-known citizen.)
- Establish a special use for the money if possible. It is up to your creativity to describe an exciting special program if you are going to use the money as general funds.
- Choose a Chairperson. It may be your director or a board member or both. But it should be someone who himself or herself is a major donor.
- Establish Benefits. No tote bags here. High dollar donors want to receive "insider" benefits. If you have a special entrance or dining room or special parking privileges to offer, so much the better. If not, you must create an ambiance of exclusivity. For example, con-

sider a naming wall or put names on your stairway or garden pavers for a certain price. Offer invitations to truly special events where members will meet other important members. Even if some people live far away and cannot attend, they will appreciate being invited.

- Offer reasons for joining that make the recipient feel special. You will find such a letter for the National Gay and Lesbian Task Force (NGLTF) as Exhibit 10–1. Their high dollar program was called Bridge Builders, and it asked for gifts starting at $1,000 and more. The name was chosen because of the Task Force's coalition-building work. NGLTF's offering of benefits was limited, but it was nonetheless successful.

The Central Park Conservancy in New York City operates a high dollar program called the "Conservators," which invites donors of $50 to $999 to attend a special party hosted by prominent Conservancy Trustees (usually in elegant apartments overlooking Central Park). There the invitees (who must become Conservators at $1,000 or more to attend) will meet other Conservators. The program has been so successful that both acquisition and renewal rates in this program are quite high.

In starting a high dollar program, keep in mind that you don't have to "sell" existing midlevel donors on the merits of your organization. The reason they contribute as much as they already do is because they believe in you. What you must do, however, is convince them that they should give at a higher level. Often this means offering the donor something he or she truly wants.

The two main things that most donors want are

1. Recognition (Put their names in a truly prominent place for all to see.)
2. Insider information (Hold special receptions and hard-hat tours, send a special director's letter, offer dinner with the president, and similar events.)

As for the letter of invitation and the renewal letter, this is the time to use

- Upgraded stationery
- Personal addressing
- First class postage
- Handwritten notes or postscripts
- First names when known to the signer

1700 Kalorama Road.NW
Washington.DC 20009.2624

Jane A. Sample

Lautman & Company

Suite 700

1730 Rhode Island Avenue

Washington, DC 20036

Place
stamp
here

THE TASK FORCE
1700 Kalorama Road NW
Washington, DC 20009.2624

continues

Exhibit 10–1 continued (letter, page 1 only)

Kerry Lobel
1700 Kalorama Road.NW
Washington.DC 20009-2624

> We cannot achieve victory in isolation. We need
> bridges to unite our movement. Bridges to reach
> out to all potential allies. Bridges between the
> barriers that separate us as gay, lesbian, bisexual
> and transgendered people. And most of all, we
> need people like you who will step forward to
> become our *Bridge Builders*.

February 2, 2000

Jane A. Sample
Lautman & Company
Suite 700
1730 Rhode Island Avenue
Washington, DC 20036

Dear NGLTF Supporters,

Your steadfast support is the reason I am writing you. The time has
come for me to invite you to take a further step and become one of the National
Gay and Lesbian Task Force's (NGLTF) *Bridge Builders* with a gift of $250 or
more.

Bridge Builders are our core supporters — made up of people like you
whose deep moral commitment and generous financial support has made them
natural leaders in the ongoing struggle for our civil rights.

As you know, the civil rights of gay, lesbian, bisexual, and
transgendered people are being vigorously challenged every day in every state.

In 1999 alone, over 227 bills that harm the rights of gay, lesbian,
bisexual, and transgendered people and people with HIV/AIDS have been
introduced in state legislatures...almost 10 percent of those have been signed
into law by governors.

The fact is, many who hate us spew out their rhetoric in the halls of
Congress. They fill our airwaves with it. Some even use it as a platform to run
for President. <u>And millions of people are listening to this intolerance and hatred</u>.

Even worse, vicious attacks against gay, lesbian, bisexual and
transgendered people are on the rise. You only need to read the accounts of the
vicious murders of Billy Jack Gaither and Matthew Shepard to realize that we
are fighting a war.

(Over, please)

continues

Exhibit 10–1 continued (reply form)

NATIONAL GAY AND LESBIAN
TASK FORCE

1700 Kalorama Road, NW Washington, DC 20009.2624 T 202.332.6483 www.ngltf.org

r.s.v.p. **Acceptance Form**
Bridge Builders

[ ] **YES,** I want to become a Bridge Builder and play a leadership role in helping NGLTF connect and unite our movement and reach out to our allies. Enclosed is my contribution* of:

Please indicate the membership level you want to join. To charge your contribution, please see other side.

Bridge Builder Backer   **Bridge Builder Sustainer**
[ ] $250 or more $ _____   [ ] $500 or more $ _____

Other
[ ] $ _____

[ ] I do not wish to become a Bridge Builder at this time but want to contribute $_____ in support of your important efforts.

Jane A. Sample   CB1210
Lautman & Company   01234567
Suite 700
1730 Rhode Island Avenue
Washington, DC 20036

Please make your check payable to NGLTF and return this form in the envelope provided. If you prefer to pay by credit card, please fill in the information requested on the back of this form.

Benefits
Bridge Builders

* Any gift of $100 or more will qualify you for admission into NGLTF's special circle of Bridge Builders and entitle you to our quarterly Newsletter and our annual by state report, *Capital Gains and Losses.*

* For a gift of $250 or more, you'll also receive our monthly *Director's Report* and have your name listed in our Annual Report.

* And if you give $500 or more, you will also receive a personal letter from the Task Force's Executive Director informing you about specific gains we are making in your home state and two publications from our Policy Institute.

continues

Exhibit 10–1 continued (invitation card)

The Board of Directors

of the

NATIONAL GAY AND LESBIAN

TASK FORCE

is pleased to invite you

to membership

as a

Bridge Builder

r.s.v.p.

Courtesy of the National Gay and Lesbian Task Force, Washington, DC.

And what if the donor joins, and fails to renew? After several tries at renewing the donors (three requests, each a month apart is recommended), simply put the donors back in the regular mail stream. Or if their giving history shows consistent giving of smaller gifts, invite them to join your Monthly Donor Program (with no mention of their having previously been a high dollar donor). Another thing you might try is telephoning the donor. People are busy, and the telephone often gets a fast response.

CAPITAL CAMPAIGNS THROUGH THE MAIL

Direct mail is not usually a technique used in capital campaigns because the size of the average donor's gift (even when combined with those from others) doesn't make much of a dent in large budgets.

Most development officers use the mail in what they term a "mop-up" campaign, asking regular donors to send a large "stretch" gift in addition to their regular gift. Basically, a mop-up appeal is simply an additional special appeal earmarked for the capital campaign.

However, some capital (building) campaigns, especially those for memorials, do exceptionally well in the mail. Memorials we have helped include the Vietnam Veterans Memorial, the Japanese American Memorial, and the U.S. Holocaust Memorial and Museum.

In such cases, the entire fundraising campaign is a capital campaign designed to raise money to build a memorial or museum over a period of 2 to 10 years. Thus, every acquisition, every renewal letter, every special appeal must provide another reason for giving to build something.

There are many possibilities, including, but not limited to

- An appeal that offers exciting new benefits, and asks for a "stretch" gift to build a particular wing or area;
- A short, personal (card size) appeal announcing an extension of the campaign (asking for another gift);
- A personalized Certificate of Appreciation and letter on the occasion of groundbreaking ceremonies ("without you we couldn't have come this far");
- A letter asking for a gift of a certain size to inscribe the donor's name on a "Wall of Honor," on paving stones, or other special places;
- A progress appeal showing excavation or construction photographs;
- A letter announcing a large challenge grant from a prominent foundation;
- A request for a large gift to help sponsor a full-page advertisement in a major newspaper on opening day or similar (the donor's name to be included in the ad itself);
- A version of the Opening Day Program sent with a letter to nonattendees (I wish you could have been with me when . . .).

Each appeal must ask straightforwardly for a gift. The copy should center on how important the donor is to the person asking for the gift, "You are the reason we have been so successful," for example.

Exhibit 10–2 is a package for the Smithsonian's National Museum of the American Indian that announced Phase II of the multimillion dollar campaign. The "bad" news that the opening day had been pushed back by several years was made acceptable by announcing that the building site on the National Mall had been excavated. Photographs of the site with the nation's Capitol rising prominently in the background were included with the letter. Thus a routine event (excavation) was made into one of great (and fundraising worthy) importance.

SYNERGISTIC PROGRAMS

I wish that direct mail fundraising had another name because direct mail conjures up the wrong image. Such efforts are really donor acquisition, membership development, donor cultivation, donor development, donor/member upgrading, and so forth.

An organization's ability to communicate regularly with members and/or donors is critical to fundraising success. A healthy donor base is what foundations, corporations, and even individual donors look for in deciding whether to make major gifts. And, in turn, telling those donors how their support helps make major gifts possible gains even more support from the donor.

In one form or another, the following phrase has appeared in several campaign letters:

In addition to seeking your renewed support and that of other members like you, we ask for the help of foundations and corporations. And when I tell these potential major donors that 50,000 people just like you support our organization, they realize that our cause is important to large numbers of people. And that's when they open their hearts and their pocketbooks.

Exhibit 10–2 Capital Campaign Letter—Request for Additional Donation (pages 1 and 4 only)

Smithsonian
National Museum of the American Indian

December 2000

Dear Charter Member,

On my most recent inspection of the construction site on the National Mall where our new Museum will be built, I saw that the area had been excavated in the form of the Museum building itself. And, what may have looked like only a hole in the ground to some, looked glorious to me!

As you can imagine, this was a very exciting moment. As exciting as the moment when we completed Phase I of our fundraising campaign. As exciting as the day when the Fine Arts Commission put their final stamp of approval on the architectural design for the Mall Museum. And yes, even as exciting as the day our groundbreaking ceremonies made the front page of *The New York Times* and *The Washington Post*.

The realization of how far we've come inspired me to go up to the top floor of the National Air and Space Museum (next door to the construction site) to get a better view. Words cannot describe all that I felt or how splendid the construction site looked spread out before me.

That is why I am sending you the enclosed snapshots to evoke in you something of what I felt at that moment. And to ask you to celebrate with us as we come ever closer to our mutual goal – the opening of the Smithsonian's National Museum of the American Indian in late 2003. That is less than three years from now – years during which I hope you will maintain your Charter Membership. Because on that glorious day when we finally cut the ribbon, we want to say thank you in person.

I'd like to end this year by telling you that the hardest part is behind us . . . that it will be relatively simple to actually build the Museum . . . to furnish it . . . to finish moving our extraordinary collection to its new home . . . to plan and install exhibitions and to research and plant indigenous Native trees, shrubs and grasses. And finally, to raise the additional money so necessary to complete all of the foregoing.

But, if I told you that, I would not be telling the whole truth. And I cannot do that to a friend like you who has been such a loyal supporter.

So here, in brief, is the real story.

SMITHSONIAN INSTITUTION
PO Box 96836
Washington DC 20090-6836
aimember@nmai.si.edu Email
www.si.edu/nmai NMAI Website

continues

Exhibit 10–2 continued

We can build the Museum and install the exhibitions. We can furnish the building and create the programs for Members. We can plan the opening ceremonies in 2003 and prepare to receive thousands of visitors. But …

… We continue to need our members – for their annual dues, of course, but also for financial help over and above the dues, as we enter Phase II of our campaign starting in 2001.

You see, the tight construction market here in the Washington, DC, area has caused significant increases in the actual costs to build the Museum. It is primarily for this reason that our opening date has been pushed back to 2003. I thank you for understanding that in a project as enormous as this, some things simply could not be anticipated …

… and I remain confident that you are still as enthusiastic about this unique undertaking as you were the day you joined – that you want to help us complete the journey we began together.

If I am right, then I hope you will make an additional gift to the Museum today. And, we will keep you informed about our progress – progress we could not make without you.

Thank you, my friend, and please accept the enclosed photos with my best wishes for the New Year to you and yours.

Sincerely,

W. Richard West
(Southern Cheyenne)
Director
National Museum of the American Indian

P.S. Please send your gift today. As you count on us, we are counting on you.

Enclosures

continues

Exhibit 10–2 continued (front and back of photo card)

December, 2000

Soon we'll see NMAI rise up out of this recently excavated space on the National Mall.

Courtesy of the National Museum of the American Indian, Smithsonian Institution, Washington, DC.

Chapter 11
Production, Mailing, and File Maintenance

CHAPTER OUTLINE

- Working with Graphic Artists
- Working with Printers
- Fail-Safe Proofreading
- Mailings
- Further Thoughts on Artists, Printers, and Mail Houses
- Thirteen Money-Saving Production and Mailing Tips
- Postage and Postal Regulations

Thus far you have read about how to present your cause, lists, financial expectations, special direct mail programs, and much more. But what in the direct mail process can truly cause you problems with your superiors and even with board members?

There are three main things, and all are production related:

1. His or her mother-in-law gets duplicate appeals or receives an appeal just after she has contributed.
2. There is something about the quality of the package (paper stock, typeface, photo choice, etc.) that they hate.
3. The mail date is missed, and goes out too late to reap enough income to make the fiscal year budget.

You may have a fourth example or even more. But the fact is that the most noticed part of the entire process is what the recipient sees. And, like ballet dancing, that's as it should be. You only see the beautiful stage sets, the charming costumes, and the seemingly effortless grace and stamina that go into the dance.

Your boss, like your donor, only sees the final product—the way the envelope is addressed, whether the letter is easy to read as far as typeface and typesize are concerned, whether the photos are too dark or light, whether instructions are easy to follow, and so on. Finally, the donor (and perhaps your boss

too—certainly the mother-in-law) notices whether the reply form fits easily into the envelope, whether it is addressed to her deceased husband (when she has asked that his name be removed), whether she gets more than one of the same appeal on the same day, and whether she receives something on October 28th with a stated deadline of October 15th.

All of these pitfalls come under the general heading of Production and Mailing and File Maintenance.

WORKING WITH GRAPHIC ARTISTS

Not every graphic artist can bring the right look to your direct mail campaign. Many artists cannot resist imposing sophisticated, innovative design ideas on your package—even if it is not what you want. To get the right image for your package, engage an artist who has experience in direct mail. If you don't know such an artist, call a direct mail consultant or a nonprofit organization whose packages you admire. Don't forget to ask about cost. Ask whether the packages were successful, the artist was easy to work with, and deadlines were kept.

When you meet with the artist, be prepared to provide the following information and materials:

- The number of components in the package.
- The details and sizes of each component (but be open to the artist's suggestions).
- Photographs, logos, or other art you wish to use.

- Your timetable (The artist generally needs a week to produce the initial draft. If it is a complex piece, you may want to see multiple concepts before choosing one.)
- Formalized style requirements for your organization or at least the likes and dislikes of your president or director (or whoever has to give final approval). For example, if your organization's logo must always be used full size, don't give the artist the impression that he or she can reduce it to the size of the period at the end of this sentence.
- The written text for your package. Not only is this necessary for developing layout, but the artist should read the copy. The message and the feeling the copy evokes will provide ideas for good design.
- Any rough sketches you may have developed that could help the artist visualize what you want the final piece to look like.

This last point is very important. If you have strong ideas about how the package should look, don't hesitate to give the artist your own rough sketch. If your ideas are good, the artist will incorporate the best of them into the design and present a final layout that is exactly what you would have composed if you had the talent.

To illustrate a case in point, Exhibit 11–1 is a sample sketch of artwork we gave to the Washington, DC, designers, B&G. The sketch is admittedly crude, but they executed our instructions perfectly.

In discussing package design with your artist, be sure to emphasize the importance of the following:
- Letter copy should be typed, with short paragraphs, indented. You don't need an artist for this. We recommend testing the font you use in letters. Many organizations find that Courier font (a "typewritten font") receives a better response on acquisition mailings, while Times Roman and other "word processing" fonts work better on appeals.
- *Size of typeface.* Body copy for a letter, response card, or brochure set in less than 10-point type is too small. Don't ever let an artist convince you otherwise if you want your copy to be read.
- *Reverse-out type.* While the look of white text reversing out of a strong color can be graphically striking, it is extremely difficult to read. If you want to reverse out a small

section of your brochure for effect, go ahead. But make sure that this information isn't critical and that the type is sufficiently large to read in reverse.
- *Use of all capitals.* ALL CAPITALS ARE MONOTONOUS AND DIFFICULT TO READ. AVOID THEIR USE EXCEPT FOR SHORT HEADLINES.
- *Unusual typeface.* If the typeface is the first thing you notice in a brochure or letterhead or response card, it's not right for direct mail. The type should command you to read the written word, not command you to admire the typeface. Sans serif typefaces are difficult to read and should be used sparingly.
- *Background design.* Often artists will take a liking to an organization's logo or some other organizational component such as a church steeple or entrance gates and will use this design in a light background over which your letter is printed. Warning: Superimposing your letter over most designs, no matter how light the screen, will cut down on readability between 15 and 40 percent. Can you afford to lose that many potential donors?

Some direct mail experts assert that professional graphic design has no place in direct mail. In fact, they maintain that the entire package should have a completely homemade look. Many practitioners of the homemade look go so far as to type their letters on a manual typewriter rescued from the junk yard, and to deliberately leave in spelling and typographical errors. In general, such practices are insulting to the prospective donor. We strongly agree, however, that most charitable direct mail graphics should not look slick, expensive, or arty. In some cases you will get higher response if it looks a little "messy," that is, the contents should be on different (not matching paper) stock. You might use white paper for the main letter and other paper colors in other package components. The introduction of a jarring color note is most effective for certain types of causes. It would not be appropriate, however, in packages designed for museums, institutions of higher education, or medical facilities where the "look" of the institution must, to some extent, be maintained.

What Will It Cost?

Depending on the area of the country, art for a complete package, consisting of a typical (not type-

Exhibit 11–1 Sample Sketch from Which Final Artwork Was Done

set) four-page letter, response device, carrier envelope, and business reply envelope will cost between $1,000 and $1,500. The cost (as of 2001) includes an initial composite, final layout, and a final "print-ready" file. In major cities, the cost is usually at the higher end, depending on the job's complexity. If your package requires more than a simple design—for example, if you need a new logo or even new letterhead, a brochure, or one or more complex line drawings—the package will be more expensive.

Before you conclude your first meeting with the artist, ask that the quoted price be confirmed in writing. And remember that the best time to make changes is when the artist gives you a composite, not when the final art is presented. Naturally, you can make changes at any point, but they will become increasingly costly as you get closer to the finished product.

A word of advice: Some artists and almost all photographers base their prices on whether their work is for one-time use only. Be sure to explain that if your package is successful, you plan to reprint it over a prolonged period. Most artists will give you outright ownership of work created for you so long as you don't use it commercially (i.e., convert the work into posters, note cards, etc., which you will sell for a profit). Be especially open with artists who are creating logos, which cost more. The questions of ownership or multiple use are negotiable.

WORKING WITH PRINTERS

If you don't know a good printer, your artist can help you locate one or you can ask colleagues. It is important for you and the artist to meet with the printer when the rough design has been completed. This will enable you to learn whether your package can be produced within your budget and schedule. The early meeting with the printer is important for other reasons.

Here are a few near mistakes from which we have been rescued by conscientious printers.

- A brochure with a fanfold could not be machine inserted into the carrier envelope because there was no folded edge for the machine to grip.
- Similarly, a folded double response device had the fold at the wrong end. Yes, there is a wrong end because the grippers on the machine inserter must grip a folded edge.
- A carrier envelope face covered by a large photo would not reproduce well with standard printing. In addition, postage regulations require a "clear zone" around the postal bar code that a large photo may impede.
- A response device was too narrow for machine inserting. This error would have meant hand inserting each package—at a substantial price.
- A brochure with heavy photo coverage on both sides was specified to be printed on 50-pound offset paper on which ghost images would have shown through.

Getting Bids for Printing Jobs

If it falls to you or one of your colleagues to bid out the printing and, if you need help but your budget doesn't allow it, you have a few choices. You can sit there paralyzed and overworked, you can go back to the same guy who printed and mailed for you before (even though you think his prices are highway robbery), *or* you can get help.

There are a couple of different types of businesses that can provide the help you need.

Through a specialist firm, you can go online to a bidding network with instant budget estimators and reach out to print vendors throughout the country—vendors who specialize in the type of work your job requires. A consolidated spreadsheet with competitive bids will return over a private, secure network. You will choose a vendor and award your job(s) electronically, transmitting purchase orders to begin projects immediately. You are in charge all the way and, because of this, you will develop relationships with your vendors that will stand you in good stead. What's more, as a customer, you can interact with your peer network through an online bulletin board. It also links you with other important sites such as the U.S. Postal Service, the Printing Industries Association, and more.

If the specialist firm option doesn't describe your need because your organization isn't that small, or if you have greater needs for whatever reason, the answer to your prayers may be to hire a production management company.

When you hire such a company, it's like gaining an experienced staff for a defined period of time. The production management company almost always obtains competitive (or even lower) prices than you could afford on your own, even though they have marked the vendor's bills up to make a profit.

With a production management company, you do even less work than in the first scenario. It is suggested that you secure solid references and work closely with the company, especially in the beginning.

Two companies with whom the author's firm has worked happily are BidToPrint.com, a specialist firm, in Arlington, Virginia, and Production Solutions, a production management company, in Vienna, Virginia. The technology that enables companies to offer these services is fairly new, so there will undoubtedly be new arrivals on the scene soon, if there aren't already.

If you decide to obtain bids on your own, be sure to give each printer identical specifications: the type and weight of paper, the final size of each printed piece, the number of colors, photographs, bleeds, etc. If you are not particular about paper, you may be able to find a printer with extra carriers or paper in their warehouse you can use for less.

It is important to tell the printer when final artwork will be ready and when you need the printed materials delivered to the lettershop. Often, one printer can produce a job in less time than others. This could be because they have exactly the right press facilities for your job, paper in stock, or because business is slow.

Should all your bids come in under or just at budget, you will have to use other criteria to select your printer. Always ask for samples of similar work the printer has done for others. And check references to be certain that other clients are happy with the quality of work and the dependability of delivery.

What To Discuss with Your Printer

Be sure you and your printer are clear about these items prior to signing a contract for the job:

- Ask for written price quotations. The quote should break out how much each package item costs per thousand in addition to giving the total cost.
- Ask the printer about the company's overrun estimates. The industry standard on printing overruns (for which the client is obligated to pay) is 5 percent on quantities of 250,000 or more and 10 percent on quantities of less than 250,000. Establish whether you are willing to accept unders (fewer pieces than your order) or to pay for overs (percentage higher than your order). We recommend against it. A simple statement on your con-

tract "No overs/unders accepted" should cover you legally. (In fact, overruns usually amount to only between 2 and 3 percent.) Agree in advance that in the case of underruns the printer will have to reprint.
- Agree in advance on delivery dates, allowing some flexibility in your schedule for time to correct errors.
  — Delivery of a printer's proof or blueline, cut and folded to size
  — Delivery of a minimum of 30 hand-trimmed samples in advance of mailing to you
  — Delivery of entire job to the mail house. Be sure to specify how the mail house wants the various items packed.
- Ask the printer to provide, in advance, samples of the various paper stocks for the job. It is not sufficient to simply order 50- or 60-pound stock, as within these weight specifications, paper quality can vary dramatically.
- Ask a new printer to provide samples of direct mail materials he or she has produced for other clients. Incidentally, as with graphic artists and mail houses, it is important to call clients for references. Ask specifically about quality of work and dependability of delivery.
- Give your printer specific instructions in writing. Without written instructions, you are without recourse should something go wrong with your job. With written instructions you can usually correct a disaster—e.g., wrong color, wrong size—at no cost to you. And you can get the price of a barely acceptable job greatly reduced.

FAIL-SAFE PROOFREADING

You should proofread the typeset copy twice: once for sense and a second time backward to catch spelling and punctuation errors. If possible, use a professional proofreader. If you are not using a professional proofreader and don't know proofreading symbols, ask your artist or printer to recommend a book. The correct proof marks will enable the artist to make the proper corrections in the beginning, and will save you time and money.

The art that is supplied to the printer, usually on disk, will be "photographed," film will be made, and a positive image of the film, called a "blueline," will be submitted to you for approval. Some printers are now using technology that skips the blueline stage. You should still insist on seeing a final "print proof" prior to printing because that is an exact representation of what your piece will look like.

The proof or blueline is your fail-safe opportunity to catch elusive mistakes not discovered earlier. However, the real purpose of the proof is not to discover typos. Catching typos (or worst of all, making copy changes) at this stage is expensive and will delay your mailing.

Check your proof carefully for the following:

- Is the fold correct?
- Is the size correct?
- Are photographs (and captions) and text correctly placed?
- Are the pages consecutive (e.g., did the printer accidentally transpose pages 1 and 3)?
- Does any printing on the response card "show through" the window on the carrier envelope? (Was it supposed to?)
- Is the intensity of the ink good? (Too dark? Too light?)
- Are there "hickeys" (unattractive spots often caused by dust on the film) in the photographs (or anywhere else in the piece)?
- Are the color breaks marked correctly (e.g., are the parts that are meant to be blue actually blue and not red)?

If you find it difficult to judge printing quality by looking at a blueline, ask the printer to provide a "match print" color key. This will cost a bit more, but because it breaks out all colors, it can be well worth the additional cost—especially on a four-color printing job. For important jobs, we recommend press checks to check color and quality while the job is on the press.

When the proofs come from the printer, you'll also want to make sure the quantity, paper stock, and delivery location indicated for each component are the same as you planned.

MAILINGS

Working with Lettershops

You have come a long way. You have planned, budgeted, created, conferred with artists, negotiated with printers, and corrected layouts and proofs. Now you are ready to mail. The choice of a mail house is no less critical than the choice of an artist or printer.

There are big mailing houses and small mailing houses. There are the expensive and the less expensive. There are good and bad. In our experience, we have been unable to relate expensive to good, inexpensive to bad, or any other combination of the above. Once again, the best way to choose a lettershop is to ask your colleagues in other organizations for referrals. Then, as with printers, obtain three price bids.

A good mail house or lettershop will:

- Open your printed materials on receipt and notify you immediately if there are shortages in quantity or questions about quality.
- Call promptly if your written instructions are not absolutely clear.
- Not delay your job for another—perhaps more lucrative—job (assuming that you are on time).
- Keep you informed of well-founded rumors (e.g., a backup at the bulk mail center, a potential postage increase, fast- and slow-moving mail during certain periods).
- Mail on time—assuming that you and your printer are also on time—and advise you promptly of any delays. Note: It is useless for a mail house to deceive a customer about the drop date because the post office receipts that will be submitted with your mail house bill will verify the actual date(s) of mailing.

Your Responsibilities to the Mail House

- Obtain the correct postal permits well in advance or arrange for the mail house to do it for you. The process of obtaining postal permits is discussed later in this chapter.
- If your lettershop is doing your processing and personalization, send an advance listing, with assigned key codes, of the lists that are expected at your mail house. Send written instructions to the mail house with a sample package, inserted the way you want it. Instructions should be typed clearly and should leave no room for guesswork. Most important are the mail date and instructions on how to handle split tests.
- Send the postage check in advance. Mail houses usually require the check five working days in advance and most will not start work until it has arrived.

- Ask the mail house to send you a half dozen "live" samples right off their inserting machine. (Unlike the samples from the printer, live samples show you exactly how your mailing looks to recipients.)
- "Seed" yourself in the mailing. Make sure several pieces are addressed to you so that you will know when others receive their mail and when you may expect returns.
- Request live samples of personalization and inserted packages to ensure your instructions are understood and followed. Do not relax after you have completed all of the above, expecting that the mailing house will call you should problems arise. They might and they might not. Call to make certain your materials have arrived and that work is progressing on schedule. Then call again the day the mail is scheduled to drop just to make sure.

How To Cope with Late Mailings

Even if you have done everything humanly possible in working with your list broker, printer, and lettershop, Murphy's Law can still prevail. Let us here forewarn you of potential last-minute pitfalls. For example, suppose you discover at 5 PM on Friday that something has to be rewritten and reprinted and your mail date is scheduled for Monday. What's the problem here? The fact is, you have contracted for a particular mail date, and your material is timed to coincide with a political or social "event" that will make the mailing many times more effective.

It isn't possible to provide you with the right answer for all cases, but here are some alternatives:
- In contracting for a specific date for the use of an outside list, you have not promised to mail on that date, but within that week. Thus you have some leeway.
- If your material is dated and critical, you may wish to mail parts of your file first class, despite the cost.
- If your material is not dated and the list broker gives you permission to mail late, you should ask whether a competing organization might be mailing to the same list at the same time. If so, you should ask for a new mail date.

It is important to remember that late delivery of lists and materials can cause the same havoc. It is therefore prudent to ask your printer to print and deliver your response devices first if possible. Thus, the mail house usually can get a head start on personalization.

FURTHER THOUGHTS ON ARTISTS, PRINTERS, AND MAIL HOUSES

It is a good idea to visit your printing plant and mail house (or lettershop) in the beginning to educate yourself about techniques and meet the people with whom you will be working. This makes for a far better relationship in the long run. People who know you will be more likely to go the extra mile when a problem arises.

If your mail campaign is at an ongoing stage, and you're happy with the services provided by your artist, printer, and mail house, you might wish to give each a schedule of future mailings. The more they know about your plans, the better they can serve you. For example, your printer may be able to order a preferred paper that he or she would not have been able to get on short notice. Or, your artist will be able to warn you in advance if he or she expects to be especially busy during a certain time of year. Your mail house can schedule you in its work log. This type of planning pays off for you too, because by planning out the year, you know when you have to write a new package or start ordering lists for the next campaign.

THIRTEEN MONEY-SAVING PRODUCTION AND MAILING TIPS

1. Obtain several printing bids for the best price.
2. Ask your printer for suggestions about the most economical size for each component of the package.
3. Order envelopes from envelope manufacturers as opposed to buying them ready made off-the-shelf. (It takes longer but it's less expensive.)
4. Use standard left-hand window envelopes (as opposed to the more expensive center or right-hand windows).
5. If you are a larger mailer, order envelopes in large lots, especially the business reply envelopes, which rarely change. As for carrier envelopes with name and address printing, you can always overprint teaser copy later.

6. Confine use of two colors to the first page of your letter; and on most presses, page four will line up with page one on a four-page letter, so you can print a different color signature if blue is your second color. Otherwise use black.

7. Test partial personalization (e.g., personalize only the response card and test it against a fully personalized package, if that is what you use).

8. On house file mailings, test regular reply envelopes where the donor affixes his or her own stamp against business reply envelopes where you pay the postage.

9. "Your stamp is an extra donation" is common language on most BREs. Tests have shown that this can depress results. Test it.

10. Always presort for postal discounts.

11. Proof carefully at all stages of package development to avoid costly changes at blueline.

12. Weigh all package components before printing to avoid unexpected additional postage costs, and make sure your lettershop weighs them too.

13. Stock photos are expensive. Build up your own photo library and be sure to obtain reprint releases on all identifiable persons on photos.

Following is a helpful production checklist (Exhibit 11–2) that goes beyond what you may think about. You can copy and use it as a safeguard for each of your mailings.

POSTAGE AND POSTAL REGULATIONS

Cost To Mail

Many nonprofit organizations can qualify to mail at the nonprofit bulk rate, providing major savings from first class postage.

Because there is such a substantial savings, most organizations elect to mail all acquisitions and most renewal or special gift appeals at the nonprofit rate. However, many organizations do mail their high dollar donors (here usually classified as $250 and over) at the first class rate. First class ensures faster delivery and forwarding addresses, and also may have an impact on perceptions.

Third class postage can be live stamped, metered, or provided through preprinted indicia. Many postage tests have been conducted to ascertain whether the stamp outpulls the meter or the meter the indicia. The results? In most cases, both meter and stamp outpull the indicia and in some cases, the stamp does better than the meter. But not always. The simpler the envelope, the more important the look of the postage. Thus a commercial looking envelope with a great deal of illustration and text might do just as well with an indicia, while a simple, dignified envelope might benefit from a live stamp.

The test results have varied so widely that you should test this yourself. If in doubt, however, you will not go wrong by metering your mail with a live nonprofit stamp.

Nonprofit Bulk Rate Permits

Everything you need to know about postal permits and regulations is contained in the Postal Service Manual issued by the U.S. Postal Service.

If you do not have the manual, or if you find the information confusing, the following should be of help:

If you are a 501(c)(3) organization, it is a relatively simple matter to obtain a nonprofit bulk-rate mailing permit. Submit completed Form 3614 to your local postmaster with the following proofs of status:

- articles of incorporation and bylaws (including a dissolution statement)
- certificate of tax exemption
- samples of existing brochures and direct mail packages
- a summary of your organization's activities for the last 12 months (a financial statement is acceptable)

In addition, your application must show that the primary purpose of your organization is religious, educational, scientific, philanthropic, agricultural, labor, veteran, or fraternal, or that it is a qualified political committee. Other types of nonprofit organizations do not qualify for special rate usage.

Organizations classified as 501(c)(4) and 501(c)(6) may also obtain a nonprofit bulk-rate mailing permit, providing they are able to show that their primary purpose is one of those listed as qualifying in the preceding paragraph.

Exhibit 11–2 Production Checklist

	Yes	Notes
1. Postage permits obtained or renewed?	_____	_____
2. Written list confirmations received and checked for correct quantities, selects, and codes?	_____	_____
3. Final copy carefully proofed by professional or someone who didn't work on the project?	_____	_____
4. All copy and art approvals (your boss, the letter signer, etc.) obtained in writing?	_____	_____
5. Prototype of package made at early stage to make sure everything fits? To make sure it isn't overweight?	_____	_____
6. When reprinting old materials, copy checked for possible changes in statistics, dates, board listings, and other variables?	_____	_____
7. Instructions to printer, computer bureau, and mail house verified in writing? (Remember, nothing you said by phone can be proven.)	_____	_____
8. If inventory is to be used, have you double-checked to make sure what you need exists?	_____	_____
9. Bluelines checked for correct folds, color breaks, and size as well as text? PMS color selects verified?	_____	_____
10. Arrival of all tapes sufficiently in advance of mail date?	_____	_____
11. Postage check to cover mailing requisitioned and sent in advance to mail house?	_____	_____
12. Quantities verified by mail house immediately when delivered by printer?	_____	_____
13. Inserted samples checked prior to mailing? (Is it your BRE in the package or someone else's? Are the pieces inserted in the correct order and facing in the same direction?)	_____	_____
14. Drop count verification received from mail house within 24 hours after mail date? (Are 10 sacks of your mail still sitting at the mail house rather than at the post office?)	_____	_____
15. Sufficient funds deposited in lock box account to pay for donations returned in BREs?	_____	_____

Once you have obtained a nonprofit bulk-rate mailing permit, it is a simple matter to obtain one or more second points of entry if you change mailing agents and/or mail from more than one location. You must submit Form 3623 plus a letter on your stationery to the post office you wish to mail from. Your mailing agent can provide you with both the form and a prototype letter. There is no additional charge for this, and while the form says to allow 30 days for processing, you can usually obtain it sooner.

Standard Nonprofit Mailing Requirements

The mailing requirements for standard nonprofit mailings (as of 2001) are:

- Mailings must consist of at least 200 pieces or 50 pounds.
- Letters must be presorted by ZIP codes in packages and sacks to the finest extent possible.
- Each piece must be identical in weight, although textual matter need not be identical.
- All standard mailings must be mailed at least once a year at the post office from which the permit was issued.
- The authorized permit holder must be identified on the carrier envelope. The name and return address of the authorized permit holder must appear in a prominent location. Pseudonyms of persons or organizations may not be used. If the mailing piece bears any name and return address, it must be that of the authorized permit holder. A well-recognized alternative designation or abbreviation such as "The March of Dimes" or the "AFL-CIO" may be used in place of the full name of the organization.
- Your reply carrier enclosure must be automation-compatible.
- There are no maximum size standards for a single piece of third class mail. There are, however, maximum standards for third class carrier route presort, which are not more than $3/_4''$ thick, not more than $11^1/_2''$ high, and not more than $13^1/_2''$ long.
- As for minimum size standards, all third class mailings must be at least .007'' thick, rectangular in shape, at least $3^1/_2''$ high, and 5'' long.
- Third class mail may receive deferred service. The Postal Service has up to four weeks to process such mail and does not guarantee the delivery of third class mail within a specified time (as most fundraisers, unfortunately, know all too well).

Note: The Postal Service is constantly changing regulations. Keep abreast of them.

How To Save Money on Postage

Even if you mail first class, you can qualify for a three/five-digit presort, or better still a carrier route presort, all of which save substantial money. Although your merge/purge house or lettershop will handle the tedious job of sorting the mail according to postal regulations, it's up to you to keep abreast of any changes. At minimum, you can mail three/five-digit presort, and if you mail as much as 250,000 pieces, you can probably mail carrier route presort where the savings will be even greater. This is much the same as three/five-digit presorting except that you must sort your mail down to even smaller areas (carrier routes). Have your data processing company or lettershop run an analysis of the most cost-effective way to sort.

Bar Codes

In addition to putting bar codes on business reply envelopes, an organization should add bar codes to its carrier envelopes; otherwise the Postal Service will add less attractive bar codes to ensure deliverability.

Keeping Your List Clean

With ever-increasing postal rates, one way to make sure that you're not wasting money is to keep your list clean and make sure that all addresses are deliverable.

The most efficient way to clean your list is to mail one of your annual house appeals with the printed words:

ADDRESS CORRECTION REQUIRED

RETURN POSTAGE GUARANTEED

Please note: No copy or art can be $^1/_4''$ above or below this printed legend and type size can be no smaller than 8 point. If your appeal is undeliverable to an address, the post office will return your letter together with a new address if one is known. There is a small fee for this service, but it is a good investment when you consider how costly it is to continue to mail to undeliverable addresses.

In addition, the Postal Service offers the following service to assist customers in making sure their mail is deliverable:

The National Change of Address (NCOA). Change of address records are furnished weekly by the Postal Service to these computer facilities and can be used to update your file. The Postal Service can provide you with a list of companies (23 companies across the country) offering this service, and the charges vary from company to company.

We recommend that an NCOA be done at least annually at minimum if you mail exclusively at third class postage rates. If you mail at first class presort rates, the post office requires that you perform NCOA processing every 180 days.

Business Reply Mail

Whether you elect to receive your contributions in-house or through a bank lock box, it is usually economical to open a Business Reply Account at your local post office. The annual fee will be amortized quickly.

Here is how it works. Without such an account, your postage-due mail will be delivered to your office, where you must pay in cash each day. However, if you have a Business Reply Account, you deposit money in that account equal to your anticipated returns (plus an annual fee) and your account is then charged at a significantly reduced rate for each piece received. When your account runs low, you deposit more money. If it runs out, the post office will stop delivering your postage-due mail. A sudden slack in BRE mail should signal you to check your financial status with the post office, or better yet, monitor the account faithfully.

Everything you need to know about first class business reply mail can be found in the Postal Service manual mentioned earlier.

Printing Regulations

Any photographic, mechanical, or electrical process or any combination of such processes other than handwriting, typewriting, or hand stamping may be used to prepare the address side of business reply mail.

A business reply envelope must have a bar code, and the color of the stock may be any light color that allows the address, postmark, and other required endorsements to be readily discerned and does not interfere with the bar code reader. Brilliant colors may not be used. Green diamond borders or other borders are not authorized for business reply labels, cartons, and envelopes larger than 6″ × 11″.

Shown here are two envelopes for the Central Park Conservancy: a courtesy reply envelope (CRE) (Exhibit 11–3) that requires the donor to use his or her own stamp and a business reply envelope (BRE) (Exhibit 11–4) where the nonprofit organization pays the first class return postage.

Note that the phrase "Your stamp is an extra contribution" is used on the BRE. The use of this phrase should be tested as numerous mailings have shown that—counterintuitively—it depresses returns.

Also shown here is a CRE for the Elizabeth Glaser Pediatric AIDS Foundation (Exhibit 11–5). This envelope uses the phrase "Place Stamp Here" where the donor's stamp will go. And because there is no regulation in how an address must look on a CRE, organizations can print their name and/or logo in any format they wish.

The last illustrated envelope is a "wallet flap" for the Smithsonian's National Museum of the American Indian (Exhibit 11–6). The flap can be easily removed at the perforation line, inserted into the envelope, and sealed. The value of this format is that the confidential information contained cannot be read. While the Museum uses this envelope as an enclosure in acknowledgment letters (and while it can be regarded primarily as a gift membership form), the wallet flap is used by some mailers in their acquisition and prospect mail.

The drawback to wallet flaps is that there is more work on the receiving end in interpreting handwriting and other information than would usually be found on the imprinted response card.

Exhibit 11–3 A Courtesy Reply Envelope (CRE)

Recycled Paper
SCXZZZZZ

CENTRAL PARK CONSERVANCY
BOX 5204, GPO
NEW YORK NY 10087-5204

Courtesy of the Central Park Conservancy, New York, New York.

Exhibit 11–4 A Business Reply Envelope (BRE)

Your stamp is an extra contribution
to the Conservancy!

Recycled Paper
SCXZZZZZ

||||

NO POSTAGE
NECESSARY
IF MAILED
IN THE
UNITED STATES

BUSINESS REPLY MAIL

FIRST-CLASS MAIL   PERMIT NO. 9196   NEW YORK, NY

POSTAGE WILL BE PAID BY ADDRESSEE

CENTRAL PARK CONSERVANCY
CHURCH STREET STATION
POST OFFICE BOX 4004
NEW YORK NY 10277-0149

Courtesy of the Central Park Conservancy, New York, New York.

Exhibit 11–5 A "Place Stamp Here" CRE

PLACE
STAMP
HERE

Elizabeth Glaser
Pediatric AIDS Foundation

2950 31st Street, Suite 125
Santa Monica, CA 90405

Courtesy of the Elizabeth Glaser Pediatric AIDS Foundation, Santa Monica, California.

Exhibit 11–6 A "Wallet Flap" Reply Envelope

Please detach and return with your check payable to NMAI/Smithsonian

My name _____   Gift Recipient _____

Address _____   Address _____

City _____ State _____ Zip _____   City _____ State _____ Zip _____

Enclosed is $_____ to help support NMAI. For proper processing, please check one of the boxes below.

☐ This is a new membership at $_____. (AM104WF)   ☐ I wish to renew my membership. Membership #: _____ (R104WF)

☐ This is a tax-deductible gift donation; Check one: ☐ I am not a member. ☐ I am a member. Membership #: _____ (HGIFTWF)

☐ This is a gift membership at $20 or more. Please send a gift announcement in my name to the person listed as gift recipient.
(If giving more than one membership, please print additional names and addresses on a separate piece of paper.) (M104WFGM)

        Amount $ _____   Card Expiration Date (MM/YY) _____/_____

        Signature _____   Credit Card # _____

Place
Stamp
Here

Smithsonian
National Museum of the American Indian
PO Box 96836
Washington DC 20090-6836

Courtesy of the National Museum of the American Indian, Smithsonian Institution, Washington, DC.

Chapter 12
Computers and Service Bureaus

One of the most important relationships in the entire development process is the one you have with your donor records. The problem is that computer systems are often major sources of frustration and fear. It doesn't have to be that way. With some patience, logic, and a large dose of self-discipline, you can make your system work for you. A good donor database is imperative to *all* fundraising efforts, but because this book focuses on direct mail fundraising, we will review some of the ways you can create a powerful database and use it as the foundation for an effective direct mail fundraising program.

An important related topic, merge/purge, is also discussed at the end of this chapter, as well as in Chapter 3.

THE OPTIONS

At present, there are only two realistic options for database management: (1) an in-house system or (2) an outside service bureau. Web-based systems management is in its infancy right now, but by the time you read this, it may very well be an excellent third option, especially for smaller organizations. (Check out www.e-tapestry.com.) Each system has its pros and cons. Figuring out which is right for you is the hard part, but this chapter is designed to help.

ANALYZING YOUR NEEDS

To get the right system, first analyze your fundraising needs. Begin by taking a careful look at your fundraising strategy and programs. Remember, nobody's perfect. Many service bureaus and software suppliers would like nothing better than to have you adapt *your* fundraising strategy to *their* systems. Don't do it. Be sure that you can modify the system to your strategy. And beware—the more compromises you have to make within the system to accommodate your strategy, the less likely it is that you've found the ideal system for you. Following is a checklist of potential needs and considerations. Note those you think you will require and then discuss them with several service bureaus, software vendors, and/or consultants.

The Systems Checklist

Basic Donor Information. You must be able to store some basic information on each of your donors. How the information is stored is as important as what is stored. For names and addresses, any system will use fields for each section of the name and address. As some married women retain their given last names, a good system will allow two names in each record and will use "fields" for each section of the name and address.

- *Name:* Full name (the more fields a system uses to create the full name, the better it is). An ideal system would have a record of the name as follows:

Name 1:	Title	First Name	MI	Last Name	Suffix

Name 2:	Title	First Name	MI	Last Name	Suffix

- *Company Name, Organization Name, or "in care of."*
- *Address:* You will need at least two lines to accommodate street names at the very minimum. Three is better, especially if you have foreign addresses. Apartment number, city, state, and ZIP code should each be in separate fields. If your donors move around a lot, make sure the system permits an alternate address.
- *Country.*
- *Telephone Number:* Include fields for both home and office numbers.
- *E-Mail Address:* Leave a dedicated field.
- *Salutation:* If you plan on personalizing your mail, this is a must. Allow for several salutations that can be tailored to different letter signers (e.g., president, board chair, executive director, development director).
- *"Flag" Codes* (also known as classifications, tags, donor codes, and demographic codes): These can be used for a variety of purposes, most of which help bond and cultivate your donors by giving them individualized attention inexpensively. Make sure you have plenty of room to "tick mark" each record with individual characteristics of the donor (e.g., interest, mailing restrictions, high-dollar status, and demographic information). You will also want to be able to store the date on which the flag was applied to the file or changed.
- *ID Number:* Every record needs a unique identification number or match code. Don't let your mail go out without it!

Basic Gift Information. The most cost-effective and accurate way to predict future giving behavior is to have a complete picture of the donor's history.

Data modeling, demographic information, and other predictive enhancements described in Appendix C can add to, but never replace, past giving information. There are six basic pieces of information you should be able to store for each gift, and, you must be able to store every gift a donor makes:

- *Amount of the Gift.*
- *Date of the Gift.*
- *Source of the Gift:* Usually expressed in the form of a code that is at least six positions long. A minimum of eight is preferable. Go for length here; it will give you flexibility in the future, even if you don't use all the positions now.
- *Gift Type:* You must be able to distinguish among different types of gifts (e.g., first gift, renewal, appeal, pledges).
- *Batch Number:* Although your fundraising system may not accomplish all of your accounting needs, it is often useful to store the number of the batch in which an individual donation appears, just in case you have to find the source document in the future. This will also allow you to track when the gift was entered and who entered it.
- *Payment Type:* Is the gift part of an ongoing sustainer gift via electronic funds transfer (EFT)? If the gift was made with a credit card, you may want to know that in case the charge authorization is eventually denied.

Renewal Information. Are you going to have a renewal program? If so, the system should be able to accommodate your strategy. If you are a membership organization and have or wish to create what we call a "magazine style" (usually six- or seven-part) renewal program, you will almost certainly require a system that allows you to:

- automatically assign expiration dates to each individual record (monthly, quarterly, semi-annually, or annually)
- automatically advance the individual donor's expiration date when a qualifying gift (e.g., renewal) is received
- easily select recipients for the first notice, nonrespondents to the second notice, etc.
- allow for manual adjustments of expiration dates to handle customer service issues

Monthly Pledge Programs. You may have some donors to your organization who are so highly motivated that they will give to you every month. Can your system handle credit card payments and EFT transactions? If not now, later on you may want to send monthly bills to monthly givers who don't opt for credit cards/EFT transactions. In this case, you will need a system with the following storage and processing features:

- pledge information (initial pledge amount, upgraded pledge, dates for each)
- monthly giving history
- calculations of how much is owed
- method for calculating who is delinquent
- method for adding personalization to individual bills
- method for printing bills each month

High-Dollar Programs. Many organizations are tempted to store their high- and low-dollar files on two separate systems. It sounds logical, because the amount and kinds of information you'll want to be able to retrieve on each type of donor are quite different. But setting up separate systems—dual databases—will only add to your problems.

Dual databases often lead to an unusually high number of duplicates. Inevitably, the following scenario occurs. A major donor responds to a prospect mailing and gets added to the low-dollar file. Then the next time you do a house mailing, the VIP donor may receive both the "down and dirty" low-dollar version and a highly personalized high-dollar version. As a consequence, he or she doesn't feel very special any more. Over time, instead of upgrading VIPs, you may downgrade the size of their gifts.

It is possible to find systems that can accommodate your database management requirements for both low-dollar (renewals, appeals, monthly giving) and major donor programs. But proceed carefully. Make sure that your high-dollar file is properly cared for on your computer. In addition to the storage requirements already mentioned, here are some of the things to look for:

- ***Professional Information:*** Occupation, place of employment, position
- ***Biographical:*** Birthday, education, VIP contacts (e.g., names of corporations, foundations, important individuals whom this donor knows, contacts that might be helpful to you later as you broaden your fundraising reach beyond existing large donors). Because there are numerous research companies who will provide this information, you should make sure your database can handle a computer upload of such data. Otherwise, you may face a mountainous data entry issue.

- ***Board and Staff Contacts:*** You'll want to be able to retrieve the names of major donors your board or staff members know, whom they can cultivate and solicit.
- ***Pledge Tracking:*** To accommodate that precious big giver who pledges $25,000 in 10 installments and then asks you to remind him or her each time a payment comes due. You'll want some kind of automatic tickler file that tells you when a payment is due, the total pledge, amount paid, and outstanding balance.
- ***Solicitation Requests:*** Sometimes major donors have pretty elaborate instructions on when they want to be solicited and when they don't. Your system should be able to take care of most of this using the flag (demographic) codes. If not, make sure your high-dollar system can meet this need. You don't want to downgrade a major donor by asking for a big gift at the wrong time.
- ***Planned Giving:*** At some point, you will want to store data on planned giving prospects. If you have an aggressive planned giving program, you may want your database to link with PG-Calc or other planned giving software systems.
- ***Miscellaneous:*** Ultimately, there will be some information on major donors that you'll want to store that doesn't lend itself to compartmentalization ("Board Chair Smith met Donor Jones at a White House reception on 11/18/90. Jones expressed interest in our litigation project."). This kind of information usually ends up in a manila folder, but it would be nice if you could store small amounts of it electronically with the rest of the donor's record.

In addition to these storage considerations, the system should be able to "select" on virtually all of this information (not just individually, but in combination), so that you will be able to ask the database to output, for example:

- the names, addresses, and giving histories of the major donors who live in ZIP code 20016
- all donors who have made a pledge for the next two months, with name, address, total

pledge, amount paid, amount of next payment, and proper salutation

- all donors who live in New York City who have given a gift of $100 or more within the last two years
- all the attorneys on the file who are major donors; and so on

Finally, there is the issue of "query language," which generally refers to your ability to ask your database for information without the intervention of the people who service your system. We urge you to make sure that you can communicate with your database directly, with as few programmers, MIS gurus, or service technicians as possible standing between you and this tremendous asset known as your donor file. The reason for this has less to do with systems than with fundraising. We believe that you and the individuals in your organization who work with the major donors should be encouraged to have as much hands-on direct contact with the donors as possible. It makes for more effective fundraising.

Questions You'll Want Answers To

What follows are some of the many questions that we ask—or are asked—as we get into the process of developing a new database or converting an old one to a new system. Use this checklist as you think about your own needs. You'll find that as you look at these questions, new questions and needs you never knew existed will arise.

Gift History. Does the system give you an automatic summary of giving highlights (e.g., highest previous contribution, latest gift, annual total, and first gift)? Does the system store unlimited gift histories? It should (remember, past giving patterns are the best, cheapest way to predict—and upgrade—future gifts), but if it doesn't, how many gifts are stored? What happens to gifts that roll off the system?

Record Layout. Is there room for all the information you want to be able to retrieve later on? Can additional data elements (fields) be added later if your needs change? How much will it cost you? How much information that is stored in the record layout can be selected?

Flag Codes. How many flags can you put on an individual record? Who defines the flags: the creator of the system, or you, the client? Where do you have to go to look up flag code definitions—can they be stored in the system and displayed with an individual record when you look one up on-screen?

Updating. Updating, simply translated, means changing out-of-date addresses, adding new donors, removing contributors who are deceased or otherwise lost to you, and recording the latest giving information on the donor's record. The two basic ways to update your file are periodically (in "batch" mode), and online, in real time. Think carefully about how quickly you need to have changes made to your system, and when you'll want to access the new information.

Member Identification Number. You have two choices: either a unique ID number or a name/address "match" code. This is a code created by the computer using alpha/numeric elements from the name and address. But beware. If the address changes, the match code changes. We believe that the unique ID number is better than a match code for helping prevent duplicates from being added to your file. Whichever way you choose, make sure that the ID number or match code meets your requirements.

Specialty Programs. Can the system accommodate gift membership promotions? Member-get-a-member and membership canvasses? Premiums? Other items you might want to offer to your donors? Donor gift clubs? Levels of membership? Giving circles?

Data Entry. Who is going to be responsible for data entry? Is the system flexible enough that you can do as much of the data entry as your staff load permits? If you hire a service bureau, will they be responsible for data entry? Does the system generate reports that allow you to balance the money you key to your database with the bank control logs maintained by your lock box or caging shop?

What is the turnaround time for data entry if it is to be done by someone other than you? What is the person or company's accuracy rate? How are personnel trained and supervised? How easy is it to change (update) a record? Can you combine records easily if you find duplicate records in the system? Can address changes be made quickly and efficiently? If so, is a "data trail" established by the system so you can refer to it at a later date? Does the system contain ZIP code and source code tables to reduce the instances of human error (for example, trying to add a wrong ZIP to a city or attempting to add a gift to the file using an incorrect code)?

This may be one of the most important aspects of your computer system. Remember, garbage in– garbage out. If the chairman of the board's name is misspelled on the database, that is how every piece of mail he gets will be addressed. We've seen direct mail programs eliminated because the board got frustrated with bad data entry.

Deduping. There are two ways a system can help you keep your file free of duplicate records. The first is at the data entry state. Does the system attempt to locate possible duplicates on the file before you add a "new" name? If so, how does it work? How much does it cost? How efficient is it?

Second, the system should be able to run a program periodically (usually semiannually, although some groups choose dedupe runs more frequently) that lists potential duplicate records so you can combine those that are duplicates. How much does a dedupe run cost? How easy is it to combine records?

National Change of Address (NCOA). How does your system or service bureau interface with the postal service's database when there are address changes? By running NCOA at least twice a year, you can help keep your addresses up to date.

Record Viewing. If you are looking at a batch-update system, how can you view a record? What does the galley listing report look like? Does it have all the information on it that you will require? If you're looking at an online application, is it more expensive than batch updating? Is it worth it? If so, how long does it take to summon a record to the screen once you've accessed your file? What information is displayed?

Conversions. If you have an existing file and you are contemplating moving to another system, you will want to know exactly how the file will be "mapped over" to the new system. Does the new vendor have experience converting files like yours to its system? Does the vendor give you a detailed conversion plan? How long will it take, and how much will it cost? Does the vendor recommend a parallel run of the old system and the new system for a period of time before you go off the old system for good? What is your risk? If you choose a service bureau and it takes longer than expected—or if they flub the job— do you have to pay?

Acknowledgments. Those of us in fundraising know that thanking people for a gift is good manners—and good fundraising. How does the system handle "thank yous"? Can they be done daily, weekly, monthly? How expensive is it?

Output. How long does it take to get output (tapes, disks, printouts)? Hours? Days? It's important to know how long it will actually take to send the information you need to a disk or Zip disk. If you use a service bureau, in what form does the bureau want your requests for output? Can the system provide you with every kind of output you need? If not, are alternatives available that don't cost more? What is the processing turnaround time for standard orders? For unusual requests? Is there a charge for processing? If so, how much?

Query Language. How user friendly is it? What is the response time? Depending on your management philosophy, you may want less contact with your file, or more. But even in the former case the system should be flexible, so that it can keep pace with your changing needs.

Statistical Reports. By report, we mean not only output (labels, forms, letters, etc.), but also statistical and management reports. Can you get reports on the basic statistical information you need to analyze your mailings and make rollout decisions? At a minimum, you will need a report on each type of mailing and you may want the information organized in different ways.

For example, you'll want to be able to read acquisition mail from both the list-by-list vantage point and by package. Can the system create these kinds of reports? Can you also sort by other features (e.g., season, ranking by response rate, average gift, cost per donor)? Can the system create different kinds of reports for your house mailings, sorting by package, low- and high-dollar mailings, renewals (by notice, expire group, quarter, package)? Take a good look at the system, because you want it to do as much of the number crunching as possible; you should spend your time analyzing the numbers, not juggling them.

Every report should have the following basic information:

- quantity mailed
- date mailed
- date of first return
- date of latest return
- number of days of returns
- number of returns (money and nonmoney)
- percent response rate
- total dollars received
- average gift
- total cost of mailing
- percent cost recovered
- gross returns per thousand (or per package)
- cost per thousand (or per package)
- net per thousand (or per package)
- cost per dollar raised

Obtain samples of existing reports. Do they meet your needs? If you have a fundraising consultant, get his or her reaction, too. How often are the reports generated? How up to date are they when you receive them? How much do they cost? If you're looking for an online system, can you see some or all of the statistical information on-screen? How current is it?

Management Records. Can the system give you a comprehensive statistical picture of the entire fundraising program—a kind of an executive summary that includes the number of donors and how much money they've given in the last 3 months, 6 months, 12 months? How about state/ZIP analysis? Year-by-year trend analyses? Report by expired group (also known as renewal forecast or renewal cycle analysis)? Donor upgrade/downgrade? Lapsed donors/members? Suspected duplicates? Standard segmentation by recency, frequency, level of giving?

Select and Sort. Can the system select and sort on all the fields that are relevant to your needs? Can it select and sort on multiple fields? How about upper case/lower case? Is the system flexible enough for you?

Downloading. If you're looking at an online data-entry system, you should be able to transfer data from the service bureau's computer to your own PC via modem or the Web. How easy is this to accomplish? How much does it cost? Is the bureau flexible enough to give you what you need to work on the system locally, in your office?

Security. The security needs for batch-update and online systems are entirely different, but the basic questions you want to ask are: How is access to your file restricted? If passwords are used, who designs them; can they be changed easily? Are your files backed up frequently? Are older generations of your file kept in a secure location off-site?

Service. As we have pointed out several times, one of the principal distinguishing features among systems is—or should be—service. What do references say about the level of service? How much in-house clerical assistance, if any, will you need? Make sure this cost is included in your systems cost calculations. Are personnel—account executives and/or programmers—on staff to handle your needs? Do you want their help with some of your fundraising planning? If so, will it cost extra? How much training is provided? At what cost?

SELECTING THE DATABASE (IN-HOUSE VS. A SERVICE BUREAU)

Now that you have established your needs, you must decide whether it is more practical and economical to contract with a computer service bureau or purchase software and install it on your own system. How do you know which option is right for you? The answer depends on many things, including the size of your file, the amount of processing you will do, and how much money you are willing to spend for your own system, including training and employing the staff necessary to input information, upgrade software periodically, and maintain the system on a daily basis.

Use the checklists in this chapter throughout the process of creating or upgrading your database—while you're planning, during the vendor interview process, and even after you think you've decided which system is right for you. You may even want to consider hiring a systems consultant. You and your consultant should sit down together and lay out your specific needs and the capabilities that your computer system and software should have. If you decide to interview service bureaus, we suggest you approach three or more for serious discussions based on what you've developed through the checklists.

Only you can make the final decision. Table 12–1 will help you compare the major differences between the two. The jury's still out on Web-based management systems because not enough people are using them to get a good picture of what works and what doesn't. If you think you want to try it, make sure you're totally comfortable with the people and the system before you proceed.

In addition to these factors, you should consider the format in which you are currently keeping your data (an Excel spreadsheet? An in-house system using Access? Hand records?) and what the expenses will be, both in terms of money and staff required to convert your data. One advantage of a service bureau is that they will handle your conversion, but there is often a fee associated with this.

There are other architectural factors that you should consider in choosing the option best suited to your fundraising strategy:

Hardware Costs. Will you need to extensively upgrade your current system in order to run an efficient fundraising database? Even if you select a service bureau, you may need to upgrade your PC to properly view your data.

Software. A software program is like a knitted sweater; pulling on a loose thread may unravel a whole sleeve. So try to get software that is *comprehensive* enough to meet all your current needs and *flexible* enough to accommodate future changes in your strategy and fundraising needs. Also, *make sure*

Table 12–1 Comparison of In-House Systems and Service Bureaus

	In-House System	Service Bureau
Costs	One-time charge for purchases.	Monthly fees, plus other charges.
Training	Usually an extra fee for training.	Minimal. Service bureau does most of the work, and training should be included in fees.
Technical Expertise	You must have a solid grasp of computers and databases to make a system like this work effectively. In-house MIS staff would be an asset.	Vendor responsibility.
Flexibility	Most off-the-shelf programs offer limited flexibility. They are rarely fully customizable.	During initial setup, you can usually achieve most customer requirements at no additional charge. After setup, there may be programming charges associated with changes.
File Maintenance	Will require a staff member dedicated to maintaining the file.	Included in monthly fees.
File Manipulation	Your responsibility.	Vendor responsibility.
Upgrades	Your responsibility.	Vendor responsibility.

that the software has been *fully* tested by other users before you acquire it. Don't be a "beta" site unless you're a real computer pro and there's some distinct advantage to your organization in doing so.

Training and Vendor Support. Regardless of the type of system you acquire, make sure that you can get unlimited training both at the time you convert to the system and later on, as your staffing picture changes. Make sure training is either included in the initial acquisition cost or is, at a minimum, inexpensive. If you can't afford to teach people how to use the system, it will quickly turn into an expensive white elephant that gathers dust in the corner of your office. By implication, vendor support—both for training as well as follow-up—is essential.

Data Entry. You and your staff will either be manually entering gifts one by one, or they will be batch-keyed by you or an outside agent and put on the database through an upload. Make sure your preferred method is compatible with the system you choose.

Questions To Ask

Whether you hire a service bureau or purchase software, there are many questions you should be asking about the company with which you will be dealing.

The following questions are important and you surely will have questions of your own:

- How long has the company been in business?
- Who are the references? Are they for the exact same system you will be using or is it a different version?
- How much flexibility does the hardware/software have? Who wrote the software? Does that person still work there? Is the software easily modified? By whom? At what cost? Is the software still supported by the developers? What about future upgrades? How much will you have to pay to keep the system state of the art?

- Does the company have in-house programmers? If not, are the programmers on call? Whom do they use? How much do they charge?
- Does the company service fundraising programs similar to yours? How many do they have? For how long?
- What is the system's track record on delivery (turnaround) time? Accuracy? Specialized applications?
- What kind of training is available at time of sale? Later on? How much does it cost?
- Will the company assign a specific operations person to your account?
- How often is the system down? For how long?
- What are their security provisions? If you have multiple locations where all have access to the system, how are they protected?
- Will the company show you a sample contract? Does the contract state that you—and only you—own the file? Is there a security clause in the contract that binds the company to confidentiality of your data? Is there a "break-out" clause in the contract that allows you to change systems for any reason? Will the company cooperate in the conversion to another system if it becomes necessary?
- Can the company provide you with a sample conversion plan and schedule? Do personnel document their conversations? Will they give you the documentation?
- What is their emergency retrieval plan? What is the procedure for file backups? If you plan to use a service bureau, is there off-site backup storage?
- What is the fee structure? Can the company give you a detailed estimate of what the system will cost for the first year? What does a typical invoice look like? Are invoices itemized and easy to understand? Before you begin talking to any service providers, we recommend you talk to other organizations whose direct mail programs you admire. Ask what they use for their database and how happy they are. And don't be afraid to ask how much it costs.

There are two basic ways to obtain this information.

First, you can issue a request for proposal (RFP), outlining the various requirements you have and asking for written responses. Once you've evaluated the written presentations, you will probably want to see a live demonstration of the semifinalist systems, after which you can conclude your interviews and make a choice. (Several of our clients have asked their accounting firms to help them develop comprehensive RFPs. Where we've seen this done, it has worked well.) The other way is to go directly to the interview stage. Either way, after your questions have been answered to your satisfaction, look carefully at the experience of clients already on the system. An impressive list can be persuasive, especially if the salesperson is good. But don't enter into an arrangement based solely on charisma. Call at least four of the service bureau's or software vendor's clients— especially those in the nonprofit area. Don't be shy; ask them hard questions. Your cause is at stake.

THE MERGE AND PURGE PROCESS

How the Computer Merges and Purges

Merge/purge is the process that allows you to eliminate duplicate names when mailing to prospect lists to acquire new donors. It also enables you to eliminate duplicate names between your own donor/member file and the prospect lists to ensure that you are not sending acquisition mail to your own donors. This is done by combining many names and addresses from a variety of lists (merge) and deleting the duplicate names (purge). There are several reasons for doing this.

- To obtain accurate information on the performance of each prospect list you use, you must remove your house names, which will only serve to inflate your returns artificially. And even though some current donors or members will respond to prospect pieces, thereby inflating returns, they will often also be annoyed at receiving a prospect piece, and will not hesitate to let you know.
- You will be able to use the Direct Marketing Association's "PANDER" file, at no charge. This is the list of people who have written to the DMA, requesting that they be suppressed from all unsolicited mailings. In view of current-day privacy concerns, it is imperative that nonprofits respect the wishes of those who do not want to receive direct mail requests for donations.
- Many donors become understandably annoyed when they receive several identical

appeals within a short period of time. Such annoyance can cause you much grief when the annoyed donor happens to be a member of your organization's board and/or one of your major contributors.

Because the execution of a merge/purge requires sophisticated processing, it is a good idea to check out the service bureau that will be conducting yours. Talk to several bureaus about costs as well as their criteria to determine duplications. Obtain samples of what their system will—or won't—be able to detect as a duplicate. Today's merge/purge technology is very sophisticated. It relies on algorithmic equations and percentages of similarity between name and address fields to determine probable duplication. Thus, many records with considerable differences can be identified as duplicates, and merge/purge programs can be tailored to fit the different needs of different organizations.

For instance, the computer can be instructed to identify two records with the exact same names, within the same ZIP code, as duplicates if one record contains a street address and the other contains a post office box. Conversely, the computer can be instructed that within densely populated metropolitan areas, two records with the same names and street addresses should not be identified as duplicates until apartment numbers are checked. Most service bureaus offer a "standard" merge/purge program, which has been tested and verified with a number of organizations as the best for most of them. They can also furnish examples of the duplicates identified by their standard program for your review. By looking at the types of duplications a computer suspects, you will be able to determine whether you would have challenged the name yourself (as a duplicate) and if, perhaps, there are others you might have checked if you had looked at the files yourself. By discussing the various options with your representative, you can tailor the merge/purge to your own organizational needs.

Bear in mind that you do not have to use the same computer house that maintains your file to do your merge/purge. In fact, you probably shouldn't. There are service bureaus that specialize in merge/purge and, unless your own bureau is an expert at this process, you may wish to have different companies handle these two tasks.

Once a service bureau understands the particular nature of your needs, it can alert you to difficulties that may arise. For instance, a merge/purge for a nonprofit organization is fundamentally different from a merge/ purge for a mail order catalogue, because catalogue mailers want to mail to their house files instead of eliminating those names. Once you have selected the service bureau to run your merge/purge, you must arrange for your rented prospect lists to be delivered via FTP Web site, or on magnetic tape. The service bureau will advise you if any special format is needed. Normally, most formats are acceptable as long as the data are provided in fixed fields, and are accompanied by file layouts.

Be sure to discuss scheduling. Most merge/purges take one to two weeks after all lists have arrived (though some companies can do it in a week). It is best to provide yourself a cushion of extra time to allow for late or missing lists. (And there is always at least one list that is late.) Once the names have arrived (if they haven't, you may decide to proceed without one or two in the interest of meeting your deadline), the service bureau will convert all the data into a common format, load them into the computer, and suppress the duplicate names from list to list, including your own. What you then receive is a list made up of unique names (i.e., one mail label per individual).

Once the computer determines that a name is on two or more lists, it pulls the name as a duplicate or "multibuyer." You want to eliminate multiple uses of the duplicate, but you still want to mail to it at least once. To do this, you have to decide to which of the original lists the name will be assigned. There are several methods of doing this. Because the duplicate names will perform between 20 and 50 percent better than the rest of the mailing, each of these techniques will have a different effect on your mailing.

Proportionate Assignment. This method assigns the names to the lists in the proportion in which the duplicates were pulled out. If a list had a high percentage of duplicates, it will get the same high percentage of reassigned names. If a list had a low percentage of duplicates, it will get a low number of reassigned names. This method keeps the relative strength of the lists close to what they were before the merge (i.e., the lists with the most duplicates will still have the most duplicates).

Ranking by Block. This method allows you to decide beforehand if one group of lists will receive a large proportion. This is most often done in the case of new test lists, about which you have no return information. The theory is that the multi-names are a part of the new list and are necessary to compare that list's returns with the rollout lists on which you already have results. However, this will distort the performance of the lists that receive the smaller proportion of duplicate names. Therefore, we don't recommend this method, unless you have some other reason to offset the loss of valid list returns.

Priority Assignment. This method allows you to decide on an individual basis which of the lists will receive a larger proportion of duplicate names and which of the lists will receive a smaller proportion. Sometimes there are specific reasons to give greater or less priority to specific lists. For instance, if some lists are rented on a net name basis, these lists should be given the least priority in duplicate assignment, so that as many names as possible will be pulled off these lists, thereby lowering the list rental costs.

In all of these methods, the duplicate names being reassigned are the names that reduplicated from list to list only. You would not want to reassign the names that are matched to your house file, asthe elimination of those names from your mailing is one of the primary reasons for conducting the merge/purge.

The Advantages of Merge/Purge

There are other advantages to be realized from a merge/purge, including:
- Postal automation regulations make it almost impossible to qualify for discounts without doing computerized postal presorts. The cleaner your list is going into the presort (usually done at the lettershop), the better your postal discount.
- You can segment the file and mail different packages to different parts of the country by having your output split by ZIP code or sectional center (the first three digits of the ZIP code).
- You can conduct multiple package tests by having the service bureau skim off a certain number of names from all of the unique names and split them into several lists. These "created" lists can be used to test different package components or other elements. Since this list is made up of an accurate cross-section of all continuation lists, it is an accurate representation of the entire mailing. However, you must take an accurate cross-section of the entire mailing, which would be no less than 10,000 (10M) names per individual package test. The process to achieve this is called taking an "nth select" (where a decision is made to select every 10th, 20th,

or 30th name and thereby ensure a statistically reliable presentation as opposed to taking the first 20,000 names on the list, which would all be from the same section of the list). For example, begin with a total list order of 150,000 names from 10 lists of 15,000 each. A duplication rate of 20 percent will suppress 30,000 names and leave a net output of 120,000 names. Before this list is resorted back into the original input lists, have the computer skim off a cross-section of 20,000 names. This leaves 100,000 names in the original input lists and two test panels of 10,000 names each. You can then use these test panels to test various packages against the control. Exhibit 12–1 shows a step-by-step guideline.
- You can split each of your lists in half, or by a specific number of names (5,000 minimum), to test different packages or messages on specific lists.

Costs of Merge/Purge

Most service bureaus charge additionally for each step in the processing. Obtain a price list and discuss the costs with your representative before deciding which tests, if any, you wish to do. Also ask the company to suggest other types of processing done for clients. Chances are they have additional procedures that they perform regularly for others that may be just right for you.

But remember, the main savings for a merge/purge come from:
- not mailing unnecessary duplicates
- postage discounts for large mailings

Additional processing will drive your costs up and make it harder for the mailing to recover its expenses.

The Merge/Purge Report

The merge/purge report you receive following the mailing (be sure to ask for it in advance) contains much valuable information. For example, a good indicator of what will prove to be your most successful lists are those that have the highest duplication rate with your own file. Look also for lists having high duplication rates among the prospect lists. Duplication is a good indicator of a strong list. Now check whether your mail file is concentrated in any

Exhibit 12–1 Step-by-Step Guide to Testing

Merge/Purge—Input 10 lists × 15M names each	=	150M
Duplication Rate of 20%–30M duplicate names	=	−30M
Total Merge Net Output		120M

Have the computer skim off 20M names from the remaining 120M and sort them into two lists of 10M each. You then have the remaining names sorted back into their original input lists.

Names in original input lists without duplications	=	100M
Two lists of 10M each (which represents a cross-section of all of the input lists) without duplication	=	+20M
Total Mailing		120M

Mail the control package to the 10 input lists. Mail a different package or test variation to the new cross-section lists. This will allow you to compare the results of several different test packages in one mailing.

specific area of the country (specifically small ZIP clusters). If so, you will want to consider doing geographic test mailings of those ZIPs with the heaviest concentration of duplicate names.

MAILING DUPLICATE NAMES: THE VALUE OF "MULTIBUYERS"

Many mailers traditionally hold a copy of the list of duplicate names from a merge/purge and mail the duplicates two to four weeks after the first mailing has gone out. These names are key coded separately so that you can tally how well this "list" works for you. The reason that it usually works well is because these donors appeared on two or more of the lists you carefully selected for the mailing. This may indicate a higher interest in causes such as yours. By mailing

to these multidonors twice, you double the chance that a prospect will contribute. The multidonors can pull as much as 15 to 50 percent better than the original mailing!

HIRING A FIRM

Many mail houses and lettershops offer merge/purge services. Some do the job very well, while others do not. Don't assume that because your mail house or lettershop is good, that they are also experts at merge/purge. Call for specific references about their merge/purge capabilities.

In addition to your regular resources there are firms specializing in merge/purge. We only know one firm good enough for special mention: Triplex, in Novato, California.

Chapter 13
Telemarketing and Why People Love It

At a time when America's mailboxes are stuffed with competing direct mail appeals, when person-to-person solicitation becomes more difficult because of a scarcity of volunteers and sheer distance in our mobile society, the telephone has come of age. Its capacity to improve response rates, increase the size of average gifts, upgrade donors, and return inactive donors to a more active status is being proven each day by an increasing number of nonprofit groups.

The telephone—like the letter—is an extension of the individual, the instrument or medium through which an organization's case for support is clearly and effectively stated. Truly, when it comes to direct solicitation and cultivation of donors, the telephone is the next best thing to being there.

SOME COMMON CONCERNS

Before we proceed, let's address a few common concerns. *The telephone is intrusive. Its use will anger those whom we call.* Unlike direct mail, a telephone call does not slip silently through the letter slot. Its presence is announced by a bell, sometimes a persistent ringing bell. When used properly, however, the telephone fundraising call can be like a friendly call from a neighbor or friend. And that's the trick to making successful use of the telephone.

Here are some suggestions to keep the telephone from being resented.

Select the Audience

The key to keeping the telephone from being intrusive is to carefully select the audience to be called. Generally, telefundraising is best suited to *existing* donors. They are *already* part of the family, and your telephone call may actually be welcome. Like a good appeal letter, the well-conceived telephone campaign is designed to:

1. thank the donor for previous support
2. convey information about an immediate and pressing need
3. ask specifically for a gift
4. thank the donor again

The economic reality is that a properly conducted telemarketing effort is very cost-effective. Admittedly, uncontrolled and unplanned use of the telephone is wasteful. But the same can be said for mail, volunteer solicitation, and other types of fundraising. Most of us initially view the use of the telephone as an expensive medium because we have all been taught since childhood to be watchful of long-distance charges. But like the photographer's film or the printer's paper, the long-distance phone charge is only a small part of the total cost that makes up a successful effort.

The cost of telephone campaigns should be measured by the same standard as all other fundraising techniques, and the question is not how much you spend to raise money but how much money you raise in proportion to the amount you spend. Well-run in-house telephone fundraising efforts generally produce cost/income ratios far superior to those enjoyed by mail alone.

How can a telemarketing professional answer your donors' questions?

If you already have a satisfactory relationship with a direct mail firm, you are more likely to place confidence in a telemarketing firm. You know that the firm's principals will help educate the callers about your organization. Of course they can't answer every question (could you?), but they are well trained and given answers to the most commonly asked questions. In the event of not knowing an answer, the caller will tell the questioner that someone will get back to them. (This is what you would have a volunteer do, too.)

As for the calling script, which is the equivalent of a direct mail letter, the professional knows best how to position the case. But as with the direct mail letter, you have final approval and final sign-off on the letter that goes out with the pledge confirmation. The advantage to calling is that if anything changes (either organizationally or a world event that will be distracting), you can temporarily suspend calling. You can even change the script midstream for any reason. Telefundraising's versatility and mobility make it quite attractive to many organizations, especially those in the public spotlight and in the news.

Timing the Call

Make your calls at reasonable times. The hours of 6:30 PM through 9:00 PM are the best. In fact, it has become law that such calls cannot be made after 9:00 PM. Other good times are Saturday and Sunday afternoons. And, for some organizations whose constituencies tend to be at home during the day, the daytime hours are just fine.

Style

Be polite and friendly. Telemarketing is often dismissed without even a test by some fundraisers who mistakenly equate it with those telephone boiler rooms selling underwater real estate. Nothing could be farther from reality. A well-thought-through telephone effort run by knowledgeable telefundraisers is no more intrusive than a personal visit from a volunteer of the organization.

Substance

Listen to what the donor/member is saying. If he or she says "absolutely not," don't put him or her in the "maybe" batch. If he or she says never call after 8 PM, note his record accordingly. If he or she says "yes," show some excitement. It may be your 100th call, but it's his or her only such call.

Although many organizations run their telephone campaigns themselves, there are dozens of professional telefundraising firms that provide a range of fundraising services. They generally can provide them at a cost lower than the expense incurred by an organization in setting up its own program. (You can ask your colleagues for recommendations.) You can also get a list of firms providing telemarketing services for fundraising by writing the Direct Mail Marketing Association, 6 East 43rd Street, New York, New York 10017.

You will want to interview several firms, check references, and listen to the callers actually soliciting for another organization. Once you have chosen your telefundraising firm (or several firms for a test if your list is large enough), you will want to make certain that it is registered in those states where it will be soliciting on your behalf. Your nonprofit must be registered too. (See Appendix D for more information on state registrations.)

Whether you hire a professional firm or decide to do it yourself, here are some applications of telemarketing that are particularly beneficial.

PRECALL YOUR DONORS

Tests have demonstrated that your mail has a better chance of being opened, read, and responded to if you first call the recipient alerting him or her to the fact that a mailing is on its way. The technique is called preselling or precalling. Its purpose is simple: to pique the attention and interest of the reader even before the mail arrives, to ask the reader to watch for the mailing from a particular organization and give it preference over other mail. The results of this technique speak for themselves. An increase in the net income from a mailing of between 30 and 50 percent is possible.

The technique and the message are relatively simple: "Hello, Mr. Smith, this is Dan Jones. I'm calling from Jack Frost's office at the Association of Associations. He put a letter in the mail to you tonight and asked that I call and ask you to watch for it. He thinks you'll find it of great importance." What you have done by using the precall or presell technique is to let the prospect know that something out of the ordinary is occurring. He may not know what it is or what the letter is about. And, in many ways that's just fine. Now he is curious. Your letter will be opened while others lie in anonymity on the kitchen table. Precalling is not for every mailing. In fact, it should be used selectively. Generally, use the technique only for your own house file and use it infrequently. You want to protect the novelty because that's what makes it an effective technique.

POSTCALL YOUR DONORS

Akin to precalling is the technique of making the telephone call once the mailing piece has been received. However, there are important differences in the reasons for the use of the postcall:

- Unlike the precall, which is designed to get the mail opened, a postcall is designed to lift the response rate or the size of the average gift. Or both.
- The postcall is far more of a sales approach than the precall. Here the prospect has already received (and hopefully read) the basic message. It is the job of the telefundraiser to come in after the mailing and reinforce the message of the letter—to provide additional information and urgency and negotiate with the donor over the size of the gift.
- Use of the postcall requires careful timing to ensure that the donor receives the letter before the phone call but not too far ahead of the call that memory of the message is dimmed.

The results of the postcall can be far more spectacular than those of the precall, particularly where gift size is concerned. We'll cover this process of substantial upgrading later. The postcall can be made either as part of a carefully orchestrated campaign involving a series of letters and phone calls or as a one-time follow-up to a specific mailing. In the case of a one-time mailing and use of the precall versus the postcall techniques, you may want to do some testing to see which works best for you. There are no universal rules.

REINSTATE YOUR DONORS

As you know, the economics of direct mail fundraising are such that the most expensive part of the process involves the acquisition of new donors to replace those who no longer give. The telephone has proven to be a remarkably cost-effective way of reinstating or renewing donors who have failed to renew through direct mail efforts alone. Following a direct mail series of six of seven renewal notices, it is likely that somewhere between 10 and 15 percent of a lapsed or expired group of donors can be reinstated by telephone. And they can be reinstated or renewed at far less cost than the organization normally would spend to acquire a new donor to replace one lost through direct mail attrition.

Just as important is the fact that once reinstated or renewed by telephone, these donors can then be put back into the direct mail program. Their performance in future years will be virtually identical to those who never strayed from the direct mail program in the first place. As a general rule, telephone renewal or reinstatement programs are run at the end of the direct mail renewal cycle. But even that can be tested. Response rates and average gifts often can be im proved dramatically by putting the telephone solicitation into the middle of the renewal process. As in the case of precalling and postcalling, the renewal or reinstatement call revolves around the use of a direct mail piece. Generally, the most effective use of direct mail lies in a mailing that follows the reinstatement phone call.

THE DIRECT MAIL/TELEPHONE CAMPAIGN

Until now we have covered the use of the telephone primarily in one-time applications. The one-time use makes the telephone no less effective, but there are other more sophisticated uses. Let's begin by seeing how the telephone can be used in soliciting larger gifts than those that conventional direct mail can attract. There's no question that in a perfect world any development director or fundraiser would prefer to have trained volunteer solicitors making face-to-face calls on specially selected prospects.

But it's not a perfect world. And from a fundraising standpoint, it's growing even more imperfect. Volunteer solicitors are scarce and growing scarcer. The geographic spread of most organizations' donor constituencies makes organizing expensive and time consuming. Enter mail and telephone! By trying to replicate as nearly as possible the essential dynamics of one-on-one fundraising through the use of direct mail and telephone, you can accomplish much.

A campaign built on mail and telephone uses the mail as a cultivation and information device and the phone for the actual solicitation phase. Generally, these campaigns consist of two or more letters mailed before the actual telephone solicitation takes place. The purpose of the mailings is to state the case for support, provide a sense of urgency, and to introduce the fact that the prospective donor will be receiving a telephone call.

Following the initial mailings comes the all-important phone call or calls. The purpose of the phone call is to make certain that the prospect understands the information conveyed through the mail, has his or her questions answered, and is then solicited. As in face-to-face fundraising, the process of solicitation often involves more than one call. And remember, the process of negotiation over size and timing of the gift is key. Because many mass donor bases contain no more information about donors than the size and frequency of their previous contributions, the role of the phone solicitor becomes paramount. It is the solicitor's job to identify interests, aim high enough when it comes to the amount of the suggested gift, and carefully keep the prospect interested while the size of the gift is discussed or negotiated. Once the solicitation is over, follow-up mailings come into play to confirm and collect the telephone commitment.

As in all telephone/mail campaigns, the audience being addressed has a direct bearing on the efficiency of this process. One generally can expect the "best" part of a mass donor base to perform best by mail/phone. Those parts of a donor base that are marginal by mail generally will be marginal by mail/phone as well. In all fundraising—and telephone fundraising is no exception—it's critically important that the fundraising manager understands the efficiencies of the technique being used. The telephone has the capacity to take the best part of a donor file and upgrade it substantially. It also has the inherent weakness of being overused as in the case where the telephone is applied indiscriminately across a file when mail or other techniques may be more efficient for some portions of that file.

If the telephone is employed properly in conjunction with mail, substantial upgrading of small gift donors is possible to a degree unimagined by mail alone. The trick is not to go overboard and use the telephone where mail could be used just as effectively in generating the same net income. The successful campaign based on telephone and mail should make it pos-

sible for you to upgrade a small donor base substantially. It is not unusual to find that somewhere between 5 and 10 percent of a mass base that normally contributes $25 to $50 can be upgraded to gifts ranging from $300 to $1,000 and even more.

TELEPHONE TESTING AND DONOR INFORMATION

Until now, we have addressed the use of the telephone to solicit gifts to renew contributions. But for the direct mail practitioner, there are other applications.

Testing Copy Approaches

As market researchers and political pollsters learned long ago, the telephone is a remarkable research tool. Consider testing your copy approaches through telephone interviews before committing to mail. This is particularly true when your own donor file is concerned. A few hundred telephone calls randomly selected from your active donor files often can guide you to the most effective and efficient house appeals.

Membership Alerts and Donor Information

Many organizations have members and donors who do more than give money; they are active participants in the work of the organization. This is particularly true for those groups that engage in lobbying. The use of an incoming 800 number can be used to provide information and request timely action. The prerecorded message delivered by a computer-driven dialing mechanism can be used to reach thousands quickly and inexpensively. Generally, these techniques are not techniques of fundraising, but ones of urgently imparting information and initiating action.

REACH OUT AND ASK SOMEONE

Is telephone fundraising for you? Probably. Like all direct response media, the telephone can be tested and its benefits and problems can be discovered readily. With the public's growing acceptance of telemarketing, you owe it to yourself and your organization to learn what hundreds of successful fundraisers have already discovered—the telephone can add an exciting and profitable dimension to your program.

Chapter 14
The Future and Fundraising on the Internet

CHAPTER OUTLINE

- Internet Strategy
- Developing a Website
- Driving Traffic to the Site
- Acquiring New Donors/Members
- Testing
- A Final Word of Caution

It is impossible to predict with any credibility the future of electronic fundraising 10 years hence. The Internet, online giving, and other forms of giving in a paperless world are changing far too rapidly for that. But, I do believe that 10 years from now the following will be true:

- Direct mail will still be with us (although I don't know about the discounted postal rate for nonprofits).
- Monthly donors programs via electronic funds transfer (EFT) will increase and, because of their growing acceptance, more nonprofits will benefit from them. Simultaneously, more nonprofits will have Planned Giving programs and more planned gifts will be transacted.
- The baby boomers, of which there are many, will begin retiring, en masse, and minorities will become majorities. Both groups will produce donors to replace those older people now on your file.
- Laws concerning privacy via the mail, phone, and Internet will alter the way we exchange and rent direct mail and Internet lists, as well as the way we telefundraise.
- It will be easier to donate via the Internet, but this medium will not in any way eclipse direct mail.

The Internet is the subject that currently draws

thousand of fundraising conference attendees to presentations. It's the medium everyone treats like a knowledgeable adult, when, in fact, it's only a young child learning to talk and walk. And 10 years from now, it still won't be an adult, although it will have changed as rapidly as a child outgrows shoes.

So as you read this chapter, bear in mind that this writer believes that because of all this, some "how to" advice may be outdated in one year, never mind in 10. Keeping up with the subject is important, but don't put all your eggs in this basket. Wait till they hatch.

Everybody's talking about it, but is anybody really doing it?

There is a complicated answer to this question: yes and no. Large, well-known organizations that specialize in disaster relief, such as the American Red Cross, are doing quite well in Internet fundraising. Some activist causes that run campaigns based on newsworthy events, such as the American Civil Liberties Union and Common Cause, are also doing well on the Net because of their high visibility, even if only for short periods of time. But for the most part, we now can say with some amount of certainty that the Internet is highly unlikely to replace direct mail fundraising as a major source of income for most organizations. Why? Well, it's mostly because the website just sits there, waiting for people to visit. And unless you have a compelling reason for people to search for and visit your site, it's unlikely anyone except the truly committed donor is going to visit your home page. That's why disaster relief organizations do well. When there's an earthquake, flood, hurricane, or other well-publicized natural catastrophe, people all over the world want to help. The Internet offers an instant means of gratifying that desire. Instead of waiting for the right organization to get an appeal in the mail, the savvy Internet users will find the organization they want to help. But for the most part, it will be a high profile organization like the Salvation Army, Catholic Charities, or the American Red Cross.

Disease organizations do well because people who have a disease themselves, or have a loved one who is struggling with a specific disease will often use the Internet for research and information. As a result, the organization finds willing donors who are not on direct mail lists. These people are giving because they are interested in a very specific cause—and for them, it's easy to give this way. For advocacy groups, it's also about people who are interested in a newsworthy topic finding the website; in essence, it's always there when activists want to find out what's happening with a particular cause.

But even if you're not in disaster relief, diseases, or activist issues doesn't mean you shouldn't have a fundraising website. It just means you need to examine carefully why you have one and what you should expect from it. If you decide that you can afford to take donations online, don't expect it to be a cash cow. Right now, all it really will be is a convenience to your donors—and a little extra money from "accidental" visitors who somehow arrive at your site. But, you never know. One of those Internet donors might want to make a major gift. Or become a monthly donor. Or, maybe they'll make a one-time gift of $25 and you'll never hear from them again. In this way, it's like direct mail. You can't really control who's going to respond or how.

INTERNET STRATEGY

If you believe that your organization is perfect for online fundraising, now's the time to develop an Internet strategy—a plan for using the Internet to further your organization's mission and goals.

Your Internet strategy must include, at a minimum, answers to the following questions:

- What are our short and long-term organizational goals, and how will using the Internet help us accomplish them? What organizational problems will the Internet help solve? What problems might it cause or exacerbate?
- How does the Internet fit into our current educational, fundraising, program, membership, strategic plans, etc.?
- What are our specific goals for the Internet itself? Fundraising? Education? Member benefits?
- Who will be responsible for carrying out the Internet strategy and keeping it up to date?
- How much will it cost, and what are the sources of funding?
- What is the exit strategy if using the Internet doesn't meet expectations?

DEVELOPING A WEBSITE

Unless you're a technological wizard with lots of time on your hands, creating a website from scratch is not a job for most. We strongly recommend finding a savvy consultant to help you through the maze of domain names, programming, Web hosting, and secure servers. In order to put your website up, you'll need to have a domain name—a Web address. It can be your name (e.g., [organization name].org) or anything you want it to be, so long as someone else hasn't already registered and paid for the name. In order to get a domain name, you have to register it with one of the many Internet agencies located on the Web. It will cost about $35 each year to maintain your name. Visit http://rs.internic.net to get further information and a comprehensive list of places to register, or let your consultant help you.

Other technical issues include who will design your site, what language it will be written in, and where the server for your site will actually reside (Web hosting). And, if you are going to take donations over the Web, you'll need a secure server to protect the integrity of credit card transactions. These are highly technical issues for which you should have creative and technically complete solutions. Make sure you discuss them with your consultant.

To locate a consultant, check with the Association of Fundraising Professionals or the Direct Marketing Association for some recommendations as to reputable consultants. And make sure to get references. Remember, before you call a consultant, make sure you know why you want a website: fundraising, advocacy, education, forming alliances, or other reasons. What you want to do with your site will determine what it should look like and how complex it is.

Another website issue is deciding who's to be in charge. The information technology department may want to control it, while the communications department may want to design it. But if it's a fundraising website, you should be part of the process, because fundraising on the Web is very similar to fundraising in the mail. Your response device needs to look like a response device. Your fundraising message needs to be direct and easy to read. You need to have an immediate (electronic) thank you so the donor knows you've received the online transaction—and you should also send a traditional acknowledgment through the mail.

Another important issue for fundraising on the website is visibility. If the goal is fundraising, don't bury your first fundraising message three layers down in the website. It must be easily accessible on the home page and easily recognizable. If it doesn't say "Donate now" or "Become a Member Today" or "Here's How You Can Help," then you aren't sending the right message. The Web may be a "cool" medium in terms of attracting people to a particular site, but it's a "hot" medium in terms of immediacy. If people don't find what they're looking for (or what you want them to find) right away, you've lost them. It's like getting people to open the envelope in the mail. You've got about five seconds to get their attention. Even less on the Web.

But this isn't a book about creating a website—it's a book about fundraising. So suffice it to say, when you're developing your website, don't forget to use your fundraising expertise. Make sure you have a mechanism for capturing a donor's name, address, and giving history. And if you somehow end up with two separate databases (one for online names and one for direct mail names), one of the databases (preferably the one for direct mail) must be designated as primary. It is imperative that the two databases be compatible, and that there is a system to updating the main database regularly.

DRIVING TRAFFIC TO THE SITE

Let's assume you have a functional website with a secure server to take donations online. How can you increase the number of people who visit your website? That's not an easy question and the answers are constantly changing. In the early days of the Internet, the answer was "banner advertising." Today, so many banners offer sweepstakes and free airplane tickets and commercial products that most people regard them as the advertising they are—and ignore them. For the most part, the Internet user is a pretty sophisticated consumer. So you'll want to come up with other strategies. Following are a few time-honored strategies that every organization should use.

Linking

If you've ever clicked on a highlighted area of one website that immediately takes you to a new and different website, you've used a *link*. One way you can increase traffic to your site is by having links from other appropriate sites. Make a list of those you want to link with, and contact all of them. It won't be an easy task, but well worth the time spent.

Search Engines

You'll want the big search engines (Yahoo, Google, Alta Vista, Goto, Hotbot, Excite, etc.) to list your organization when someone searches for it on the Web—and even when they search for information about your *kind* of cause. There are two strategies for making sure that you pop up when someone asks a general question that your organization can answer.

The first is to make sure you have precise "metatags" on your site. These are programmed into the top of your home page, and use short descriptions of who you are and what you do. For example, you might use words like "charitable organization," "charity," "nonprofit" and "not-for-profit" as metatags. But you'll also want to be more specific about what it is you actually do: "prevent child abuse," "feed the hungry," "cancer research," "environmental action," etc. This will require some creative thinking on your part, and some good programming on the part of your Web consultant.

The second technique is to call the search engines directly (or contact them via e-mail) and register with them. Thus, when someone asks for information on the Web that pertains to your group, they'll make sure your name pops up under the right classification.

E-Mail Solicitations

If you want to send e-mails to your donors, you must obtain their permission. Once you have permission from your donors to write to them via the Web (called an opt-in), you can write to them via the Internet, asking for their help, just like you do in direct mail. For some causes—not all—this is an effective tool. As in direct mail, you'll have to test it to find out if it works for you. Stanford University recently did a controlled study about this very technique, and those alumni who received e-mails had overall better giving histories than those who didn't. But this might not prove true for you.

How do you go about getting permission? Well, you have to ask for it. You can do that by asking for an e-mail address on regular mail or in your newsletter or other correspondence, and by sending an e-mail confirming that the donor has given his or her permission. Or, you can ask people to register when they enter your site. As part of the registration process, ask for an e-mail address, and permission to "keep you informed about our progress via e-mail." But if you don't have permission, don't communicate by e-mail.

E-Newsletters

Finally, there's the question of e-newsletters. If you're going to have e-donors, you're going to need an e-newsletter. It's an excellent way to keep your donors informed—and can inspire them to return to the website to make another gift. But the newsletter needs to be timely, informative, and professional. It doesn't have to be long, and it can include a fundraising solicitation, as well as links back to your main site. In fact, if you have to scroll down too far to get to the good stuff, it's too long. Two screens' worth is probably just right.

ACQUIRING NEW DONORS/MEMBERS

Currently, e-list brokers aren't particularly sophisticated or knowledgeable about lists, unlike direct mail brokers. Few have knowledge of whether the names on their lists are responsive to Internet fundraising appeals—or to any appeals at all. So beware if your Internet strategy relies heavily on acquiring donors through the use of rented Internet names. Unless you have a great deal of money to invest, wait until there are better ways of acquiring qualified e-mail addresses.

TESTING

Testing on the Internet is just like testing in direct mail, except the technical mechanism is different. If you want to test two different offers, you set up two separate places for the response to be received (called landing pages). If you want to test two different headlines, you have to set up two different landing pages. Additionally, you must devise a mechanism for key-coding the response when it gets to the landing page, so you can capture the information in your database. It's a complicated technique, worthy of a consultant's time and energy. Otherwise, how are you going to tell which offer did better? And just like in direct mail, you can test only one thing at a time—and your universes have to be identical.

A FINAL WORD OF CAUTION

Because things are changing so rapidly in this volatile medium, by the time you read this book, what works and what doesn't will probably have changed. So, like any good fundraiser, limit your exposure by testing and have a realistic set of benchmarks for success before you begin. What should those benchmarks be? Well, since this is brand new, uncharted territory, no one really knows. But make sure that you can afford to view all of the money it costs to experiment in Internet fundraising as an investment, with no monetary return. You may create a fabulous educational website—something your organization really should have—but you may not be a good candidate for raising money on the Web.

As with direct mail, even when we don't know exactly what to expect, we set goals: "In order to continue this project, we need to acquire X number of new donors" or "we need to net X amount of money," or "we can only lose $X per new donor acquired." Create some bottom lines that are right for you before you venture out into this brave new world. At least you'll know what you're trying to achieve, even if you don't always get there.

Chapter 15
The Acknowledgment Program

CHAPTER OUTLINE

Getting that first gift from a new member/donor is only the start in building a good donor base. Success can be measured only by whether the donor renews subsequently. And the first step toward keeping him or her lies in sending a prompt acknowledgment.

SEND A MEMORABLE ACKNOWLEDGMENT

Too many organizations allow copywriters to write warm, human acquisition or renewal copy, but when thanking the donor, they tend to send overly corporate and ponderous letters. Writing the acknowledgment letter is actually simple. All one has to do is "copy" the wording in the appeal letter to which the donor responded. After all, that wording was well received initially, prompting the original contribution. For example, if you ask for money to buy toys and clothing for children at Christmas, your thank you letter should remind the donor why he or she gave in the first place. For example, "I wish you could have heard her squeals of delight when Clarissa opened the gift your generosity made possible," or "Imagine the relief a homebound senior feels when she receives the help your generosity made possible."

Compare the opening sentences of the two acknowledgment letters below:

1. On behalf of the board and officers of the St.

George Care Center I wish to thank you for your generous gift of $100. As we enter our 75th year of service to community, your support is more important than ever before if we are to continue.

2. Your gift of $100 arrived today and was joyously received! Certainly your generosity brings us even closer to our 75th Anniversary Campaign Goal, but the goal isn't what's important. What's important is the people we serve. Your continued support tells me that you have confidence that we are doing a good job, and it is trust like this that inspires my staff and me on our darkest days.

The difference between the two thank you letters is that the second makes the reader feel valuable and engaged with the organization. The first, while technically fine, is strictly a corporate-style acknowledgment. Regardless of your special technique for thanking high dollar donors, smaller donors are equally entitled to friendly, warm acknowledgments rather than corporate-style "please find enclosed" letters.

PERSONALIZE ACKNOWLEDGMENTS

If you have a relatively small file, you can separate the various categories of donors manually. One category, for example, may be to separate donors who make more than one gift in a year. If your list is large, instructions to your computer bureau will determine which category receives which letter. When acknowledging gifts to special appeals, be sure to set up a system wherein the planned use of the gift is highlighted.

The directors of several organizations with whom I work review every gift of over $100 and more (this amount can vary from organization to organization) along with the donor's history of giving. He or she then pens a short note on each thank you letter, simultaneously personalizing it (if she or he knows the recipient) by marking through the more formal salutation and writing in the person's first name. Please note that such personalized letters of any type must be mailed first class. Form letters can be mailed third class collected in batches of 200. This is admittedly exceptional personalization, but, as you might suspect, the organization's donor loyalty and renewal rate is extraordinary.

FULFILLING BENEFITS AND PREMIUMS

If you have offered benefits or premiums and they are too large or bulky to enclose with the thank you letter, reference them in the acknowledgment copy in any event. For example, tell the donor that his or her membership card and decal are enclosed, and that his newsletter will be sent under separate cover.

WELCOME MEMBER KITS

Some organizations call their new member acknowledgment letter and enclosures a "Welcome Member" kit. Whether or not the kit contains 3 or 20 items, you can not only call it a kit, you can print those words on the carrier envelope and help bond the new donor to your organization. Welcome member kits can contain any or all of the following: membership card, official pin, newsletter, decal, premium for joining such as cards, additional literature about the organization, a bequest or planned giving brochure, free admission tickets (if appropriate), and more. Frankly, you don't really need as many treasures as are cited here, but the word "kit" does convey real membership and it may well bond donors over time.

PROMPTNESS IN ACKNOWLEDGMENTS

Some nonprofits are proud of the fact that they are able to turn acknowledgments around literally overnight. Certainly that is better than a late "thank you," but I'm not sure donors regard this as a plus, because such speed may make your organization seem like a factory. Acknowledgments should, of course, go out promptly. One week is ideal, two is acceptable, and three weeks shows you have good manners, but are poorly organized. More than that raises questions in your donor's mind about overall management ability.

If problems with your service bureau or any other type of problem delays the acknowledgment process (or the sending of promised premiums) by more than four weeks, send a simple postcard of apology and a promised delivery date. Mail order catalogues do this routinely, and almost always deliver on the promised date. It restores one's faith.

WHAT SIZE GIFT TO ACKNOWLEDGE

Some organizations thank everybody. Some only thank $15 and over donors. Some write letters only to $250 and over donors and send postcards to the rest.

What Should You Do?

It is proposed that you acknowledge all donors of $5 and over even if you never receive another gift from them, but that you not computerize or mail to donors of less than $5. If your base dues level is $20, for example, you can try to renew $10 or $15 donors at the higher amount with some success. Segment and key this part of the file to see how many donors upgrade to your desired basic level. Remember, you want every donor to be cost-effective to maintain.

ASKING AGAIN IN THE ACKNOWLEDGMENT

A much-debated topic is whether to ask for a second gift in the thank you letter. Recent donors, believe it or not, are the best prospects for second gifts, even if they are first-time donors. To take advantage of this fact, some organizations enclose another reply envelope with the acknowledgment. In fact, some organizations have designed "Memorial" reply envelopes similar to a regular contribution envelope, which provide the opportunity to make an "In Memory Of" or "In Tribute To" gift in the name of a specified person. The acknowledgment letter often suggests that the donor keep the envelope on hand until there is occasion to use it. Far more aggressive acknowledgment programs ask directly for another gift in the thank you letter that includes a "tear off" response form at the bottom and a reply envelope.

What Should You Do?

It is wise to read your mail from member/donors regarding complaints about your acknowledgment program (and everything else). It is also a good idea to keep track of the income you earn from acknowledgments. (Don't simply lump it with all white mail. White mail should be mail that cannot be identified by source.)

There is no hard-and-fast rule on asking again in the acknowledgment. It is suggested that if your organization already sends frequent appeals (say, 10 annually) that you not ask in the acknowledgment, but that you do enclose some type of return envelope. If you ask infrequently (less than 4 times annually), you may wish to ask again in your acknowledgment letters.

FORMAT OF ACKNOWLEDGMENT LETTERS

The size of the acknowledgment letter is not important. Put it on conventional letterhead with no envelope teaser copy so that it looks like a real communication. The letter, generally, is no longer than one page with good margins, preferably signed by the sender of the request letter. If another person signs the thank you, try to include the name of the sender as in "Roger Smith joins me in thanking you...."

Thank you letters to new donors can be a bit longer than letters to past donors. It isn't because you appreciate past donors any less, but because new people know less about you and, having just given, are probably more receptive to additional information.

Other Enclosures

Use acknowledgment letters as a reason to send additional literature, which hopefully you haven't sent with the appeal for fear of diluting its impact. For example, a renewal letter isn't a good place to include a bequest brochure. Nor, for that matter, should you enclose an order form for any item (no matter how relevant), an invitation to an event, or

anything else that will divert the prospect from giving at this time.

Do not, in any way, dilute your message so that the donor has to think about two things or to mistake your appeal for anything other than what it is—a gift request. Including a second message will dramatically lower returns.

Bequest Acknowledgments

Acknowledgment letters are the perfect vehicles for bringing your deferred giving program to the attention of member/donors. People tend not to like thinking about wills and bequests, so tread lightly in the copy. But, if you have a brochure, include it, and in the letter, say something like the following: "Because so many members have asked about the possibility of putting the XYZ organization in their wills, we thought you might be interested in the enclosed brochure that shows how you can support your favorite causes even after you are gone. Keep it in a safe place and refer to it when you make or change your will."

Keep the request message simple and make it the shortest part of the acknowledgment letter. You can't track the results of such letters, but you can be sure that the reminder will pay off big in the future. Most bequests don't come from major donors, but from small, regular donors who perhaps don't give a lot now only because they don't know what the future holds.

TELEPHONE ACKNOWLEDGMENTS

Why not pick up the phone and thank your higher dollar donors? Higher dollar doesn't mean the pace-setting gifts, but are donors who give significantly more than the average person, or the ones who upgrade a gift substantially. There are many reasons and you will not only enjoy the conversation, your donor will be grateful that his or her gift is so appreciated and it will inspire future loyalty.

The telephone acknowledgment has several advantages: (1) It sets you apart from organizations that thank the donor only at higher give levels; (2) it bonds the donor to your organization and inspires future giving; and (3) the telephone conversation provides an unequalled opportunity to learn more about the donor and also to learn more about what donors think about your organization and your fundraising program.

To be certain, a few donors or members may express displeasure and even annoyance at having been called. Reasons for this negative reaction vary, but you will still have learned something about this particular donor (that is, never telephone). Fortunately, such donors are in the great minority, and you must not let one negative experience spoil the potential of so many good ones.

LEGAL ISSUES

It is important that you check all issues concerning tax deductibility with your organization's attorney. Bear in mind, that the Internal Revenue Service requires that donors receive statements for tax-deductible contributions of $75 or more. It is in your acknowledgment letter to these $75-plus donors that the following phrase should appear, "No goods or services were received in return for your contributions." If goods or services were received (for example at a dinner), you must calculate what the costs actually were—even if underwritten—and the amount must be stated clearly in the acknowledgement.

LAST THOUGHTS

Acknowledgments are part of the overall fundraising process. Donors who feel appreciated and well-informed are far likelier to renew, upgrade, and even to leave a bequest to your organization. Never underestimate the importance of saying thank you.

Appendix A
Why People Give

As I stood in line waiting to vote recently, I struck up a conversation with a new friend. When I happened to mention that I worked with the United States Holocaust Memorial Museum, she whipped out her Museum Membership Card. To my amazement, so did two other people in the line.

Not long before that I had been reading the obituary page when these words leapt out of an otherwise unremarkable notice. "The deceased was a Charter Member of the Smithsonian's National Museum of the American Indian."

These incidents are cited for the purpose of stating why people give (either in person or by mail). While many reasons are given by various authors, I believe people give for one of two basic reasons:
1. The first is called "What's in it for me" or WIFM.
2. The second is "Interest in the Cause."

Admitting to be motivated by the first category does not make one a selfish person. In most cases, the donor responds to both reasons. But if he or she already supports a number of charities, some criteria must be used to evaluate whether or not to take on a new cause. And let's face it, we craft our fundraising appeals offering special perks because we work in a competitive arena.

For example, some organizations offer opportunities to hobnob with important people . . . use special dining privileges . . . attend certain functions . . . and so on. Not to mention offering membership cards, discounts, magazines, tote bags, and the like.

If the donor is truly interested in your cause, the WIFM is that you give him or her reading material (magazines or newsletters) so that he or she can stay informed. And donors will contribute even more if you offer them access to insider information or a behind-the-scenes look at what's going on in their field of interest.

What's in it for them can range from having their name permanently listed in a public place to having it listed in your Annual Report. The point is that the donor is recognized and feels like an "insider."

Now some people think that if you have simply crafted a good letter for a worthy and tax-deductible cause, people will give.

This is rarely the case. Tax deductibility, of course, matters to the person making a very large gift (say $1,000 or more). But the average direct mail donor gives far less money, and tax deductibility is only important in that it may seem to lend credibility to the cause.

As for contributing because it's a good cause and well-crafted appeal, just look at the facts. People are inundated with good appeals for good causes all the time, and there are just so many causes one can contribute to. So even if you get the prospect to say yes the first time you write (because it is a good appeal and a good cause), he or she may never renew. That is why first time renewal rates are only about 50 percent or a bit more. Half the people who were seduced eventually realized that their real interests lie somewhere else. That is one reason why some people give multiple gifts to others and only one gift to you.

Also in the category of WIFMs are the donors who give to a cause because they have experience in that field. If the case is medical in nature, they may give out of fear that they will get the disease or someone they love has or had the disease. If the cause is educational in nature, they may give because their own alma mater hasn't asked them and you have. If the cause is about domestic animals, they may give because of a strong attachment to their own pet. If it is about disadvantaged children, they may give because they were disadvantaged as a child, and so on.

So just because there is something in it for the donor, compassion also plays a major part in giving—especially when it comes time to renew or give again.

FOCUS GROUPS

Focus groups have become popular in various arenas and are used to predict public reaction to various types of new products, political candidates, and even nonprofit causes.

They are useful, relatively inexpensive tools that should be taken with a grain of salt. If you don't know what a focus group is, here is a brief description.

A focus group company (with good references and past experience in your area) assembles a group of approximately 15 pre-interviewed individuals in a room with a one-way mirror. Hopefully, participants are direct mail donors to your organization or other causes; otherwise the information they give you is far less useful. The focus group leader, with your help, has prepared a list of questions and has engaged the participants in conversation. These people are not usually told the name of the sponsoring organization (yours) until toward the end of the two-hour session.

You and your colleagues sit on the other side of the one-way mirror, and if you aren't too noisy the participants can't hear you, but you can hear and see them. For an additional fee of about $500 (Focus

Groups range from $2,500 to $4,000 each), you can have the session recorded on video to show back at the office.

What you want from a focus group is some direction on copy platform so that you can put together the most compelling direct mail pitch possible. You will learn, for example:

- whether people have heard of your cause/organization and if so, what they think of it
- what they think of your competitors
- whether they currently use or can imagine using your services
- whether they would contribute to your cause/organization
- whether benefits would inspire their giving (and if so, what benefits in particular they would like to receive)

Usually, more than one focus group is needed to learn if present members/donors think differently than prospects. And if you are a national organization, you will probably want to hold focus groups in different parts of the country to learn if people on the East Coast have very different opinions from West Coasters or Midwesterners.

The trouble with focus groups is—well, we won't go so far as to say people lie, but it is true that most people want to present their best face. Thus, most individuals will answer questions by saying what they believe makes them look good.

For example, almost inevitably focus group participants claim that they want absolutely no benefits in return for their contribution—that they want every cent to go to the cause. However, for most organizations, in testing of certain benefits versus none, the benefit offers are far more successful. And such careful tests produce quantifiable results as compared to what people "say" on camera. (Besides, they know you are behind the one-way glass.)

However, if the focus group leader is good and if he or she has a "good" group of people, you can receive some excellent guidance. But be certain to test information of which you are uncertain in the mail, remembering that people are capable of fibbing—just a little.

Appendix B
Data Modeling

Data modeling is often touted as a means of "making your database perform better." There's some truth to that, but only if you really know what you're doing—and only if you have a large database.

A data model is nothing more than a mathematical equation that describes how the characteristics of a person, or a household, *relate* to the way they behave. A model can be constructed using Regression, Logit, Probit, CHAID, or a Neural Network. Characteristics in the model often include demographic and psychographic information (age of donor, presence or absence of children in the household, ZIP code), and information about the donor's relationship with the organization (length of time on file, the number of gifts given, frequency of contributions, dollar amount of contributions).

For direct mail, typically either a response model or a performance model is created. A response model is an "either or" model used to predict who is more likely to respond to a campaign. A performance model predicts a behavior along a continuum; for example, how many dollars each donor is likely to contribute in the next year. In both cases, the predictive model uses "weights" applied to each characteristic in the model and the known behavior patterns of others with similar weights to predict behavior. After a model is constructed, it can be applied to a larger group of people, or households, to *predict* their individual behavior. The larger group of people/households can then be divided into segments (each receiv-

ing a "score"), based on the type of behavior they are predicted to exhibit.

The problem with data modeling for direct mail is that there's no way in this formula to predict emotion. Why does a donor give to a cause? Because he or she cares about it. And knowing a donor's age, or income, or whether he or she has children won't tell you whether mom died of cancer or he or she believes in civil rights or cares about your cause.

Very large files (500,000 or more records) can help aggregate some of the obvious factors for improved giving. For example, it can help locate better prospects for you on a large compiled list or locate lapsed members/donors on your own file who have a better chance of responding. But while it may increase response rates marginally (increasing it, say, from 4.5 percent to 5 percent on a lapsed reinstatement mailing), modeling won't double your rates. And it's expensive to build a rigorous, statistically valid model. If an organization wants to use demographic or psychographic data in the model, it must first purchase the data overlays. This alone can cost $10,000 for a 100,000-record file. Then, hiring someone to build a model can cost upwards of $25,000 and often as much as $50,000. Very rarely do the incremental improvements made in direct mail as a result of the model exceed the cost of creating the model. What's more, such models grow old quickly and must be updated every 18 months or so, as more data are collected.

Thus far, data modeling and data overlays are discussed only as they pertain to direct mail. However, these same tools can be used to locate potential major donors or planned giving prospects on your file. In this instance, an outside firm will append a variety of information to your database. This information can include age, income, whether the donor owns a home, has a driver's license, is registered to vote, etc. Some overlays include more extensive financial information, such as whether the donor is on the board of directors of a major corporation, for example. You can also purchase information about donors who have made major gifts to other organizations. Naturally, the data won't include the name of the organization or the exact amount of the gift.

This overlay information can be used to create a response model for the file to find people predicted to say "yes" to a major donor solicitation. As with direct mail models, the records will each receive a "score" based on whether the model predicts respon-siveness. Some systems use ranges from 1 to 10; others score from A to E, with "1" or "A" having the best potential for major giving, "2" or "B" being a planned giving prospect, etc. Scoring of this type can help identify good prospects for personal solicitations of major gifts—and one or two large gifts can pay for the model.

Consider the following, however. Experienced fundraisers have long practiced a more sophisticated form of modeling (to use the term loosely), and that is to mail to lists with constituencies similar to their own donors. Some mailers are disappointed when a merge/purge produces a high (25 percent or more) duplication rate. Instead, they should be ecstatic because this high rate portends great success as it evidences *interest*. On the other hand, mailing to people targeted by overlays indicates only *potential* and will most likely raise results only marginally.

As stated earlier, you can't predict a donor's heart. And, donors don't give because they are wealthy; they give because they care.

Appendix C
State Registration Regulations

It's the law. If you solicit funds in any of the 39 states requiring registration, you must register and report to them. Generally, exceptions are made *only* for religious, government, educational institutions, and hospitals. If you are already in the mail but have not registered, do not be afraid to register now (fearing that you have already broken the law). Most states want you to register and will be helpful even after the fact. Although some may issue fines, they will certainly be lower fines than if they come after you.

Actually, state registration isn't as difficult as it sounds (at least it isn't any more) thanks to the work of several organizations. Most notable of these organizations is the Association of Direct Response Fundraising Counsel (ADRFCO), which has worked for many years to get a unified state registration form approved. As of this writing, 35 states have signed on to the use of a unified form and only 4 of the 39 states requiring registration insist that their own form be used. A listing of the 39 states requiring registration follows.

States Requiring Registration

Alabama	Maine	North Dakota
Alaska*	Maryland	Ohio
Arizona*	Massachusetts	Oklahoma
Arkansas	Michigan	Oregon
California	Minnesota	Pennsylvania
Connecticut	Mississippi	Rhode Island
District of Columbia	Missouri	South Carolina
Florida*	Nebraska	Tennessee
Georgia	New Hampshire	Utah*
Illinois	New Jersey	Virginia
Kansas	New Mexico	Washington
Kentucky	New York	West Virginia
Louisiana	North Carolina	Wisconsin

* These states do not accept the URS (Unified Registration Statement) and separate registration forms must be obtained.

ANNUAL REPORTING

In addition to registration, which establishes a baseline for your organization's governance and finances, many states require that you renew and report annually on your organization's finances and fundraising results. States requiring annual reporting will not automatically request the information. It is up to you to comply with each state's annual needs and deadlines (which will be stated in their original documents). Many states have annual fees and late fees, so be certain to file on time.

HOW TO REGISTER

The URS is the best place to start. The URS is a project of the National Association of Attorneys General and the National Association of State Charities Officials. The most recent version was released in November 2000, and includes the supplemental forms required by the six states requiring same. You can download a complete filing kit from the URS website at www.nonprofits.org/library/gov/urs. You may also obtain it by contacting one of the following organizations: ADRFCO, DMA Non-Profit Federation, or AFP (formerly NSFRE). See Appendix E for addresses, phone, fax, and e-mail numbers.

To obtain registration forms from the four non-participating states, you are again referred to the URS website, which is a superb site for all matters pertaining to state registrations.

REGISTRATION REQUIREMENTS

You will find that while the registration form is unified, different states require different information and documentation. In general, be prepared to submit the following:

- the completed (and sometimes notarized) form
- completed additional forms (for 6 states)
- IRS Determination Letter

- contracts with professional fundraisers
- organizational bylaws
- Form 990 for the previous year
- financial audit
- fee (if applicable)

REGISTRATION COSTS

Registration fees vary from state to state, with some states levying no fees at all while other states charge according to the amount of money raised. For example, if yours is a national organization raising $1 million annually, registration fees will cost about $3,000 per year as of January 2001.

In addition to the fees, you must absorb ongoing clerical and professional expenses for maintaining registrations. If yours is a local organization or one soliciting in a limited number of states, this may not be overly burdensome. But if yours is an organization soliciting nationally, it may be helpful and economical to engage a firm specializing in state registrations. You may wish to speak to one or more of the several firms listed at the end of this chapter before making a final decision.

REGISTRATION FOR FUNDRAISING FIRMS

Yes, your fundraising consultants and telemarketers must also register—and at far greater cost. For them, there is no URS, and they must register on a state-by-state basis and must even post surety bonds in some states.

It's a two-way street. If counsel registers in one state and the nonprofit fails to register or renew there, counsel will be notified that they cannot serve clients who are mailing in said state. If they do, and are discovered, they and you are subject to legal action. Conversely, if the nonprofit registers and counsel does not, the state will advise the organization that their counsel is in noncompliance and that they may not mail.

Companies Providing Registration Services

Coates & Hutchinson, P.C.
PO Box 561
Odenton, MD 21113-0561
(410) 672-6339

Copilevitz & Canter
423 W. Eighth Street, #400
Kansas City, MO 64105
(816) 472-9000

Labyrinth, Inc.
932 Hungerford Dr #16B
Rockville, MD 20850-1751
301-340-2030

Nonprofit Service Group
1250 24th St NW, 4th Floor
Washington, DC 20037-1124
(202) 466-6620

Perlman & Perlman
220 Fifth Ave, 7th Floor
New York, NY 10001
(212) 889-0575

Webster, Chamberlain & Bean
1747 Pennsylvania Ave, NW, #1000
Washington, DC 20006-4604
(202) 785-9500

Appendix D
Donor Privacy Considerations

It is human nature to want to be in control of one's own name and address, and for that reason alone, many of our donors request that theirs not be exchanged or rented (they will incorrectly use the term "sold").

If you exchange or rent your list even occasionally, it is strongly suggested that you offer your members/donors several opportunities annually to "opt out" of this practice. And if your donor avails himself or herself of the opportunity to not be part of the rental or exchange, you must "flag" his or her computer record with a "DNE" (Do Not Exchange) code, and honor that code at all costs.

In addition to setting up a system on your database, it is suggested that each time you obtain an acquisition/prospect list (whether through rental or exchange), that you have this and all other lists in the mailing run through the "preference file" maintained by the Direct Marketing Association. The preference file consists of the name and addresses of everyone who has written to the DMA requesting that they never be sent unsolicited offers by anyone, including nonprofit organizations.

Compliance with these privacy measures can show that our industry is honorable and self-regulating; thus far harsher rules can be averted. While some percentage of your donors will "opt out," it is far better than the alternative that could result from loss of confidence in our industry.

Following is a list of Privacy Rules put out by the Association of Direct Response Fundraising Counsel (ADRFCO).

- Maintain an "opt-out" system, whereby donors are informed of list rental/exchange practices and are afforded a reasonable opportunity to withdraw their names from such uses. *(The opportunity should be provided quarterly.)*
- Maintain an in-house suppression file to honor "don't mail to me" requests from the general public from prospects who have self-identified as a result of a prior solicitation.
- Provide all donors/members with an opportunity to opt-out of listings in the organization's publications. *(For example, publications that honor donors for a certain size gift through a listing of their names.)*
- Make every reasonable effort to honor donors' requests regarding frequency and types of mailings. *(If he or she says once a year, stamp the envelope of the one appeal you send accordingly.)*

---

* Bold italics explanations are the author's and not part of the ADRFCO rules as written.

Courtesy of the Association of Direct Response Fundraising Counsel, Washington, DC.

- As appropriate in the circumstances, utilize the Mail and/or Telephone Preference Service, administered by the Direct Marketing Association, as a suppress list for all acquisition efforts.
- Establish and maintain procedures and standards for approving or rejecting list rental/exchange requests.
- Ensure that a regularly updated, duplicate copy ("fire file") of the donor list is maintained and that it is readily available and accessible at all times, under any circumstances.
- Protect the donor file against unauthorized use with a "decoy" system (*i.e., misspell your name or that of a friend to make sure no one uses your list who shouldn't, or **when** they shouldn't*).

If you would like more information, or if there are some rules you do not understand, please contact the ADRFCO directly (listed in Appendix E).

LANGUAGE AND LOCATION FOR "OPT OUTS"

The most commonly used place in your package for providing "opt out" language is on the front of the reply card. The phrase can be included as an optional check off box in the same size type as *"Here is my gift of $_____."*

You can also offer the "opt out" option in your acknowledgment letters, in which case every one of your donors in a given year will be offered this opportunity annually. It is necessary, of course, to give the donor a BRE or some other way to reply. The most common language reads something like the following:

Because it is so hard to locate other generous people who share your concern for (cause), we occasionally exchange lists with other carefully screened nonprofit organizations. If you do not wish to receive letters from others, please check here, and we will abide by your wishes.

Appendix E
Organization Resources

Name	Member Type & Requirements	Benefits *
Association of Fundraising Professionals (AFP) (formerly NSFRE) 1101 King Street, #700 Alexandria, VA 22314-2967 P (703) 684-0410, x458 F (703) 684-0540 www.afpnet.org	• Individual memberships for over 20,000 national members • Local (chapter) membership required—call national office for those near you • Signing Code of Ethics required	• Certification (CFRE) preparation courses • Education (local luncheons, meetings and international conferences) • Job bank • Library and resource center • Mentoring • Networking • Newsletter and magazine • Scholarships
American Association of Fundraising Counsel (AAFRC) 10293 North Median Street Indianapolis, IN 46290 800-46-AAFRC or P (317) 816-1613 F (317) 816-1633 www.afirc.org	• Corporate memberships for fundraising consulting firms only • Code of Ethics and Standards of Practice required • Sponsorship required	• *Giving USA* (Publication) • Networking with member firms • Summer Institute
Association of Direct Response Fundraising Counsel (ADRFCO) 1612 K Street, NW, #510 Washington, DC 20006-2802 P (202) 293-9640 F (202) 887-9699 ADRFCO@aol.com	• Corporate memberships for direct mail fundraising firms only • Signing Code of Ethics required	• Advocacy • Luncheon meetings • Monthly bulletins and other publications • Networking • State regulations
The Direct Marketing Association (DMA) 1120 Avenue of the Americas New York, NY 10036-6700 P (212) 768-7277 F (212) 302-6714 www.the-dma.org	• Organizational memberhips for the borad direct marketing industry	• Educational seminars and conferences • International awards • Library and resource center • Postal rates and regulations • Preference list • Privacy issues • Student internships

DMA Nonprofit Federation 815 15th St. NW, #822 Washington, DC 20005-2201 P (202) 628-4380 F (202) 628-4383 www.federationofnonprofits.org	• Organizational memberships for nonprifits, and consulting firms that must first belong to DMA (see preceding org.)	• Awards to individual achievers and nonprofit organizations • Conferences • Newsletter • Postal rates and regulations • Regulatory issues
Direct Marketing Association of Washington (DMAW) ** 7702 Leesburg Pike Suite 400 Tysons Corner, VA 22043 P 703-821-DMAW F 703-821-3694 www.dmaw.org	• Indidividual memberships • Focus on Mid-Atlantic region	• Educational seminars • Industry awards • Job bank • Monthly luncheons • Networking • Scholarships
Direct Marketing Fundraisers Association (DMFA) 224 Seventh Street Garden City, NY 11530 P (516) 746-6700 F (516) 294-8141 www.dmfa.org	• Individual memberhips • Fundraising focus • Primarily NYC members, but not all	• Job bank • Monthly luncheons • Newsletter • Package of the Year contest • Scholarships • Seminars and workshops • Special events
Women's Direct Response Group (WDRG) 18402 Beech Lane Triangle, VA 22172 P (703) 221-1594 F (703) 221-2618 www.wdrg.org	• Individual memberships for women (and men)	• Job bank • Luncheons and meetings • Networking • Newsletter by e-mail • Scholarships • Woman of the Year award

*   Primary benefits listed; others may be available. Membership directories available for all organizations.

**   Other Direct Mail Associations exist throughout the country under the national leadership of the DMA. To find the one nearest you, call the DMA headquarters at (212) 768-7277.

Appendix F
List Brokers Specializing in Fundraising

List brokers are not all the same, although their fees should be. You need a broker with knowledge in the nonprofit field. A listing of the best-known such brokers follows:

- A.B. Data Corp., 8050 N. Port Washington Road, Milwaukee, WI 53217 (specializing in Jewish donor/membership lists)
- American Mailing Lists Corp., 7777 Leesburg Pike, Falls Church, VA 22043
- American List Council, 88 Orchard Road, Princeton, NJ 08543
- Atlantic List Co., 2425 Wilson Blvd., Suite 500, Arlington, VA 22201-3385
- Bernice S. Bush Co., Springdale Lists, 3 Corporate Park Drive, Suite 200, Irvine, CA 92606-5113 (specializing in religious donor/ membership lists)
- Catholic Lists, 100 Stevens Ave., #410, Mt. Vernon, NY 10551
- Carol Enters List Co. (CELCO), 9663-C Main Street, Fairfax, VA 22032
- Coolidge Company (see MSGI Direct)
- List America, 1202 Potomac Street, NW, Washington, DC 20007
- LISTCO, 1276 46th Street, Brooklyn, NY 11219 (specializing in Jewish donor/membership lists)
- Listworks, One Campus Drive, Pleasantville, NY 10570-1602
- May Development/Direct Media, Inc., 200 Pemberwick Road, P.O. Box 4565, Greenwich, CT 06830
- Millard Group, 85 Old Kings Highway North, Darien, CT 06820
- MSGI DIRECT (see nationwide locations listed below)
  - MSGI DIRECT (CMG Direct), 187 Ballardvale Street, Suite B110, Wilmington, MA 01887
  - MSGI DIRECT (Formerly the Coolidge Company), 25 West 43rd Street, New York, NY 10036-7491
  - MSGI DIRECT (Formerly Media Marketplace), 140 Terry Drive, Newton, PA 18940-0500
  - MSGI DIRECT (Formerly Metro Direct), 333 7th Avenue, 20th Floor, New York, NY 10001
  - MSGI DIRECT (Formerly Stevens Knox Associates), 304 Park Avenue South, 6th Floor, New York, NY 10010
- Names in the News, 1300 Clay Street, 11th Floor, Oakland, CA 94612-1429
- National Fundraising Lists, 1670 Village Green, Crofton, MD 21114
- Omega List Co., 1420 Spring Hill Road, #490, McLean, VA 22102
- Preferred Communications, Inc., 5201 Leesburg Pike, Falls Church, VA 22041
- Religious Lists, 86 Maple Avenue, New York, NY 10956
- RMI Direct Marketing, Inc., 42 Old Ridgebury Road, Danbury, CT 06810-5100

Appendix G
Telemarketers Specializing in Fundraising

Angeles Communications
425 E. Colorado Street
Suite 600
Glendale, CA 91205
818–637–5227

Aria Communications
717 W. St. Germain Street
St. Cloud, MN 56301
800–955–9924

Direct Advantage Marketing
5601 Hobart Street
Pittsburgh, PA 15217
412–521–2500

Facter Direct, Ltd.
4751 Wilshire Blvd.
Suite 140
Los Angeles, CA 90029
323–634–1999

IDC
2920 N. Green Valley Parkway
Building 5–521
Henderson, NV 89014
702–450–1000

InfoCision Management Corporation
325 Springside Drive
Akron, OH 44333
330–668–1400

Meyer Associates, Inc.
14 Seventh Ave., North
St. Cloud, MN 56301
612–259–4000

MSGI Direct
1728 Abbot Kinney Blvd.
Venice, CA 90291
P 310–301–1999

NPO Direct Marketing, Inc.
12555 W. Jefferson Blvd.
Suite 325
Los Angeles, CA 90066
310-822-8833

Public Interest Communications
7700 Leesburg Pike
#301
Falls Church, VA 22043
703-847-8300

Share Group
99 Dover Street
Somerville, MA 02144
617-629-4500

The Smith Company
4455 Connecticut Avenue, NW
#600
Washington, DC 20008
202-895-0900

Telefund, Inc.
1129 State Street
Suite 3E
Santa Barbara, CA 93101
805-897-1180

Compiled with the assistance of Avalon Consulting Group, Washington, DC.

Appendix H

EFT Service Providers

CHI Cash Advance
325 S. Highland Avenue
Briarcliff Manor, NY 10510
212–862–0500
888–CHI–0500
914–923–0500
www.chi-cash-advance.com

EFT Corporation
2911 Dixwell Avenue
Hamden, CT 06518
800–338–2435
www.etransfer.com
email: eft@etransfer.com

FINET(Financial Electronic Transfer, Inc.)
500 W. Lincoln Trail Box 998
Radcliff, KY 40159–0988
800–360–2218
270–351–2165
www.gopay.com

Payment Solutions
P.O. Box 30217
Bethesda, MD 20824
301–996–1062

Beacon Financial Group, Inc.
1501 Commerce Avenue
Carlise, PA 17013
717–249–8800
1–800–DO–DEBIT
www.bfgi.com
email: info@bfgi.com

Appendix I
Recommended Reading

Hatch, D. et al. 1999. 2,239 *Tested Secrets for Direct Marketing Success*. Chicago: NTC Business Books.

Johnston, M.W., ed. 2000. *Direct Response Fundraising: Mastering New Trends for Results*. New York: John Wiley & Sons.

Lautman, K.P., and Goldstein, H. 1991. *Dear Friend: Mastering the Art of Direct Mail Fund Raising*. 2d ed. Rockville, MD: Fund Raising Institute. Out of print but recommended—borrow one or try the library.

McKinnon, H. 1999. *Hidden Gold: How Monthly Giving Will Build Donor Loyalty, Boost Your Organization's Income, and Increase Financial Stability*. Chicago: Bonus Books.

Smith, G. 1996. *Asking Properly: The Art of Creative Fundraising*. London: White Lion Press.

Warwick, M. 2001. *How To Write Successful Fundraising Letters*. 2d ed. New York: John Wiley & Sons, and other books by Mal Warwick.

Appendix J
Glossary of Direct Mail Fundraising Terms

ACQUISITION MAILING: A mailing to prospects to acquire new members or donors (also called PROSPECT MAILING).

APPEAL: A mailing to current donors asking for a gift above and beyond basic dues (also called Special Appeal).

THE "ASK": The amount of money requested.

AVERAGE GIFT: A dollar amount calculated by dividing the total number of gifts made into the total dollar amount received.

BANG-TAIL: Envelope with a large flap that can be used as an order form (also called WALLET FLAP).

BLEED: Term used by artists and printers of art, photographs, or other design elements that run off the edge of the paper, leaving no border.

BLUELINE: A specially processed photograph of an artist's design reproduced on blueprint paper and cut and folded to resemble the final product. A blueline is the printer's final proof.

BULK RATE MAIL: Non-first class (second, third, or fourth class) mail that qualifies for special postage rates lower than first class postage.

BUSINESS REPLY ENVELOPE (BRE): A self-addressed envelope that does not require postage to be paid by the sender; the receiving organization guarantees payment of postage on receipt (also called POSTAGE PAID ENVELOPE).

CAGE: Refers to the intake of contributions at a bank or other company where donors' money is received, sorted, and batched by mail code and other specific criteria; processed for fulfillment of benefits and/or premiums; banked; and (optionally) acknowledged. (The term *cage* refers to the outmoded practice of literally locking workers in a metal cage or room and searching them upon leaving to prevent theft. Today's caging clerks do not work under lock and key, but the companies for which they work are bonded against theft and loss.)

CAGING COMPANY: A bank or bonded company engaged by the organization to process contributions from donors. *See* CAGE.

CALLOUT: Excerpt from the text (usually a letter or brochure), set apart graphically from body copy to highlight important points.

CAMERA-READY ART: A perfectly positioned artist's mechanical (usually produced electronically) containing the copy, the placement of correctly sized HALFTONES, screens, and any other artwork, as well as COLOR BREAKS indicated for the printer.

CARRIER ENVELOPE: The outside envelope that contains the appeal letter and other components of a direct mail PACKAGE.

CARRIER ROUTE PRESORT: Sorting mail before delivery to the post office (according to U.S.

Note: Words set in SMALL CAPS are defined elsewhere in the Glossary.
Source: Copyright © Kay Partney Lautman.

Postal Service regulations) so that it is bundled into individual carrier routes in order to qualify for discounted postage rates (abbreviated as Car-rt-sort).

CHESHIRE LABEL: A type of label to which names and addresses are transferred by means of a heat process. Most Cheshire labels are printed four across. Once the most common means of addressing direct mail, many lettershops no longer offer this means of addressing.

CLEAN LIST: A mailing list that has been updated, removing deceased donors, etc., and to which address changes have been made.

to CLEAR: A request for the use of another organization's list for your prospect mailing either through rental or exchange. A list clearance is typically done through a list broker.

CLOSED FACE ENVELOPE: A plain envelope that, regardless of size, does not have a window.

COLD LIST: A prospect list that has not been tested previously by your organization. *See also* PROSPECT.

COLOR BREAK: Indications on a BLUELINE or a color key that show where each of the colors used in the printed piece appears.

COMPUTER FILL-IN: The personalized elements of a preprinted letter, etc., included by using a computer process (e.g., the recipient's name, amount of previous gift, etc.).

CONTINUATION MAILING: A second, third, fourth (and so on) mailing to larger quantities of lists that have been tested first in modest quantities. *See also* ROLL-OUT.

CONTROL PACKAGE: A PACKAGE (usually acquisition) that has performed successfully and remains in use. It is against this "control" that new package ideas are tested.

COST RECOVERY: This measures a mailing's success by calculating what percentage of the cost was made back through contributions. It is calculated by dividing the total income by the total expense (Total Income/Total Cost).

COURTESY REPLY ENVELOPE (CRE): A self-addressed reply envelope requiring that the sender pay the postage.

DATA CARD: A one-sheet description of the list available through list brokers and list managers. It provides the name of the organization, the size of the list, some information on the list (how it was acquired, how many 0–12-month donors are available, etc.), special segments that are available, and the cost.

DECOY: A bogus name and address placed in an organization's HOUSE FILE and sometimes in prospect files. *See also* SEEDING LISTS.

DEMOGRAPHICS: The study and application of social and economic characteristics and/or data; those characteristics of a population that are measured by variables such as age, sex, marital status, family size, education, geographic location, and occupation.

DIRECT MARKETING: A broader term than direct mail, also encompasses telemarketing and e-mail.

DISCLOSED AGENTS: Third parties such as consultants who, by agreement with an organization, place orders for printing, lists, or other services that the organization is legally obligated to pay.

DMA PREFERENCE FILE: A database of people who have requested the Direct Marketing Association (DMA) to notify member organizations "do not mail anything to me." Mailers who abide by the DMA ethical guidelines use the list as a suppression for all prospect mailings. The preference file is sometimes called a "pander file."

DONOR UPGRADE REPORT: A computer report showing the number of donors who have increased the size of their donations as a result of a particular effort.

DUMP AND LAYOUT: Printed information showing contents and format of a magnetic tape, FTP transmission, or other data transfer.

ELECTRONIC FUNDS TRANSFER (EFT): A method whereby a donor instructs his or her bank to make an automatic monthly (or other set period) deduction from his or her account, earmarked for the charitable organization of his or her choice.

FANFOLD: A piece of paper that has been folded back and forth like a fan leaving no double edge for the insertion machine to grip.

FIVE-DIGIT PRESORT: Sorting mail before delivery to the post office (according to U.S. Postal regulations) so that it is bundled into individual five-digit ZIP codes in order to qualify for discounted postage rates.

FOCUS GROUPS: A research tool through which a group of similar people (donors, members, prospects) are brought together and asked questions about your organization or initiatives you are planning.

GALLEY: A computer printout listing donor information such as names, addresses, and any other information that is stored on the computer (e.g., date of first donation, largest donation, most recent donation).

GEOGRAPHICS: The study of markets by using geographic analysis, principally regions, states, counties, and localities. Specifically, geographics entails the study of markets by SMSA (standard metropolitan statistical area), ZIP code Sectional Center, or other territorial designation.

HALFTONES: Printer's term for photographs.

HAND-MATCH INSERT: The process of hand-inserting personalized PACKAGE elements (e.g., inserting a personalized RESPONSE DEVICE or certificate of appreciation into a CLOSE FACE ENVELOPE).

HAND-TAMPING: The process of tamping (or gently striking) the end of a batch of stuffed, sealed PACKAGES to be certain that the name and address are lined up with the envelope's window.

HICKEY: Accidental spot or mark that mars the appearance of a BLUELINE.

HOUSE FILE: The names and addresses of active and recently lapsed donors and members of an organization.

INDICIA: A permit to mail that has been typeset and printed at the same time as the envelope. The indicia (which indicates that postage has been paid) appears in the upper right-hand corner of the outside envelope, which otherwise would be stamped or metered.

KEY: The numbers, letters, or a combination of the two (generally up to five digits) affixed to the mail label or RESPONSE DEVICE to indicate the list from which the donor name originated.

LASER LETTER: A letter that has been personalized through a process where laser beam, toner, and fuser lay images on continuous computer forms.

LAYOUT: The hand-drawn or digitally created composition of copy, art, and photographs, which indicates approximately how the finished product will look.

LETTERSHOP: The service bureau that addresses, inserts, sorts, bags, ties, and delivers your mailing to the post office. Lettershops often have printing capabilities, unlike mailing houses, which receive materials from the printer and take the mailing process from there.

LIFT NOTE: An additional appeal, usually smaller in size than the main letter and usually signed by someone other than the signer of the main letter, which is enclosed in the direct mail PACKAGE (also called Endorsement Letter).

LIST BROKER: An agent who brings the renter (list owner) together with the buyer (mailer) to arrange the rental or exchange of a mailing list (or part of a list).

LIST EXCHANGE: The exchange of donor lists between two organizations on a name-for-name basis to enable each organization to mail to the other's constituency.

LIST RENTAL: An arrangement through which one organization can pay a set price for 1,000 (or increments thereof) names from another organization for a one-time use.

LIVE SAMPLE: A sample PACKAGE that comes off the inserting machine with all components inside, sealed and stamped.

LIVE STAMP: A postage stamp (first class or nonprofit) affixed by hand or machine to a CARRIER ENVELOPE.

MACHINE-INSERTING: The mechanical process of inserting the letter, brochure, RESPONSE DEVICE, and other enclosures into the CARRIER ENVELOPE.

MAIL DROP: The delivery of bundled, bagged, or postage-affixed mail to the post office.

MAIL HOUSE: *See* LETTERSHIOP.

MAILING CLUSTERS: Groups or *clusters* of ZIP codes, which are grouped together by DEMOGRAPHIC or PSYCHOGRAPHIC similarities.

MERGE/PURGE: A computer operation that merges two or more files of names in a matching process to produce one file free of duplicates.

MONARCH SIZE STATIONERY: Stationery that measures $7\frac{1}{4}'' \times 10\frac{1}{2}''$.

MONITOR SERVICE: A service company that maintains a network of DECOY or bogus names by which mailers can track use and/or theft of their mailing lists.

MONTHLY DONOR PROGRAMS: *See* SUSTAINER PROGRAM.

MULTIDONORS: Often called multibuyers, these are donors or buyers found on more than one list obtained for a mailing. A donor who appears on a large number of lists is considered a better prospect than one who appears on only one list.

NIXIE: An undeliverable piece of mail returned to the sender by the post office.

NTH SELECT: A process used to select a smaller number of names from a larger file to get a total random sampling of the entire file.

NONPROFIT POSTAGE: A special reduced postage rate accorded to qualifying nonprofit, tax-exempt organizations.

OPT-OUT: Giving a donor or prospect the choice not to receive mail from an organization(s).

OUTPUT: The final result after the information or data have been processed by a computer.

OVERLAYS: DEMOGRAPHIC or PSYCHOGRAPHIC characteristics that are purchased and added onto your database of donors.

OVERPRINTED ENVELOPE: An envelope that already has been printed with the name and address of the mailer, and then is reprinted with an additional message or art.

OVERS: Overruns of printed materials; generally 10 percent is allowed according to industry standards.

PACKAGE: The total direct mail appeal; all components of the mailing.

PIGGYBACK MAILING: The inclusion of one organization's appeal in the PACKAGE (or invoice) sent by another organization.

PILOT MAILING: A first-time mailing by an organization to determine whether a direct mail test campaign will be successful. *See also* TEST MAILING.

PLANNED GIVING: The application of sound personal financial and estate planning concepts to the individual donor's plans for lifetime and testamentary giving (usually bequests).

POSTAGE PAID ENVELOPE: *See* BUSINESS REPLY ENVELOPE.

POSTCALLING: Calling a potential donor after he or she has received your direct mail appeal.

POSTING: Recording direct mail gifts by date, mail code, and amount.

PRECALLING: Calling a potential donor before he or she has received your direct mail appeal.

PREMIUM: An incentive to give in the form of a gift offer.

PRESSURE-SENSITIVE LABELS: Mail labels, which are hand-applied and do not require water or machinery for affixing.

PRINTOUT: A printed copy of any information or data from a computer.

PROFITABILITY RATIO: The ratio of net profit to gross income, which is determined by dividing the gross income into the net profit (the amount remaining after costs have been deducted).

PROSPECT: A name from a COLD LIST; a potential donor who has never contributed to the organization.

PROSPECT MAILING: *See* ACQUISITION MAILING.

PSEUDO-TELEGRAM: A mailing PACKAGE designed to resemble a telegram and thus convey a sense of urgency.

PSYCHOGRAPHICS: The means of classifying consumers based on their activities and interests. It specifically deals with the study of lifestyle, behav-ioral, and personal traits as they apply to consumers and within an identified market.

RECAPTURE MAILING: A mailing designed to reenlist the interest and support of lapsed members or donors (also called Reenlistment and/or Reinstatement).

RENEWAL MAILING: A mailing to donors or members requesting renewed support, especially renewal of membership dues.

RENEWAL RATE: The percentage of current donors who give again in the next fiscal year.

RESPONSE DEVICE: A form bearing the name and address of both the organization and the prospective donor (coded by list or file segment), on which the recipient indicates the size of his or her gift (and any other information requested) and returns it with his or her check.

RESPONSE RATE: A statistical measure of the success of a mailing, calculated by dividing the number of responses by the number of pieces mailed (number of responses ÷ number mailed). The rate can be compared to projections and to past responses to determine the success of a mailing.

REVERSE-OUT TYPE: Type that is dropped out of a solid area so that the background appears dark and the type light.

ROLL-OUT: *See* CONTINUATION MAILING.

SECTIONAL CENTER (SCF): A geographic area defined by the first three digits of the ZIP code (e.g., 100–101 for New York City, 600–606 for Chicago).

SEEDING LISTS: The insertion of real or fictitious names and addresses on a list to protect it from misuse or theft and to monitor delivery.

SEGMENTATION: Grouping donor names by characterizations such as gift recency, frequency, and dollar amount. Also called file segmentation.

SELF-MAILER: A self-contained package without a separate carrier envelope or reply envelope.

SERVICE BUREAU: Usually refers to a computer service bureau that offers a full range of computer services.

SINGLE/DOUBLE/TRIPLE RESPONSE DEVICE: Single: one panel, $8^{1}/_{2}'' \times 3^{1}/_{2}''$; double: two panels, $8^{1}/_{2}'' \times 7''$ total size; triple: three panels, $8^{1}/_{2}'' \times 11''$ total size.

SOURCE CODE: A code or key in the form of numbers and/or letters that specifies the list from which a contribution was generated. *See also* KEY.

SOURCE CODE REPORT: An analysis of source codes (or KEYS), which indicates the profitability of all lists used in a mailing.

SPLIT TEST: The testing of a variable in the mailing by splitting the list (on an nth selection) and keying the response devices or envelopes to learn whether one approach works better than another.

SUSTAINER PROGRAM: A program wherein donors pledge to make a gift each month for which they are billed (also called Monthly Donor Program).

TEASER COPY: A brief message, usually a sentence or phrase, designed to pique the interest of the reader. This is most frequently used on CARRIER ENVELOPES.

TELEFUNDRAISING: Raising funds by telephone. *See also* TELEMARKETING.

TELEMARKETING: Raising funds or selling products or services by telephone.

TEST MAILING: A mailing in which a test of any nature is conducted; can also apply to an organization's first time mailing. *See also* PILOT MAILING.

TEST PANEL: Each component of a split test.

TURNAROUND TIME: The time elapsed between the beginning of a job (or an element of a job) and its completion.

TYPEFACE: A style of lettering or font.

UNIQUE NAMES: Net names generated after a MERGE/PURGE has identified and deleted duplicate names.

UNIVERSE: The total number of names on a particular list; also the total number of names in a particular list market.

UPDATING: Adding, changing, or deleting information on a master file of donor records to bring it up to date. See also CLEAN LIST.

UPGRADING: A special appeal or renewal requesting a larger contribution than the donor's previous one.

WALLET FLAP ENVELOPE: *See* BANG-TAIL envelope.

WHITE MAIL: Mail (including BREs and CREs) received by an organization that is not keyed or coded, thus preventing attribution of any gift to a particular list or campaign.

WINDOW (BETWEEN MAILINGS): The period between the use of a list by two different mailers or the period between campaigns by a single organization.

WINDOW ENVELOPE: A carrier envelope that shows the name and address through a cutout, or window, in the envelope.

ZIP STRING: A run (or string) of mail data in ascending ZIP code order beginning with East Coast addresses and ending with West Coast addresses.

Index

About the Author

Kay Partney Lautman, a Certified Fund Raising Executive (CFRE), is President of Lautman & Company, a fundraising firm in Washington, DC. The award-winning firm specializes in membership and donor development. Prior to starting her own firm, Ms. Lautman was President of Oram Group Marketing; before that, she was Associate Director of the World Wildlife Fund.

Ms. Lautman has originated and conducted successful fundraising campaigns for numerous organizations, including the Vietnam Veterans Memorial Fund, United States Holocaust Memorial Museum, American Society for the Prevention of Cruelty to Animals, Smithsonian's National Museum of the American Indian, AARP Andrus Foundation, Ronald McDonald House of New York, and the Jane Goodall Institute.

Ms. Lautman is the recipient of several prestigious awards. In 1985, the Washington DC Chapter of the National Society of Fundraising Executives (NSFRE) named Ms. Lautman "Outstanding Fund Raising Executive." In 1994, the Women's Direct Response Group named her "Woman of the Year," and the Non Profit Council of the Direct Marketing Association (DMA) gave her a Lifetime Achievement Award in 1996.

Ms. Lautman is co-author of the best selling book, *Dear Friend: Mastering the Art of Direct Mail Fund Raising*, published by The Taft Group in 1984 (now out of print). She is also a frequent speaker at fundraising seminars and conferences.